WOMAN VERSUS MAN
SOCIO-LEGAL GENDER INEQUALITY IN PAKISTAN

WOMAN VERSUS MAN
SOCIO-LEGAL GENDER INEQUALITY IN PAKISTAN

RASHIDA MOHAMMAD HUSSAIN PATEL

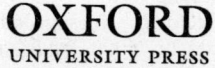

OXFORD
UNIVERSITY PRESS

OXFORD

UNIVERSITY PRESS

Great Clarendon Street, Oxford OX2 6DP

Oxford University Press is a department of the University of Oxford.
It furthers the University's objective of excellence in research, scholarship,
and education by publishing worldwide in

Oxford New York

Auckland Bangkok Buenos Aires Cape Town Chennai
Dar es Salaam Delhi Hong Kong Istanbul Karachi Kolkata
Kuala Lumpur Madrid Melbourne Mexico City Mumbai Nairobi
São Paulo Shanghai Taipei Tokyo Toronto

Oxford is a registered trade mark of Oxford University Press
in the UK and in certain other countries

ISBN 0 19 579895 3

Typeset in Times
Printed in Pakistan by
Mas Printers, Karachi.
Published by
Ameena Saiyid, Oxford University Press
Plot No. 38, Sector 15, Korangi Industrial Area,
Karachi-74900, Pakistan.

CONTENTS

PREFACE

Ideology

Pakistan was created to be a separate homeland for Muslims. Yet, it has evolved as an ideological Islamic State. Islam is the State religion. Vast majority of the people are Muslims. Religion has a strong hold. There is limited movement towards secularism for the State. Islam is considered a complete code of life.

The Objectives Resolution, which has been described as the *ground norm* of Pakistan, was the preamble to the successive Constitutions of the Islamic Republic of Pakistan of 1956, 1962, and 1973. The Martial Law regime, by Presidential Order, in 1985 added Article 2A to the Constitution, according to which, the Objectives Resolution became a substantive part of the Constitution. It declares, among other things, that sovereignty over the entire universe belongs to Allah Almighty alone and is to be exercised by the people within the limits prescribed by God. It envisages the observance of the principles of democracy, freedom, equality, and social justice as enunciated by Islam. It provides that Muslims shall be enabled to order their lives in the individual and collective sphere in accordance with the teachings and requirements of Islam as set out in the Quran and Sunnah. It also protects the rights of minorities, guarantees fundamental rights, including equality of status, opportunities and before law; social, economic and political justice and freedom of thought, expression, belief, faith, worship and association, subject to law and public morality.

The Objectives Resolution coupled with other Islamic Provisions of the Constitution, namely the Islamic Ideology Council and the setting up of the Federal Shariat Courts with powers to determine and strike down any law or provision of law which is repugnant to Islam, has made Islam the basis for all laws. This means that the reinterpretation of the Quran and Sunnah, the primary source of Islamic Law, are the key factors for progress and change. Not much has been achieved for the people specially the women of Pakistan. Obscurantist attitudes, adherence to historical accreditations, and persistent adherence to age-old wrong interpretations by jurists of mediaeval times continue to hold the fort. Held back by the human element, Islamic Law has not matured to meet the present-day needs.

The increasing misinterpretation and misapplication of the pristine principles of Islam are taking a heavy toll on the lives of women. The so-called Islamization process during the Martial Law regime of President Ziaul Haq in the late seventies and early eighties brought in the Zina (adultery) Ordinance in 1979 and the Qanoon-e-Shahdat Ordinance (law of evidence) in 1984, which are detrimental and derogatory to women. Customs, traditions, and laws are confining women to be subservient, meek, and suffering. Education, training, health, and family planning facilities are lacking. Rape, *karo kari*, and domestic violence have become frequent. Poverty is increasing.

Reform

The Muslim Family Laws Ordinance 1961 and the Family Law Courts Act 1964, since their inception were found to be ineffective. NGOs have consistently called for reforms. Through the Pakistan Women Lawyers' Association (PAWLA) I had research and studies undertaken. Based on the findings of these studies PAWLA forwarded recommendations for reforms to successive governments. In the year 2000-01, the Pakistan Law Commission recommended amendments to the Act, which incorporated certain reforms demanded by PAWLA. The amendments were studied and some of them were found detrimental to women. The President of Pakistan and his Ministers were contacted by PAWLA, pointing out the defects in the proposals, which have to some extent been remedied before they became Law. The Ministry of Women Development and the Ministry of Law and Justice brought forth a comprehensive draft for amendments to the Family Law Courts Act, which was approved by the cabinet.

After I had given the manuscript of this book to Oxford University Press for publishing, on 1 October 2002, by an Ordinance, the military government of President General Pervez Musharraf brought in important changes to the Family Law Courts Act 1964. I sent in the changes to be incorporated in this book. As they are recent, we need to see their effective propagation and implementation.

Unfortunately, the condition of life of the people, especially of women, has deteriorated. The justice system has failed. Poverty and crime have increased. I felt the urgent need to recount and analyse the contemporary socio-legal issues with a view to spell out ways and means to improve the situation. This book is an effort for positive change towards understanding and improving the life and laws in Pakistan, which is my life's mission. Not all the topics have been covered, as I wanted the book to be in print at the earliest. Besides I have only dealt with Muslim laws and have not been able to include personal laws as applicable to Hindus, Christians, and Parsis. I expect to cover the remaining topics in a subsequent book.

I have had some comments and support from friends and colleagues. I especially thank Dr Sabiha Syed, Imtiaz Kamal, Farida Moten, Faiza Asad, and Ameena Saiyid, Yasmin Qureshi, and Daleara Jamasji-Hirjikaka of Oxford University Press. My appreciation to Mr Ghufran Hussain Farooqi, who worked on the manuscript and patiently prepared the drafts, redrafts, corrections, and references on the computer.

RASHIDA MOHAMMAD HUSSAIN PATEL
F-21/1-A,
Block 8, Clifton,
Karachi 75600, Pakistan
Tel: 92-21-5866013-14
Fax: 92-21-5866013
Email: rashida59@hotmail.com

INTRODUCTION

Pakistan emerged as a sovereign state on 14 August 1947 as a result of the division of the Indian subcontinent, which was ruled by the British. Pakistan is a huge country. The terrain is vast and diverse. It has agricultural lands, deserts, mountains, and rivers. It touches the Hindukush mountains in the north and extends to the Arabian Sea. It has a border with Iran in the west, with Afghanistan in the north-west, India in the east and south-east, and the Arabian Sea in the south. There is a common border with China alongside Gilgit and Baltistan in the north.

The population is over 140 million people and is fast increasing. The are more males than females. Statistics show 48 per cent females and 52 per cent males. The rural population is around 68 per cent, whereas the urban population is around 32 per cent, which is rapidly rising. Literacy is low with vast differences within different urban/rural and male/female population. Health facilities are limited and inadequate.

It has a patriarchal system with widely diverse socio-cultural conditions. The economy is predominantly agricultural with expanding industry. Development has been slow and faltering. The social sector has been neglected. The need for electricity, sewage, and potable water is not met in most areas, especially in rural areas, resulting in grave hardships.

The country has urban societies, rural communities, and tribes. Tribal lords rule the tribal areas, often using *jirgas*, applying their own laws. Tribal feuds are a problem. In rural areas large land holdings are concentrated in the hands of a few, while the majority of the people are agricultural workers under the influence and control of landlords.

Crimes are high, law and order is poor. Law and the judicial system are dilatory with long delays. Poverty is rampant and rising. There are considerable differences in incomes of the very rich and the very poor; the rich and the poor; the upper middle class and the lower middle class; the rest are all too poor.

In this milieu, women are the poorest of the poor and the most oppressed of the oppressed. The majority of women are controlled and dependant, playing the role of daughter, wife, mother, sister with severe family constraints. Most women have several children, constantly work within the home and outside without monetary recompense, but some women are gainfully employed outside the home.

By contrast to the majority of poor, illiterate, dependant women, there are several women who are educated, independent, professionals, holding important influential posts, supporting their families or themselves, some rich, some poor, some housewives, some working women. Recently women have been elected councillors and Members of Parliament, with wide roles to play with limited resources and serious handicaps.

In these difficult conditions of life, men and women are struggling to move forward towards progress and prosperity.

ABBREVIATIONS

APWA	All Pakistan Women's Association
BHU	Basic Health Units
CEDAW	Convention for Elimination of Discrimination Against Women
CIA	Crime Investigation Agency
CLC	Criminal Law Cases
CPLC	Citizen Police Liaison Committee
CPR	Contraceptive Prevalence Rate
CrPC	Criminal Procedure Code
CS	Central Statute
DHH	District Headquarters Hospital
DLR	Dhaka Law Reports
EDO	Executive District Officer
FCR	Frontier Crimes Regulations
FIR	First Information Report
FPAP	Family Planning Association of Pakistan
FSC	Federal Shariat Court
GNP	Gross National Product
IC	Indian Cases
IEC	Information, Education, Communication
IUCD	Intra-Uterine Contraceptive Device
JUI	Jamiat-e-Ulema-e-Pakistan
Kar/Khi	Karachi
KMC	Karachi Municipal Corporation
Lah	Lahore
LHW	Lady Health Worker
MCH	Maternal and Child Health
MFLO	Muslim Family Laws Ordinance 1961
MLD	Monthly Law Digest
MLR	Monthly Law Reports
MMR	Maternal Mortality Ratio
MOH	Ministry of Health
MOPW	Ministry of Population Welfare
NGO	Non-Governmental Organization

NIPS	National Institute of Population Studies
NLR	National Law Reporter (Published by the National Law Reporter, Urdu Bazar, Lahore)
NWFP	North West Frontier Province
PBUH	Peace be upon Him
PAWLA	Pakistan Women Lawyers' Association
PCPS	Pakistan Contraceptive Prevalence Survey
PDHS	Pakistan Demographic Health Survey
PFFPS	Pakistan Fertility and Family Planning Survey
PHC	Primary Health Care
PLD	Pakistan Law Digest (Published by the All Pakistan Legal Decisions, Nabha Road, Lahore)
PLJ	Pakistan Law Journal
PMA	Pakistan Medical Association
PO	President's Order
PPC	Pakistan Penal Code
PPP	Pakistan Peoples Party
PRHFPS	Pakistan Reproductive Health and Family Planning Survey
PSC	Pakistan Supreme Court Cases
PSYB	Pakistan Statistics Yearbook
PWA	Progressive Women's Association
RHC	Regional Health Centre
RI	Rigorous Imprisonment
S	Section
SAARC	South Asian Association for Regional Cooperation
SC	Supreme Court
SCJ	Supreme Court Judgment
SCMR	Supreme Court Monthly Review (Published by Malik Muhammad Saeed at the Pakistan Educational Press, Lahore)
SD	Shariat Decisions (Published by National Law Reporter, Urdu Bazar, Lahore)
SHO	Station Head Officer
SMS	Short Message Services
SO	Section Officer
TBA	Traditional Birth Attendants
TFR	Total Fertility Rate
THQ	Tehsil Headquarters
UN	United Nations

UNCEDAW	United Nations Convention for Elimination of Discrimination Against Women
UNHRC	United Nations Human Rights Commission
VAW	Violence Against Women
VBFWW	Village-Based Family Welfare Worker
WHO	World Health Organization
WP	West Pakistan

1

MARRIAGE LAWS

Marriage is an all-encompassing part of women's lives. Laws governing marriage are extremely important for women. Life and laws cannot remain static. A forward movement is essential for survival and progress.

Background

In the Indian subcontinent, the British rulers chose limited interference with the laws governing the personal life of Indians. Religious laws, tempered by customs, subject to a few statutes, were applied to the people of the subcontinent. Personal law has not been completely codified in matters relating to marriage, divorce, dower, inheritance, succession, and family relationships. For Hindus, the Hindu Law was applied, for Muslims the Muslim Law was applied, for Christians the Christian Law was applied, and for Parsis, the Parsi Law was applied. In Pakistan there has been practically no change in the antiquated personal laws of Hindus, Christians, or Parsis. Some changes have been brought in the marriage laws governing Muslims by statutes and by rulings of superior courts.

Statutes

For Muslims the important enactments brought in under British rule were the Muslim Personal Law (Shariat) Application Act of 1937[1] and the Dissolution of Muslim Marriages Act of 1939.[2] The 1937 Act was meant to dislocate customs and make Muslim Law applicable to Muslims, but the Act did not fully serve its purpose. The Dissolution of Muslim Marriages Act of 1939, to an extent, provided some relief for Muslim women from customary law or misinterpreted Muslim Law by declaring the grounds and rights of divorce to the wife. This was to correct the Hanafi doctrine as applied by courts, according to which the wife had no right to divorce. The Act still continues to be applied, practically in its original form, except for certain amendments by the Muslim Family Laws Ordinance 1961.

The Guardians and Wards Act of 1890[3] was enacted to oversee questions of custody and guardianship of children. The primary criterion is the welfare of the child, with the qualification under section 17 that in appointing or declaring the guardian of a minor, the court shall be guided—consistently with the law to which the minor is subject—by what appears to be in the best interest of the minor.

Apart from the limited spheres of these enactments, the Muslims of pre-partition India continued to be governed in their family relationships and inheritance by Muslim laws modified by customary laws, as interpreted or misinterpreted by legal decisions, thereby bringing into operation the Anglo-Muhammadan Law.

'The principles of Muhammadan Law were applied by the judges of the pre-partition phase of Indian history, keeping in view their notions of equity, good conscience, and public policy on the one hand, and the rules of Muslim Law proper as they could be gleaned from the writings of the old commentators of our law on the other.

'Anglo-Muhammadan Law is thus a "cross-breed", a compromise, and represents but a halfway house between the forces of progress and conservatism.'[4]

Law Reforms in Pakistan

Following the birth of Pakistan, several enlightened Muslim men and women launched a movement for change in the misunderstood Muslim Personal Law to divest it of traditions and customs, and to deconstruct the Anglo-Muhammadan Law as misinterpreted by decisions of the superior courts during British rule.

Muslim Personal Law (Shariat) Application Act

After Provincial Acts on the subject, the West Pakistan Muslim Personal Law (Shariat) Application Act 1962 was enacted, which covered the whole of West Pakistan except the tribal areas. The purpose of the Act was to make the uncodified Muslim Personal Law applicable to Muslims subject to statutes in family matters and inheritance. Section 2 of the Act reads as follows:

> Notwithstanding any custom or usage, in all questions regarding succession (whether testate or intestate), special property of females, betrothal, marriage, divorce, dower, adoption, guardianship, minority, legitimacy or bastardy, family relations, wills, legacies, gifts, religious usages or institutions including waqfs, trusts, and trust properties, the rule of decision, subject to the provisions of any enactment for the time being in force, shall be the Muslim Personal Law (Shariat) in cases where the parties are Muslims.[5]

Thus, the Muslim Law became applicable to Muslims in Pakistan, subject to statutes in force.

Muslim Personal Law is applied by courts in accordance with the sect to which an individual Muslim litigant belongs. The Muslims of Pakistan are divided mainly into two sects, namely the Sunnis and the Shias. The Sunnis are divided into four sub-sects, following the four Imams, Abu Hanifa, Malik, Shafe'i, and Ahmed-bin Hanbli. The majority of Muslims are Hanafi Sunnis.

Muslim Family Laws

In 1961, in response to continuous pressure from women's organizations, the Muslim Family Laws Ordinance 1961[6] was promulgated.

The Ordinance brought in some reforms which will be discussed in the relevant chapters. It was a half-hearted attempt at best, and did not activate the legal reforms as envisaged by the Rashid Report on Marriage and Family Laws, though it was purported to be based on the recommendations of the Commission on Marriage and Family Laws.[7] It was supported by forward-looking men and women but opposed by the orthodox section.

Nikahnama/Marriage Contract

An important innovation under the Muslim Family Laws Ordinance 1961,[8] is the registration of marriages and the use of the prescribed form of *nikahnama*.[9] Previously, nothing was put down in writing and the nikah was often oral. A proposal for marriage and acceptance at one meeting, in the presence of two witnesses, were considered the essentials of a Muslim marriage. According to some exponents of Shia Law, witnesses are not required and the spouses themselves could contract a valid marriage.

The registration of marriages was introduced in 1961. This had become a necessity. In certain cases, the factum of marriage was often alleged, and its proof was based merely on oral evidence, which created uncertainty and confusion.

For example, when a person was accused under section 498 of the Pakistan Penal Code of abduction of a female, his defence often was that he had married the woman concerned of her own free will, and as there was no machinery for the compulsory registration of marriage, the factum of marriage became difficult to decide. In cases where a married woman was abducted, the defence plea was that the husband having divorced her, the accused had legally married her, and as there was no set procedure for registration of divorce, the court had to rely on oral evidence. The change in the law has not really changed the situation. The system for registration of marriages is defective, and unregistered marriages are accepted in law. For centuries oral marriages without any documentation were the order of the day. The law has still not seeped down to the public, especially in rural and underdeveloped areas.

With the promulgation of the Zina Ordinance in 1979, the registration of marriage has become extremely important. In the majority of cases, the plea by the arrested couple is that they are married to each other. Even where nikah has taken place, the man and woman may not have a copy of the *nikahnama*, which leads to their arrest.

The proper registration of marriages has become absolutely essential.

For the first time in 1961 it became obligatory for the parties to use the prescribed standard form of *nikahnama*. Unfortunately, few people have taken note of the importance and contents of the prescribed form. A number of educated young girls, who have been married after 1961, when asked whether they had noted the contents of the *nikahnama* at the time of marriage, replied in the negative.

Too much sentimentality is attached to marriage; besides, its arrangements are usually entirely the parents' responsibility. The bride is too often absorbed in the frivolous demands of making a trousseau and on the wedding day sits with head bowed low, unconcerned about the practicalities of the *nikahnama*. There are so many traditional rituals being performed that the bride and her family have little awareness of the contractual nature of the marriage and possible rights and obligations, which can be included in the marriage contract.

Standard *Nikahnama*

The standard *nikahnama* requires furnishing of facts such as the date and the place of the solemnization of the marriage, details about the bride and the bridegroom, i.e. name, father's name, residential addresses, and ages.

A clause questions whether the bride is a maiden, a widow, or a divorcee. There is no such clause in respect of the bridegroom, which is a serious lacuna and should be suitably amended.

There is a clause pertaining to the amount of dower, and to whether any portion of dower was paid at the time of marriage and whether any property was given in lieu of the dower, and the details thereof.

There is also a clause pertaining to special conditions, if any. With reference to this clause it may be noted that marriage under Muslim Law is a contract and special conditions can be part of the marriage contract provided they are not contrary to Muslim Law and are not against public policy.

Clause 18 of the *nikahnama* asks whether the husband has delegated the power of divorce to the wife and if so, under what conditions. The husband can delegate his right of divorce to his wife, and such a delegation of right is known as Talaq-i-Tafwiz.

Clause 19 of the *nikahnama* questions whether the husband's right of divorce is in any way curtailed. These two clauses have been included in the *nikahnama* as a progressive step towards the security of the wife. If the right of divorce is delegated by the husband to the wife, she becomes an equal to the husband in exercising the right of divorce. If the husband's right of divorce is suitably curtailed, the wife is protected against the unjust use of right of divorce by the husband.

Clause 20 questions whether any document was drawn up at the time of marriage relating to dower, maintenance, etc.

Normally clauses 17 to 20 of the *nikahnama* are not seriously considered by the parties at the time of marriage and the protection that can be made available to the wife is bypassed. One often sees a line drawn through these clauses in most *nikahnamas*, showing that they have been dismissed without consideration due to cultural and social pressure, though these clauses in the *nikahnama* can ensure better terms in the marriage contract for the wife.

Clauses 22 and 23 relate to whether the bridegroom has an existing wife and whether permission from the relevant authority to contract another marriage has been obtained.

The *nikahnama* is required to be signed by the bridegroom or his vakil, if any, the witnesses to the appointment of the bridegroom's vakil, the bride, the vakil of the bride, if any, witnesses to the appointment of the vakil by the bride, and the witnesses to the marriage, and must also have the seal and signature of the registrar.

The registration of nikah and the use of the standard *nikahnama* if properly utilized and effectively administered can be extremely valuable to give definition to the fact of marriage and terms and conditions of marriage. This can ensure a secure legal status for the wife in the marriage and protect her.

Parents and the parties to the marriage are rarely aware of or guided to fill up the columns. The maulvi performing the nikah does not subscribe to the wife being given the rights. He is disinclined and often refuses to include these rights for the wife. Often, he terms them as un-Islamic. The nikah registrar and persons performing the nikah must be informed that it is their duty not simply to fill the formal columns of the *nikahnama* as a routine but to realize that their function in the finalization of the *nikahnama* is very important because rights to succession, property, maintenance, dower, divorce, legitimacy of children, and several other rights flow from validity of the marriage. A sense of responsibility has to be demonstrated by the nikah registrar before authenticating the nikah, by making proper enquiries as to competency of the parties to understand the nature of their acts, their ages, and whether or not they are acting of their free will and without any compulsion.

In our society, the girl is normally given in marriage by her parents and in their absence by the nearest blood relation and that too mostly at her ordinary place of residence. If this solemn ceremony is performed by the persons not answering the above description and at a place other than the ordinary place of residence of the girl behind closed doors under mysterious circumstances a heavy duty is cast on the nikah registrars to thoroughly confirm and probe into the circumstances under which the marriage was being solemnized before authenticating the same. If the registrar fails, he can, to a great extent, be held responsible for the complications that follow in addition to running the risk of being involved in litigation, both civil and criminal.[10]

The indication herein is to put constraints on the woman's right to marry according to her choice. However, a major aspect of the role of the nikah *khawan* or person performing the marriage is to work towards protecting the rights of the parties, especially oppressed women, to benefit uneducated women and their families through the proper and positive use of the *nikahnama*.

Training

There is a need to train and sensitize the nikah registrars concerning their duties before granting them the licence. Special training must be given to the registrars and persons under their jurisdiction performing the nikah so as to ensure the proper benefits of the *nikahnama* for women.

The Pakistan Women Lawyers' Association (PAWLA) has produced a video film wherein the benefits that can accrue to women by proper use of the standard form of *nikahnama* (marriage contract) have been explained point by point in detail. This educational video, with Urdu and Sindhi versions, has been well received. It has been shown on television and to several groups of women all over the country. Yet much more needs to be done.

Attitudes and customs take a long time to change. One of the officers of PAWLA who was in charge of video films, gave top priority to screenings of the afore-mentioned video. Yet, when she was getting married, she and her family refused to negotiate any of the clauses of the *nikahnama*, as they were afraid that they would lose the *rishta* or proposal. People are still unaware of the Islamic concept that marriage is a contract in which conditions can be incorporated.

Machinery for Registration of Marriage

For registration of marriage the Muslim Family Laws Ordinance 1961 and rules[11] thereunder authorize the Union Council to appoint nikah registrars. It is authorized to supply to every nikah registrar a bound register of the *nikahnama* in the prescribed form along with a seal.

The registers must contain fifty *nikahnamas*, consecutively numbered and each *nikahnama* must be in quadruplicate.

When performing the nikah the nikah registrar is required to complete the *nikahnama* in quadruplicate with signatures of the parties, witnesses, and vakils, and place his seal on it. The original has to be kept intact in the register. The duplicate and triplicate of the *nikahnama* are to be supplied to the bride and the bridegroom respectively, and the fourth copy must be forwarded to the Union Council for preservation and registration.

The quadruplicate of the *nikahnama* forwarded by the nikah registrar is to be preserved in the office of the Union Council or designated authorities, until such time as the completed register containing the originals is deposited by the nikah registrar in such office.

The completed register is required to be preserved permanently and indexed by the Union Council. The index and the registers are open to inspection. Copies from the index and the nikah register can be made available to the public on payment of prescribed fees.

When a person other than the nikah registrar solemnizes the marriage, he is required to fill in the prescribed form of *nikahnama,* which can be purchased loose, complete it, obtain the necessary signatures, affix his signature, and ensure delivery of the same to the nikah registrar of the ward where the marriage is solemnized.

Where a marriage is solemnized outside Pakistan by a citizen of Pakistan, the prescribed form of *nikahnama* or marriage contract is required to be delivered to the consular office of Pakistan in the country in which the marriage is solemnized for forwarding to the nikah registrar of the ward in which the bride permanently resides. If a marriage is solemnized by a person who is not a citizen of Pakistan, the duty of filling in and dispatching the *nikahnama* falls on the bridegroom, and if he is not a citizen of Pakistan, on the bride.

At the time of promulgation of the Muslim Family Laws Ordinance in 1961, the Basic Democracy system was prevalent in Pakistan. The procedures prescribed by the Ordinance were linked with the functioning of the Union Councils, which were small local units catering to a limited number of people living in close proximity. However, since the abolition of the Basic Democracy system in Pakistan, the functions and procedures of the Muslim Family Laws Ordinance 1961 suffered great setbacks. Most of the records and functions of the Union Councils had been transferred to municipal officers and to the offices of commissioners or deputy commissioners.

In many instances it was difficult to locate the relevant records of nikah registers and obtain the necessary copies. There is always the danger of interpolations where proper records are not carefully maintained.

Maintaining Records of Marriage

There is a dire need for an effective system for the registration and record keeping of Muslim marriages. The Muslim Family Laws Ordinance 1961 has provided under section 5, legislation for the compulsory registration of marriages. In August 2001, under the Devolution of Power Policy which led to the setting up of local councils, several duties, including the registration of marriages and issuing of marriage certificates were assigned to the Union Administration. The Union Administration is to be composed of the Union Nazim as the head, and Union Secretaries.[12] It is necessary that they are trained for the proper registration of marriages and ancillary duties of record keeping. These processes must be transparent and the procedure should make it impossible to interpolate or change the entries.

Registration of the *nikahnama* can have beneficial effects. Under the Transfer of Property Act 1882,[13] any transfer of immovable property has to be registered, though this is not essential under Muslim Law. The courts have accepted the evidence of the *nikahnama* duly registered as proof and registration for transfer of immovable property in lieu of dower, even where there is no other registered document for the transfer of the property. The Supreme Court has held that:

> Nikah of parties in the form prescribed under the Muslim Family Laws Ordinance 1961 and the rules framed thereunder and registered with the nikah registrar in accordance with prescribed mode had evidentiary value as transfer of immovable property.
>
> *Nikahnama* being a public document executed by a Public Officer, certified copy whereof was sufficient for proof of its contents unless its rebuttal was effected through cogent evidence. Dower deed by which immovable property was purported to be transferred was thus not considered to be compulsorily registered under the Registration Act 1908, and the wife was entitled to claim immovable property on the basis of the *nikahnama* wherein the same was incorporated in lieu of dower.[14]

Proof of Marriage

The written *nikahnama* can be proved in court by the registrar or by one or more of the witnesses. It is not necessary for all the witnesses to the *nikahnama* to come to court to prove the *nikahnama*. One or more of them and/or other witnesses can prove the nikah.[15]

In the absence of direct proof, the presumption regarding Muslim marriage has been raised and acted upon in instances where there has been prolonged and continuous cohabitation as husband and wife, valid acknowledgement by the man of the paternity of the children born to the woman, and acknowledgement by the man of the woman as his wife. Unless the conduct of the parties had been inconsistent with the relationship of husband and wife, the marriages have been accepted as valid without formal proof of nikah.[16]

Marriage of Prostitutes

'No hard and fast rule can be laid down on the subject of presumption regarding a prostitute's marriage when it is sought to be proved by acknowledgement and/or prolonged cohabitation. It will not be correct to say that no presumption at all shall be raised in cases of prostitutes. On the other hand it seems just and proper to hold that a presumption could be raised but it would remain rebuttable. This approach is not only desirable but also necessary.'[17]

The well-known rules of Muslim jurisprudence are in favour of legitimizing marriage rather than stigmatizing... 'Allah in His wisdom may accept *Tauba* at any time, and there was no bar for a woman who had been a prostitute to go through the process of *Tauba* and lead a normal married life with a view to advance Allah's purpose, and Islam leaned in favour of legitimization, rather than stigmatization.'[18]

Non-Registration of Marriage

Registration is evidence of marriage. Non-registration can raise doubts about the factum of marriage, especially where the parties refute it. According to court records, appellant Mst Nasim Akhtar was tried for the alleged murder of Muhammad Ashiq, purported to be her husband, by the Sessions Judge Rawalpindi, who convicted and sentenced her to transportation for life.

On appeal, the learned division bench of the High Court held:

'The appellant when examined, denied the fact that she was the wife of Muhammad Ashiq deceased and produced a certificate Exh. D.B. from the Chairman of the Union Committee Tench Bhata showing that her marriage with the deceased was not recorded in the office of the Union Council.

'She denied all the other allegations and pleaded that she was sleeping on the night of the incident when at about 2.30 a.m. she felt that somebody was picking at her clothes. When she woke up she saw that the deceased wanted to criminally assault her.... No evidence was examined in defence.'[19]

With regard to the factum of marriage it was held:

> It must not be forgotten that at the relevant time the Muslim Family Laws Ordinance was in force and every marriage was to be recorded in a register maintained by the registrar of marriages. The fact that this marriage was not entered in the office of the Union Council coupled with the discrepant evidence on this point, we are of the view that the claim of the prosecution that Muhammad Ashiq deceased was the husband of Mst Nasim Akhtar was incorrect and that there was no matrimonial string between the two. It may be that it was a clandestine marriage or that Mst Nasim Akhtar had illicit intimacy with the deceased.

Basing their decision on the finding that two false witnesses to the occurrence were introduced by the prosecution, the learned judges held:

> Therefore, from the statement of the appellant and the fact that the dead body was found in her apartment make us believe that what happened is this. That the deceased, who had a liaison with the appellant, went to her apartment without her permission and tried to share the bed with her and on her refusal criminally assaulted her and in this struggle the appellant inflicted injuries on the deceased....
>
> In the circumstances, the next question is whether the appellant has exceeded the right of self-defence. Bearing in mind the fact that there was no other person in the house at that time, it was natural for the appellant to think that the only way in which she could prevent her criminal assault was to anticipate Muhammad Ashiq deceased from carrying out his design. It was apparently with that object in view that she attacked Muhammad Ashiq with an adze. It may be that she could have stopped after inflicting only injury, but placed as she was, it was certainly difficult for her to judge whether what she had done was enough to serve her object, i.e., preventing the deceased from committing the rape on her.

That accounts for her inflicting more injuries on the deceased. We are of the view that even if she was a woman of lax morals and was assaulted by the deceased without her consent she had a right to cause injuries to the deceased.[20]

The appeal was allowed and Mst Nasim Akhtar was set free. The case illustrates the extent of the right of self-defence of a woman who is in danger, and also the finding on the topic under discussion, namely the effect of non-registration of marriage as possible proof against the factum of marriage.

In a number of cases the courts have held that failure to register a marriage does not invalidate it.

'The section (section 5 of the Muslim Family Laws Ordinance 1961) makes it absolutely necessary that the marriage solemnized under Muslim Law shall be registered. The solemnization of marriage if validly effected might not be affected by non-registration of marriage. But the non-registration of marriage causes a doubt on the solemnization of the marriage itself.'[21]

Registration of nikah is not necessary for proof of nikah, as under Muslim Law, nikah can be performed by proposal and acceptance of marriage in the presence of witnesses. Non-registration only attracts penalty under S.5(4) of the Ordinance. 'Non-registration of marriage, would not invalidate marriage as in Muslim Law nikah can be performed by offer and acceptance in the presence of witnesses. Non-registration of marriage attracts only a penalty under S.5(4) without invalidating marriage.'[22]

Registration of marriage is not considered necessary for the validity of marriage. The contract of marriage in Islamic Law need not be proved through a written document. If nikah is not registered, then either two witnesses can be produced in support of factum of nikah or the man and woman (husband and wife) may together certify factum of marriage.

The Federal Shariat Court has also held that: 'Marriage plea by accused facing charge under S.10(3), Zina (Hudood) Ordinance 1979, should not be rejected on grounds that the marriage was not registered in accordance with the Muslim Family Laws Ordinance 1961. It was held that non-registration would attract penalty under S.5(4) Ordinance 1961, but there would be no error in the nikah itself.'[23]

The West Pakistan Family Law Courts Act 1964

The above law was enacted to establish Family Courts to expeditiously settle and dispose of family cases. This purpose was not really achieved, as no separate Family Courts were established and the jurisdiction under the Family Law Courts Act was exercised by the existing Civil Courts. Civil judges even of the third class were designated as Family Court judges. The judges were inadequate. There were lacunae in the law and the powers of the court were limited. The procedure for execution of decree was extremely faulty.

The Pakistan Women Lawyers' Association (PAWLA) made several recommendations to the governments of Benazir Bhutto of the Pakistan Peoples Party and Nawaz Sharif of the Pakistan Muslim League (N) calling for reforms, especially amendments to the Family Law Courts Act to make it effective. There was little response. The pressure for reforms was continued on the military government of President Pervez Musharraf. Only very recently, by Gazette of Pakistan notification dated 1 October 2002, an Ordinance LV of 2002 to further amend the Family Law Courts Act 1964, was enacted.

Amendments to Improve the Law

The noteworthy changes under this Ordinance are as follows:

An important innovation is the addition to section 10 on Pretrial Proceedings of the Family Law Courts Act of 1964, whereby it is 'provided that notwithstanding any decision or judgment of any court or tribunal, the Family Court in a suit for dissolution of marriage, if reconciliation fails, shall pass decree for dissolution of marriage forthwith and shall also restore to the husband the Huq Mehar received by the wife in consideration of marriage at the time of marriage.'

Under the above amendments the procedure for dissolution of marriage by way of khula has been considerably simplified and expedited. The proviso narrows down the amount of return of the Huq Mehar by specifying the Huq Mehar as received by the wife 'at the time of marriage'. In the standard form of *nikahnama* there is a clause as to the amount of Huq Mehar and whether the Huq Mehar or any part of it was paid at the time of marriage. This becomes direct proof, which can be easily produced in cases of controversy. Formerly in cases of khula the court could determine the benefits received by the wife which the wife is required to forgo in consideration of khula. This at times could extend to property and jewellery given by the husband even after the marriage. There were superior court rulings laying down that on the passing of the order of the court for dissolution of marriage by way of khula, it becomes effective and return of benefits are civil claims which can be subsequently recovered.

The recommendation of the Pakistan Law Commission that 'in a suit for dissolution of marriage on the sole ground of khula, the court shall pass decree on restoration of marriage benefits, as determined by the court', has not been incorporated in the amendments as it would have been highly detrimental to women. PAWLA had taken strong exception to the proposed amendment by the Pakistan Law Commission as it would be inequitable and give undue benefit to the husband, whose supposed right of talaq without payment of Huq Mehar was not proposed to be curtailed by the all-male commission.

The present amendment though it makes it mandatory that the wife returns the Huq Mehar has clearly defined and restricted it to 'Huq Mehar received' by the wife in consideration of the marriage at the time of marriage. This makes the amendment beneficial to women desiring khula.

In section 7 of the Family Law Courts Act relating to institution of suits, a provision has been added for consolidation of issues at the option of the wife. A proviso has been added that 'provided that a plaint for dissolution of marriage may contain all claims to dowry, maintenance, dower, personal property and belongings of wife, custody of children and visitation rights of parents to meet their children'. This can end multiplicity of litigation, though it can also mean delay in deciding cases of appeals, due to the large number of issues involved.

Besides the Ordinance changes the word 'may' to 'shall' in section 8 of the Family Law Courts Act, making it compulsory for the Family Court to fix the date of not more than 30 days for the appearance of the defendant. It has also provided for service by courier. The courts have in fact been using courier services but this will add to the legality of service by courier.

The Ordinance has amended section 9 of the Family Law Courts Act relating to written statement, whereby in a suit for dissolution of marriage by the wife, 'a defendant husband where no earlier suit for restitution of conjugal rights is pending can in his written statement claim decree for restitution of conjugal rights against his wife'. Similarly 'a defendant wife may in the written statement to a suit for restitution of conjugal rights make a claim for dissolution of marriage including khula which shall be deemed as a plaint and no separate suit shall lie for it'.

The following subsections 7 and 8 have also been added:

(7) The notice of passing of the *ex-parte* decree referred to in subsection (6) shall be sent to defendant by the Family Court together with a certified copy of the decree within three days of the passing of the decree, through process server or by registered post, acknowledgement due, or through courier service, or any mode or manner as it may deem fit.

(8) Service of notice and its accompaniment in the manner provided in subsection (7) shall be deemed to be due service of the notice and decree on the defendant.

This addition will be useful in deterring the common practice of challenging *ex-parte* decrees after considerable time which has been a source of grave harassment to women and children. This coupled with amendment 1(b) (iii) for changing 'reasonable time' to 'thirty days of service of notice under section (7)', will give definiteness to decrees.

Section 12-A of the Family Law Courts Act has been amended, requiring that cases be disposed of within a period of six months and where a case is not disposed of within six months, an application can be made to the High Court for necessary direction.

In section 13 of the Family Law Courts Act for endorsement on decrees in subsection (iii) the words 'not exceeding 30 days' have been inserted after the words 'within the time specified by the Court'. This amendment will limit the time to be specified by the Court for enforcement of decree up to a maximum of 30 days. However, a number of recommendations made by PAWLA for the enforcement of decrees have not been incorporated in these amendments, which need to be pressed for reforms.

Section 14 of the Family Law Courts Act relating to appeal has been amended. The clause 2(b) now provides that no appeal shall be entertained in cases where a Family Court passes a decree for dower or dowry not exceeding 30,000 or maintenance of Rs 1000 or less per month. A new subsection (3) has been added specifying 'that no appeal or revision shall be entertained against an Interim Order passed by the Family Court and (4) that the Appellate Court referred to in subsection 1, shall dispose of the appeal within the period of four months'. This is no doubt a measure to end delaying tactics for prolonging litigation in family suits. However the parties' rights under the Constitution of Pakistan to file writ petitions before the High Court cannot be curtailed. Provision should also be made for requiring the High Court to dispose of such Constitution petitions within a short time.

Section 16 on Contempt of Family Courts has been widened to include a clause 'bb' which covers any person who 'misbehaves with any person in the court premises, or uses abusive language, threats, or uses physical force or intimidates in any form.'

The new sections 17-A and 17-B inserted in the Family Law Courts Act are as follows:

'17-A. Interim order for maintenance - At any stage of proceedings in a suit for maintenance, the Family Court may pass an interim order for maintenance, whereunder the payment shall be made by the fourteenth of each month, failing which the Court may strike off the defence of the defendant and decree the suit.'

The need for powers to the Family Court to pass interim orders for maintenance in suits by the wife and or children has been long felt. During the time that the courts take deciding these cases the wife and children were often left destitute. Though there was a High Court ruling allowing the Family Court to grant interim order of maintenance the Family Court hardly ever did so. Besides such orders could not be easily implemented. The new section 17-A also provides that when such an order is not complied with the Court may strike off the defence of the defendant (husband/ father) and decree the suit. This will go a long way in providing relief to the wife and children.

'17-B. Power of the Court to issue commission—Subject to such conditions and limitations as may be prescribed, the Court may issue a commission to

(a)   examine any person;

(b)   make a local investigation; and

(c)   inspect any property or document.'

Section 19 of the Family Law Courts Act has been clarified so that only Rs 15 is chargeable as Court Fees for any kind of suit and appeal under the Act.

A new Section 21-A has given Family Law Courts further power as regards interim order pending suits. The Family Court may pass an interim order to preserve and protect any property in dispute in a suit and any other property of a party to the suit, the preservation of which is considered necessary for satisfaction of the decree, if and when passed. The above amendment should prove extremely effective for recovery of monies and properties in cases for recovery of Huq Mehar, dower, dowry, and personal property of the wife. Previously the Family Courts had no such powers, which are normally in practice for civil cases. With these powers, the defendent can now be prohibited from disposing of his property to frustrate orders and decrees of the Court.

In Section 25-A of the Family Law Courts Act it has been added that '(2a) where a Family Court remains vacant or the presiding officer remains on leave or absent for any reason, except due to vacations, for more than thirty days, a District Court may, either on the application of any party or of its own accord, by order in writing, transfer any suit or proceedings from such Family Court to another Family Court in a district or to itself and dispose it of as a Family Court.

'(2b) On the application of any of the parties and after notice to the parties and after hearing such of them as desire to be heard, or of its own motion without such notice, the Supreme Court may at any stage transfer any suit, appeal, or other proceedings under this Act pending before a court in one province to a court in another province, competent to try or dispose of the same.' This amendment will facilitate transfer of cases where the Family Court is vacant thus reducing delays. It will also make it possible for the Supreme Court to transfer family cases from one province to another.

In Section 25-B of the Family Law Courts Act for stay of proceedings by the High Court and District Court, the proviso has been added that 'Provided that the stay application shall be finally decided by the District Court or the High Court, as the case may be, within thirty days failing which the interim stay order shall cease to be operative'. Formerly interim stay was obtained against an order of the Family Law Courts and the interim stay operated for long periods. Under the amended section the interim stay can remain in force for a maximum of thirty days, which should force appellants and courts to dispose of stay applications at an early date.

Additions have also been made to the schedule of the Family Law Courts Act: namely after dissolution of marriage the word 'including khula' has been added, after custody of children has been added 'and the visitation rights of parents to meet them', and the new serial number 9 has been added 'for personal property and belongings of the wife'. In this manner the jurisdiction of the Court has been extended and enhanced to provide relief to women.

Support and Strength

Females are entitled to maintenance from their males, under the law. Before marriage the father is liable to maintain his daughter.

After marriage the wife becomes entitled to *nafka* maintenance from her husband. The liability of the father or husband is not always fulfilled, especially in poor families. Social and economic dependence make women subservient and subordinate.

The main plank of the argument that women are inferior to men in Islam is derived on the basis of misinterpretation of the following Quranic verse:

> *Men are the protectors*
> *And maintainers of women,*
> *Because God has given*
> *The one more (strength)*
> *Than the other, and because*
> *They support them*
> *From their means...* (4:34)

In this verse the Arabic word *qawwam* has been misinterpreted to mean male supremacy in a majority of translations. In some commentaries the Arabic word *qawwam* in the verse is used in the sense of a ruler, or master, or a person having authority. In other commentaries, however, the word *qawwam* is interpreted as meaning a guardian or the head of a family. The commentaries in which the concept of dominion or sovereignty is advanced appear to be based upon the old conceptual trends.

According to Dr Asma Berlas, Assistant Professor, Chair, Politics Department, Ithaca College, New York: 'The word strength, which is in brackets, has been added by the translator. Though the Quran does not use sex and gender to discriminate against women, the translators have confused biology with social constriction holding that as women are biologically different it means that women are socially and legally inferior to men. They have disregarded divine antilogy. The nature of God, *Tauhid* oneness, the notion of un-representability of God, the notion of divine justice places God beyond sex and gender.'

The root word of *qawwam* in Arabic is *qawwma*, the words *qawwma ala* will, therefore, mean to provide for someone, to support someone, or furnish someone with the means of subsistence. *Qawwma ala* will, therefore, mean a provider, a supporter, or furnisher for another with the means of subsistence.

> It also means a manager, caretaker, custodian, or guardian. It is for this reason that Abdullah Yousuf Ali has translated the word as meaning protector. Pickthal has translated it as in-charge, which is the same thing as caretaker or guardian. Arberry interprets it as one who manages the affairs of women.
>
> The meaning of *qawwam* as a provider and protector is very much included in the verse, and discarding the concept of the male as sovereign and having full dominion over the life and property of the female is against the Quranic injunctions in which the life and property of all, including that of women is sacrosanct.[24]

From the above-quoted verse of the Quran ensues the concept, commonly understood and accepted, that it is the duty of the father, husband, and son to maintain the women of the household. The women are not bound to go out and earn or spend their own means. The liability of maintaining the children from the wedlock is that of the father.

Historically, the concept of men as protectors and maintainers of women is based on the premise of the physical strength of the male. In the social and economic conditions prevalent in Arabia at the advent of Islam, physical strength was essential for protection, therefore the males protected the females. Besides, it was normally the men who were earning and therefore it became their duty to maintain the women. However, there are a number of cases cited in the history of Islam of women working, running businesses, and earning.

In the same Surah Nisa of the Holy Quran it is stated:

> ...*to men*
> *Is allotted what they earn,*
> *And to women what they earn.* (4:32)

Evidently women are as free to work and earn as men are. There is no limitation or precondition for a woman working and earning. Where a woman works and earns she may not require to be maintained by the man. In the present day the mental capacity of a person has become important and mere physical strength does not provide protection. In the changed circumstances women may no longer require to be protected and maintained by men.

According to Dr Riffat Hassan:

> It is assumed by almost all who read Surah 4, verse 34, that it is addressed to husbands. The first point to be noted is that it is addressed to *ar-rijal* (the men) and to *an-nisa* (the women).... The orders contained in this verse were not addressed to a husband or wife but to the Islamic ummah in general.... The first sentence is not a descriptive one stating that all men as a matter of fact are providing for women.... it is in fact a normative statement pertaining to the Islamic concept of division of labour in an ideal family or community structure....
>
> Continuing with the analysis of the passage, we come next to the idea that God has given the one more strength than the other. Most translations make it appear that the one who has more strength, excellence, or superiority is the man. However, the Quranic expression does not accord superiority to men. The expression literally means 'some in relation to some', so that the statement could mean either that some men are superior to some others (men and/or women) or that some women are superior to some others (men and/or women). The interpretation that seems to me to be the most appropriate contextually is that some men are more blessed with the means to be better providers than are other men....[25]

When a large majority of women come forward for education, training, and work outside the home, it may not be necessary for men to protect or maintain women, and both men and women can share the responsibility of protection and maintenance of the family.

Presently in Pakistan, men continue to be the protectors and maintainers of women. In marriage it is unequivocally accepted that it is the husband who is required to maintain his wife and family.

Law of Maintenance

According to Muslim Law, on marriage the husband becomes liable to maintain and fulfil the needs of his wife. The father is responsible for sustaining his children. The mother bears no responsibility. Maintenance is the right to food, clothing and lodging, and all personal expenses, from the father or husband even if the wife has means of her own. The husband is obliged to maintain his wife and children in a manner befitting his social and economic status. *Nafka* in Muslim Law has a wider meaning than mere providing of food and clothing. It also includes proper lodgings and many other miscellaneous items and expenses that the wife normally incurs. In case a wife refuses to live with her husband without justification, his obligation to maintain her ceases.

The Dissolution of Muslim Marriages Act 1939 placed an obligation on the husband to maintain his wife, who was entitled to seek a decree for dissolution of marriage in the event of his failure to maintain her. After this enactment, the maintenance could no longer be called an ex-gratis grant.[26]

Maintenance under section 9 of the MFLO 1961 is a personal right of the wife. It matures into property when a decree for its enforcement has been passed. It forms part of her estate and is inheritable on her death.[27]

Maintenance of Divorced Wife

Unfortunately in Pakistan, not only has religion been politicized, but pseudo-religious interpretations are put forward to exploit and perpetuate un-Islamic laws, practices, and norms. Today's clergy-oriented feudal Islam is dominated by obscurantist attitudes, which misinterpret the Quran.

A serious misconception is that a divorced wife is not entitled to maintenance. In Pakistan, Quranic law ensuring rights to women is circumvented, so that women are denied their rights. To cite an example, the Quran clearly says:

For divorced women,
Maintenance (should be provided)
On a reasonable (scale).
This is a duty
On the righteous. (2:241)

Unfortunately, this divine revelation is ignored by the male-made Muslim Law. A divorced woman has no right to maintenance from her ex-husband under Pakistani Law as presently applicable.

In the famous Shah Bano case, decided by the Supreme Court of India, the Court held that the Quranic verses impose an obligation on the Muslim husband to make provision for or to provide maintenance to the divorced wife and that the Criminal Procedure Code was fully in consonance with the Quran. The contrary argument does injustice to the teachings of the Quran.[28]

The decision of the Supreme Court of India reinterpreting the Quran, endorsing the right of the divorced Muslim wife to maintenance infuriated the conservative section of the Muslims of India. They objected to the assumption of authority by the Supreme Court of India to reinterpret Islam, despite the fact that courts have been interpreting Muslim Law for centuries, since the British rule. There was a countrywide agitation. Subsequently, to politically appease the objectors a law was enacted which made the Supreme Court ruling redundant.

The Indian legislature enacted the Muslim Women (Protection of Rights on Divorce) Act 1986. A divorced woman who is unable to maintain herself was required to be maintained by those persons who could be heirs on her death, namely her children, parents, and other relatives and failing them, by the state waqf boards. The former husband was absolved of all responsibility of maintaining his ex-wife beyond the *iddat* period.

The question of maintenance of the ex-wife was also taken up by the courts in Bangladesh. The Dhaka High Court Division Bench *suo moto* considered the legal query as to whether the divorced wife can claim maintenance beyond the *iddat* period.

The Court, relying on the Quranic verse 2:241, held that 'a person divorcing his wife is bound to maintain her on a reasonable scale beyond the period of *iddat* for an indefinite period that is to so say, till she loses the status of a divorcee by remarrying another person'.[29]

Not unexpectedly, the Appellate Division of the Supreme Court of Bangladesh overruled this decision in Hefzur Rahman vs. Shamsun Nahar Begum, 4bMLR (AD) (1999) 41. The Court held that the word *matta* as used in the Quranic verse 2:241 was never understood as maintenance or 'provision' in the sense of legal, formal, and regular supply of necessities of life and livelihood to the wife.

It is a 'consolatory offering' or parting gift to a divorced woman as a comfort and solace for the trauma she suffers from divorce. Being a gift, it has never been judicially enforceable. The Court was also of the opinion that statutory provisions may be made for mitigating the sufferings of destitute and unjustly treated divorcee wives, as has been done in several Muslim countries.[30]

With due respect to the learned judges it is unfortunate that the male psyche is not inclined to support an interpretation of the Quran towards women's needs. The Quran supports the maintenance of the wife even after the wife is divorced. The benefits which can accrue to women are lost due to narrow male interpretations by courts and legislators.

In India and in Pakistan, even today, the right of a divorced wife to receive maintenance is not acknowledged or accepted by society and law. A wife is often untrained and not allowed to work. Even when she has training and potential, she stays at home and becomes a housewife. On divorce the wife receives only her Huq Mehar, which is usually inadequate. She has no means of support. Her family is not always willing to take on her burden. She has little alternative but to live on charity or join the world's oldest profession. The plight of the divorced wife needs to be redressed.

Maintenance of Daughters and Sons

The children of a marriage are entitled to be maintained and sustained by their father. The law is very clear on the subject that the daughter is to be maintained by her father till her marriage.[31] A child is entitled to maintenance 'if the child is getting education up to a reasonable stage of getting education which is commensurate with the existing status of the father'.[32]

> Maintenance of the child is not restricted to the period of minority. Legal right to custody of the child is irrelevant. As regards the custody of a child, the parents can have the matter decided in a Guardian Court, but it would be cruel to refuse to give maintenance to a child who was living with his mother after the termination of the period of *hizanat*.
>
> The willingness of the father to take the child and to maintain it has nothing to do with his liability to pay the maintenance, which should be irrespective of the residence of the child.[33]

Past Maintenance

Dissenting from previous authorities, in 1972 the Supreme Court allowed past maintenance to the wife within limits. Recently, the Federal Shariat Court has held contrary to this decision.
The Court held:

> It also seems clear from the authorities on Hanafi Law that neither the child nor the person who maintains it can claim past maintenance from the father unless the same has been previously fixed either by a decree of the Court or by the father himself.
>
> This proposition seems to flow from the propositions mentioned in the preceding paragraph and is supported by the exposition of the law relating to maintenance in textbooks. The *Hedaya* (Hamilton's Second Edition, p. 149) states:
>
> Arrears are not due in a decreed maintenance. If the qazi decrees a maintenance to children, or to parents, or to relations within the prohibited degree, and some time should elapse without their receiving any, their right to maintenance ceases because it is due

only so far as may suffice, according to their necessity (whence it is not so to those who are opulent), and they being able to suffer a considerable portion of time to pass without demanding or receiving it, it is evident that they have a sufficiency, and are under no necessity of seeking a maintenance from others; contrary to.... where the qazi decrees a maintenance to a wife, and a space of time elapses without her receiving any, for her right to maintenance does not cease on account of her independence, because it is her due, whether she be rich or poor.

This leaves no room for doubt that past maintenance except, perhaps, for a very short period cannot be recovered from the father by the mother who has maintained a child unless it has become due under either the decree of the qazi or agreement with the father. In view of this state of the Hanafi Law the plaintiff appellant is not entitled to a decree because she had not previously asked a court to pass a decree for maintenance against the defendant respondent and the latter himself had not agreed to pay any. The decision of the Supreme Court was based on the question as to whether under the MFLO 1961, past maintenance can be allowed. In the present case, the question is whether past maintenance can be granted to minor children under Muhammadan Law.[34]

It is not easy for deserted women to file cases for maintenance. It takes time, resources, and awareness of the laws and procedures. Cases are not decided overnight. Is the mother or her family to starve the children and deny them clothing, schooling, and medicine in the meanwhile?

All schools of thought accept the contractual nature of marriage, which results in mutual obligations including the right of maintenance of the wife and children. The Holy Quran and Sunnah are almost silent on the subject of past maintenance. According to Shafi and Shia law, a wife is entitled to past maintenance arrears. Some differences in interpretation are bound to occur. The principle of equity emphasized in the Quran has not been applied in the case by the Federal Shariat Court.

Contrary Decision

In another case the High Court rejected the contention that awarding past maintenance is contingent upon a decree of court. It held that:

> The argument seems to have been advanced oblivious of the fact that section 5 of the West Pakistan Family Law Courts Act 1964, read with item 3 of the Schedule thereof, catering for maintenance without distinguishing the period thereof in terms of past or future, has been adjudged to be in consonance with the injunctions of the Quran and Sunnah by the Federal Shariat Court, and has not been repealed and remains on the statute. The Full Bench of the Supreme Court in Muhammad Nawaz vs. Mst Khurshid Begum and others (PLD 1972 SC 302) examining the wife's right to past maintenance under Muhammadan Law, approved enunciation of the law by a Division Bench of this Court accepting claim for past maintenance.[35]

Maintenance Through Court

There are two procedures available to a wife for claiming maintenance: by filing a suit for maintenance against her husband before a Family Court and by claiming maintenance under S. 9, MFLO. Significantly, there is no provision in the MFLO for maintenance for the children.

The main problem faced by women and children, especially by poor women who come to PAWLA for legal aid, is maintenance. Often the decree for maintenance is obtained but execution of the decree, unless the husband/father cooperates, is a difficult proposition.

Legal Reforms

What is needed is more judges, better facilities in courts, convenient locations of all Family Courts, and daily hearings.

Difficulties in Execution of Decree

Formerly the execution of decree in Family cases had become very difficult, as the family courts had no power to grant injuctions or interim order for maintenance during the pendency cases.

By recent amendments to the Family Law Courts Act 1964 a new section 21A (see p. 15) gives powers to the Family Courts 'to pass interim order to preserve and protect any property in dispute in a suit and any other property of a party to the suit, the preservation of which is considered necessary for satisfaction of the decree, if and when passed'. Moreover, a new section has been added namely section 17A whereby the Family Courts have been given powers 'in suit for maintenance to pass an Interim Order for maintenance and where the defendant father/husband fails to pay maintenance, the court may strike off his defence'.

A study[36] has given the reasons for delay in execution of decrees, which need immediate consideration by the Govt. of Pakistan.

Section 13 of the Family Law Courts Act 1964 provides for certain incomplete procedures for the execution of decree.

Besides, section 17 of the Family Law Courts Act provides that the provisions of the Evidence Act 1872, and the Civil Procedure Code 1908, except sections 10 and 11, shall not apply to proceedings before the Family Court.

The Civil Procedure Code outlines in detail the procedure for execution of decrees and is particularly relevant for the execution of money decrees in maintenance cases. There have been differing opinions by the High Courts, and a legal controversy continues concerning section 13 of the Family Law Courts Act. It is strongly recommended that the law relating to execution of decree be elaborated and clarified to avoid protracted litigation.

PAWLA conducted an action-oriented study for effective enforcement of maintenance decrees.

Some of the reasons for the failure of execution processes as determined by the study are:

• Delay in obtaining decrees, resulting in accumulation of a large sum of money. This makes it difficult for the judgment debtor to pay, and he tries to evade his responsibility.

- No regular income of the judgment debtor, which can be attached.
- Service of Notice of Execution Process is dilatory.
- Male bias in the legal system.
- Judgment debtor disposes of his property as courts had no power to stop him or grant interim orders for paying maintenance.
- Appeals take long to be decided and the execution process is stayed by courts.

Recommendations for Reforms in the Law

The first need is to enhance the efficiency of the legal system. The following measures are proposed:

a) Removing delaying tactics: These include counter-litigation, filing application or adjournments, and absence of parties from the court for various reasons.
b) Ending corruption in the legal system.
c) Discouraging stay orders: Appeals/petitions should be decided within three months. There should be a guarantee for the payment of the decretal amount before stay of execution is granted.
d) Implementation powers should be vested with the family judge. By giving the court the powers of deputy commissioner and collector of revenue, the process can be made more effective, as in recovery of land revenue.
e) Avoid double service: Family cases where decree of maintenance is passed should continue as a part of the same proceedings and should not require further service to the judgment debtor by making it necessary to file a fresh application for execution as a separate suit.
f) *Bait-ul-Mal* should provide for women and children in need where the father cannot be traced or cannot support his family.

Maintenance from Abroad

As far back as 1921 it was found necessary to enact a law to ensure the maintenance of dependants who may be left unprovided for by the husband or father who chooses to reside abroad. At that time the problem arose in cases where the man went abroad, mostly to England, got married there and returned to pre-partition India, neglecting to maintain his wife and children in England, or vice versa, where the man with a wife and children in pre-partition India, resided abroad, and failed to send proper maintenance for his wife and children at home.

The Maintenance Orders Enforcement Act 1921 is meant to facilitate the enforcement in Pakistan of maintenance orders in reciprocating countries, and vice versa, for the enforcement in reciprocating countries of orders made in Pakistan for maintenance of dependants living in Pakistan. The basic feature of the Act is that it is applicable between reciprocating countries only.

Further to the 1921 Act, the Claims for Maintenance (Recovery Abroad) Ordinance 1959 was promulgated.[37] This Ordinance is in compliance with the United Nations Convention on the Recovery Abroad of Maintenance 1956. Pakistan acceded to the Convention on 14 July 1959 and provided among other things, that the Convention would have the force of law: 'Notwithstanding anything to the contrary contained in any other law, the provisions of the Convention set out in the Schedule shall have the force of law in Pakistan'.

The Convention is effective only between contracting parties and under the Ordinance, contracting party means Pakistan and any other state whose instrument of ratification or accession is deposited under Article 13 and which is notified by the Central government in the official gazette to be a contracting party.

Today, when large numbers of Pakistanis from every walk of life are going abroad to seek employment, often leaving their dependants at home, it is imperative that the practicalities of the Act be reviewed and set right. Presently, the problem of recovering maintenance from a husband or father living abroad is very acute.

A number of marriages take place between young girls living in Pakistan to expatriates abroad. Sometimes the marriages don't work out. The wife and children are sent back to Pakistan, without financial provisions. Cases have come to light where dependants here in Pakistan are left without subsistence and have no legal remedy to enforce maintenance.

It is particularly necessary to bring within the ambit of reciprocating country or contracting party many other countries, especially Middle Eastern and Arab countries. The advantages would be mutual, and dependants would be ensured maintenance even where the person responsible for their maintenance is living outside Pakistan.

Polygamy

In Pakistan plurality of wives though not common, is a constant threat to married women. It is like a sword hanging over their heads. When men attain wealth or position they are inclined to marry again, seeking younger, sociable wives. At times a man gets physically or emotionally involved with another woman, and if she is single, marriage between them may ensue. Polygamy also occurs among poor and middle-income families. It is the current religious, family, and societal acceptance of the second wife which perpetuates the practice. This causes untold misery to the first wife and her children.

Polygamy is a controversial issue. There is a misconception that Islam permits a man legally and morally to have as many as four wives at a time, without any conditions. After partition, a large number of educated women and men in Pakistan began to question whether unconditional polygamy was permissible in Islam.

The primary source of Islamic Law being the Holy Quran, the verse relating to plurality of wives needs to be considered.

If ye fear that ye shall not
Be able to deal justly
With the orphans,
Marry women of your choice,
Two, or three, or four;
But if ye fear that ye shall not
Be able to deal justly (with them),
Then only one, or (a captive)

That your right hands possess.
That will be more suitable,
To prevent you
From doing injustice. (4:3)

This verse, as is well known, was revealed after the bloody battle of *Uhad*, where a large number of males had lost their lives and several women and children were without husband and father. At present the circumstances in Pakistan are different. According to the population census of 1998, out of a total population of 1,30,579 there were 67,840 males and 62,739 females (figures in thousands).[38]

As there are far more men than women and there are fewer females of marriageable age than males of marriageable age, every male who takes more than one wife is depriving one of his fellow countrymen of a wife, and condemning him to a life of celibacy or sin, which is against the positive injunctions of the Holy Quran.

The first line of the verse lays down the precondition for considering a second wife, 'If ye fear that ye shall not be able to deal justly with the orphans' clearly spells out the circumstances under which a man can contemplate more than one wife. The treatment of orphans was to be governed by principles of humanity. A man was permitted to marry from among the orphans or the mother of an orphan if he was quite sure that in that way he could best protect the interests of the orphans. Another precondition is that if a man fears that he shall not be able to deal justly with the co-wives, 'then only one' wife is allowed. The permission for more than one wife is limited and qualified for it is clearly stated, 'that will be more suitable, to prevent you from doing injustice'. Polygamy is only permissible in very special circumstances in order to deal justly with orphans, and even in such circumstances polygamy is permissible only to persons who can deal justly with co-wives.

Equal Treatment

'The unrestricted number of wives of the "Times of Ignorance" was now strictly limited to a maximum of four, provided you could treat them with perfect equality, in material things as well as in affection and immaterial things. As this condition is most difficult to fulfil I understand the recommendation to be towards monogamy.'[39]

How many men can honestly accept the responsibility of dealing with multiple wives equally and with justice? Life and living have changed, and equal treatment to multiple wives is well nigh impossible in the present days of complex living.

The Quran enjoins:

Marry those among you
Who are single, or
The virtuous one among
Your slaves, male or female. (24:32)

'The subject of sex ethics and manners brings us to the subject of marriage. "Single" (*Ayama*, plural *Aiyim*) here means anyone not in the bond of wedlock, whether unmarried or lawfully divorced or widowed.'[40]

The Quranic verse is addressed to both men and women, enjoining marriage with a person of the opposite sex who is single. There is a clear restraint from marrying a person who is not single.

The concept of marriage, as advocated in Islam, is a monogamous union between one man and one woman, and forcefully illustrated by the Prophet (PBUH) by interlacing his fingers, illustrative of the oneness of the partners. Yet, there is a prevalent misconception that polygamy is sanctioned by Islam up to a maximum of four wives. The so-called Islamic permission for more than one wife is being misused and the condition of equal treatment to co-wives is not adhered to, except in rare cases. As a consequence, there is a reaction against polygamy.

In Pakistan the voices raised against polygamy reached a rare height in the 1950s when a Prime Minister, Mohammad Ali Bogra, in the presence of his dutiful wife and sons, took for a second wife his wife's secretary. The uproar was both social and political. Crowds of women gathered outside the Prime Minister's house to protest. The result of the protest was the appointment of a Commission on Marriage and Family Laws.

Commission's Recommendations and Dissent

The Commission recommended that it is incumbent on the State to prescribe a procedure, which would prevent people from taking advantage of this permission uninhibited by any restrictions. It is a universally accepted maxim that prevention is better than cure. It would be in the interests of justice and in conformity with the spirit of the Holy Quran that a man contemplating taking a second wife should present himself before a court to explain the circumstances, which according to him, justify his taking this step. There may be some cases in which there may be a justification and in such rare cases, the court could permit a man to take a second wife only on the condition that in the matter of maintenance and other treatment no injustice is done to the first wife and her children. The Commission is of the opinion that this step will greatly curb the unrestricted and uncontrolled practice of polygamy, which causes so much distress in family life.[41]

Maulana Ihtasham-ul-Haq Thanvi, one of the members of the Commission, wrote an exhaustive Note of Dissent against the findings of the Commission, especially relating to polygamy. He concluded that the Quranic injunction is general and there is no restriction or restraint on marriages up to the limit of four wives. This being the position, it would be an interference in the revealed religion if the plurality of marriages is declared to be unlawful or any restriction is imposed on it.[42]

However, the Commission's report unanimously accepted that family laws, as presently applied, were the result of misinterpretation of Islam and the resultant laws were un-Islamic, and that the existing judicial machinery was slow and dilatory, leading to delay and distress, and therefore the need for reforms was accepted.

The publication of the report on Marriage and Family Laws, along with the note of dissent, brought in its wake serious political controversies between the enlightened and the orthodox sections. A social problem was made the bane of religious confrontations and turned into a political issue. The orthodox sections were not prepared to let anyone but themselves be considered the fountain of all knowledge of Islam and let the power of interpreting and applying religious laws slip from their hands.

In the face of political controversy, the 1956 Report of the Commission on Marriage and Family Laws was shelved. The civilian government of the time was not willing or strong enough to take a positive stand on this vital issue.

Reforms in Family Laws

Liberal activists and women's organizations continued their struggle for reforms in family laws. In 1961 Field Marshal Mohammad Ayub Khan,[43] the President of Pakistan, promulgated the Muslim Family Laws Ordinance 1961,[44] bringing reforms in family laws. The Ordinance was enthusiastically welcomed by women, especially the All Pakistan Women's Association (APWA), the premier NGO at that time, which had spearheaded the movement for reforms in family laws.

During the regime of President Ayub Khan the Ordinance was time and again challenged on the public platform and attacked in the Provincial and National Assemblies. It was thanks to the efforts of the President of Pakistan, and the support of women and women's organizations and the progressive members of the Assemblies, that the Ordinance survived.

Unfortunately, the Ordinance was aligned with the unpopular newly introduced system of Basic Democracy,[45] and it was through the Chairman and councils formed under Basic Democracy that the Muslim Family Laws Ordinance was enforced, which fact added to its unpopularity.

The Ordinance sought to provide relief through adjudication by the Arbitration Council, which consisted of one representative from each of the parties to the disputes, that is a representative of the wife and a representative of the husband, and the Chairman of the Union Council of the relevant area, under the Basic Democracy system.

The system of Basic Democracy introduced by the then President of Pakistan, did not find favour with the majority of the people of Pakistan for various political reasons, and was repealed. All local councils constituted/elected under the Basic Democracy system were abolished with the discontinuance of the system. Elections and appointments to the local councils had been suspended or abolished from time to time. Municipal officials or others had been appointed to perform the functions of the Chairman under the Muslim Family Laws Ordinance 1961. For instance, in Karachi the vice-chairman and other officials of the Cantonment Board have been appointed for the Cantonment areas. Officials of Karachi municipalities have been appointed in other areas of Karachi to register and conduct the cases, at the KMC offices on M.A. Jinnah Road and at the Civic Centre.

The MFLO 1961 was ineffectual, especially as regards section 6 of the MFLO. The procedure for permission for a second, third, or fourth wife has been often ignored.

As local council elections, under the Devolution of Power 2000, have been finalized and local councils are functioning, the powers of the Chairman and Union Councils under the MFLO 1961 have been assigned to the newly elected Chairman (Nazim) and the councils.

Even though the Ordinance sought to give effect to certain recommendations of the Marriage and Family Laws Commission, it fell far short. This Ordinance was an acceptance of certain principles for reforms and initiated remedies and controls, though partially and ineffectively. The main attack against the Ordinance was the restriction it placed on polygamy.

Section 6 of the Ordinance provides that no man, during the subsistence of an existing marriage, shall, except with the previous permission in writing of the Arbitration Council, contract another marriage, nor shall any such marriage contracted without such permission be registered under this Ordinance. Thus polygamy is restricted to the extent that a man desiring plurality of wives has to submit an application for permission to the Chairman of the Union Council, stating the reasons for the proposed marriage and also stating whether the consent of the existing wife or wives has been obtained.

On receiving an application the Chairman is required to call upon the applicant and his existing wife or wives, each to nominate a representative on the Arbitration Council.

The Council may grant such permission if it is satisfied that the proposed marriage is necessary and just. The Council has to record its reasons, and also lay down the conditions, if any, subject to which the permission is granted. The Council may refuse, for reasons to be recorded, to grant the permission applied for.

The Arbitration Council has general powers to decide what is just and necessary for granting permission to marry again, and has to consider such circumstances as sterility, physical unfitness for conjugal relations, wilful avoidance of a decree for restitution of conjugal rights, or insanity on the part of an existing wife. Any person aggrieved by a decision of the Arbitration Council may file a revision application before the Collector.

Section 6 categorically lays down that no man shall contract another marriage (polygamous) without the permission of the Arbitration Council. Yet, the Ordinance does not specifically lay down that a marriage during the subsistence of an existing marriage, without the permission of the Council is illegal, void, or voidable. It provides monetary compensation by immediate payment of *mahr* (dower) to the existing wife and penal action against the husband. If any man contracts another marriage without the permission of the Arbitration Council, he becomes liable to pay immediately to the existing wife or wives the entire amount of the unpaid dower, whether prompt or deferred, and is punishable upon complaint and conviction with simple imprisonment, which may extend to one year, or with a fine up to Rs 1000 or with both.

However, if restrictions on polygamy are to be effective the law should go further and lay down that if another marriage is contracted during the subsistence of a marriage, without prior permission from the relevant judicial authority, such a polygamous marriage shall be illegal and void *ab initio*. Only in this manner will the wife and children be protected against arbitrary and unjustified polygamy and the wife shall be secure from the threat of a co-wife.

For some time the provision for penal action for violation of the Muslim Family Laws Ordinance 1961 and its rules had become ineffective as no authority had been appointed to perform the functions of the Union Council. Rule 21 required that for offences under the Ordinance, a complaint can only be filed by the local council. As all local councils were abolished, no court could take cognizance of any offences under the MFLO 1961 for a considerable time. Rule 21 was amended in Punjab in 1986 and in Sindh in 1988.[46] For the words 'local council' the words 'aggrieved party' have been substituted. The impact is that in Punjab and Sindh the powers of the Union Councils have been assigned to the aggrieved person.

Now, an aggrieved party can file a complaint against a husband who takes a second wife without the permission of the Arbitration Council. The second wife among others is definitely a party and being an aggrieved person as also a party can institute proceedings before the Criminal Court.[47]

Significantly, a polygamous marriage contracted without the consent of the existing wife or wives is not invalid. Besides, 'Marriage not registered or contracted in contravention of S6, has been held valid.'[48]

The courts have held that where a person, while contracting a second marriage did not obtain the requisite permission, such a marriage would not become void, but the person contracting such a marriage could be visited with penal consequences contained in the Ordinance... Failure to obtain permission from the first wife or the Arbitration Council would not invalidate the second marriage.

It is common to hear men criticize women who marry married men, putting the blame for polygamous marriages on women. This is hardly fair as the law allows polygamy with the necessary permission. The law recognizes that it is not the woman who has to be penalized. It was held that under subsection 5 of S6 of the Ordinance, criminal liability will thus be incurred by the husband being 'the man' referred to in that subsection and not by the woman he married.[49]

There are court rulings on the correct forum and procedure for penalty for second marriage without permission. Courts mostly dismiss the complaint on technical grounds. In one case, prosecution was initiated at the instance of the District Magistrate. As there was no complaint from the wife, the proceedings were held to be 'without lawful authority and quashed' in writ jurisdiction.

The Federal Shariat Court, in its recent judgment on the Muslim Family Laws Ordinance 1961, has held that the provisions concerning polygamy under section 6 of the Ordinance are not in 'violation of the injunctions of Islam, since this section has not expressly declared the subsequent marriage as illegal and has merely prescribed the procedures to be followed for the subsequent marriages and punishment for its non observance'.

The Court held that:

There is no doubt that a Muslim male is permitted to have more than one woman as wife, with a ceiling of four at a point of time as the ultimate, but the very *Ayat* which gives this permission also prescribes a condition of *Adal* and the Holy Quran has laid emphasis in the same verse on the gravity and hardship of the condition which Allah Himself says is very difficult to be fulfilled......

Now section 6 of the Ordinance as framed, in no manner places any prohibition in having more than one wife. It only requires that the condition of *Adal* prescribed by the Holy Quran itself should be satisfied by the male who wants to have more than one wife. The provision for constituting an Arbitration Council, therefore, cannot in itself be said to be violative of the injunctions of the Quran as only a procedure has been prescribed as to how the Quranic verse will be observed in its totality with reference to the condition of *Adal* placed in the verse itself.

However, it may be reiterated that the status of polygamy in Islam is no command more or less than that of a permissible act and has never been considered a command, and therefore, like any other matter made lawful in principle may become forbidden or restricted if it involves unlawful things or leads to unlawful consequences such as injustice.

Misuse of the permission granted by Almighty Allah could be checked by adopting suitable measures to put an end to or at least minimize the instances of injustice being found abundantly in the prevalent society. The Arbitration Council in such circumstances would be needed to look into the disputes arising between the husband and his existing wife/wives with respect to another marriage and after taking into consideration the age, physical health, financial position, and other attending factors, come to a conclusion to settle their disputes. However, we are of the view and accordingly recommend that the Arbitration Council should figure in when a complaint is made by the existing wife or her parents/guardians. The intention is to protect the rights of the existing wife/wives and the interests of her/their children. The wife, who is the best judge of her cause, or her parents may initiate the proceedings if her husband intends to contract another marriage. Moreover, we feel that since a nikah validly performed with a wife, whether first or fourth, necessarily entails various consequences including those related to dower, maintenance, inheritance, legitimacy of children etc., non-registration of the nikah thus performed could not only be a source of litigation between the parties but would also lead to a lot of injustice to such wife/wives.[50]

The above-recommended change in law that the Arbitration Council should be brought in when a complaint is made by the existing wife or her parents would adversely affect the interests of the aggrieved wife. She may not even be aware of her husband's intention to take another wife until much after the marriage, and the whole procedure would become inefficacious. It is the husband who is taking a second wife and it is incumbent on him to seek the permission. It is difficult to understand how the judges of the Shariat Bench, who seem to appreciate the Quranic limitations to polygamy, have failed to strengthen the limitation to polygamy in the Ordinance by recommending necessary checks and balances to be brought in as amendments to section 6. On the contrary the Court has proposed an amendment, which clearly kills the purpose of law!

As an appeal has been filed before the Supreme Court Shariat Bench against the above decision, the direction of the Federal Shariat Bench will remain in abeyance and not take effect. It is now for the Supreme Court Shariat Bench to decide these issues.

Federal Shariat Court

A new chapter, 3A, Federal Shariat Court (FSC) was inserted in the Constitution in 1980.[51] Apart from appellate powers, the FSC has been given legislative powers. The Federal Shariat Court has jurisdiction to determine whether any law or provision of law is repugnant to the injunctions of Islam. The Court is required to set out in its decision the reasons for holding that opinion, the extent to which such law or provision is repugnant to Islam, and to specify the day on which the decision is to take effect. The President or Governor as the case may be, is required to bring such law in conformity with Islam. There is an appeal to the Supreme Court Shariat Bench against the decision of the Federal Shariat Court.

NOTES

1. The Muslim Personal Law (Shariat) Application Act 1937, Pakistan Penal Code, Vol. IX, p. 404.
2. The Dissolution of Muslim Marriages Act 1939, Pakistan Penal Code, Vol. XI, p. 716.
3. The Guardians and Wards Act 1890, Pakistan Code, Vol. III, p. 300.

4. A.K. Brohi, *Fundamental Laws of Pakistan*, p. 776, Din Muhammadi Press, Chundrigar Road, Karachi, 1958.
5. Act V of 1962, West Pakistan Muslim Personal Law (Shariat) Application Act 1962–PLD 1963 West Pakistan Statutes, p. 107.
6. Muslim Family Laws Ordinance 1961, CS Gazette of Pakistan Extraordinary, 2 March 1961.
7. Report of the Commission on Marriage and Family Laws, Gazette of Pakistan Extraordinary, 20 June 1956.
8. PLD 1961, CS, p. 209, Gazette of Pakistan Extraordinary, 2 March 1961.
9. West Pakistan Rules under Muslim Family Laws Ordinance 1961, PLD 1961, CS, p. 293, Gazette of West Pakistan, 19 July 1961.
10. Shah Din and others vs. the State, PLD 1984, Lahore 137, p. 139.
11. West Pakistan Rules under Muslim Family Laws Ordinance 1961, PLD 1961, CS, p. 293, Gazette of West Pakistan, 19 July 1961.
12. Shafi Mohammadi, Sindh Local Government Ordinance XXVII of 2001 Section 74, 75, 76(d), 6 August 2001, Asia Law House, High Court Compound, High Court of Sindh, Karachi.
13. The Pakistan Code, Volume III, p. 39.
14. Fazal-ur-Rehman vs. Mst Sosan Jan and others, 1989, SCMR 651.
15. Rasool Bibi vs. Waryam and Eleven others, 1992, SCMR 1520, p. 1523.
16. Abdul Majid Khan and another vs. Mst Anwar Begum, PLD 1989, SC 362, p. 367.
17. Ibid., p. 364.
18. Manzoor Hussain vs. Zahoor Ahmed and Four others, 1992, SCMR 1191, p. 1194.
19. Mst Nasim Akhtar vs. the State, PLD 1968, Lahore 841, p. 843.
20. Ibid., pp. 844 and 846.
21. Dr A.L.M. Abdullah vs. Rokeya Khatoon and another, PLD 1969, Dhaka 47, p. 51.
22. Abdul Kalam vs. the State, NLR 1987, SD 545, p. 545.
23. Ibid., p. 546.
24. Ansar Burney vs. Federation of Pakistan and others, PLD 1983, FSC 73, pp. 80 and 81.
25. Dr Riffat Hassan, 'Muslim Women and Post-Patriarchal Islam' in *After Patriarchy: Feminist Transformations of the World Religions*, edited by Cooey, Eakin and McDaniel, Orbis Books, Maryknoll, 1991, pp. 39-69.
26. Iqbal Hussain vs. Deputy Commissioner/Collector, Lahore, PLD 1995, Lahore 381, p. 384.
27. Iqbal Hussain vs. Deputy Commissioner etc., NLR 1995, SD 554, p. 554.
28. Muhammad Ahmad Khan vs. Shah Bano and others, NLR 1986, SD 171, p. 180.
29. Hefzur Rahman vs. Shamsun Nahar Begum, 47 DLR (1995) 54, p. 56.
30. Ref 4 MLR (AD) (1999) 41, quoted by Alamgir Muhammad Serajuddin, *Shari'a Law and Society*, published by Oxford University Press, p. 323.

31. Ghulam Khan vs. the District Judge, Gujrat and others, 1990, SCMR 136.
32. Mukhtarul Hassan Siddiqui vs. Judge Family Court, Rawalpindi and others, 1994, CLC, Lahore 1216.
33. Ghulam Hussain vs. Muhammad Aslam and another, PLD 1961, WP Lahore 733, p. 739.
34. Syed Hamid Ali Shah vs. Mst Razia Sultana, NLR 1991, SD 347, pp. 348-9.
35. Muhammad Akhtar vs. Mst Shazia and others, 1992, MLD 134, p. 135(A).
36. *Effective Enforcement of Maintenance Decrees*, published by Pakistan Women Lawyers' Association (PAWLA), 710, Kashif Centre, Shahrah-e-Faisal, Karachi, April 2000, p. 55.
37. Gazette of Pakistan Extraordinary,9 September 1959, PLD 1959, CS 324.
38. *Statistical Pocket Book of Pakistan 2001*, published by the Federal Bureau of Statistics, Statistics Division, Government of Pakistan, January 2001, p. 44.
39. Abdullah Yousuf Ali, *The Holy Quran with Arabic Text Commentary and Translation*. Explanatory Note No. 509, p. 179, published by Shaikh Mohammad Ashraf, Kashmiri Bazar, Lahore, First Edition, April 1934.
40. Ibid., p. 905.
41. Report of the Commission on Marriage and Family Laws, Gazette of Pakistan Extraordinary, 11 June 1956, p. 1216.
42. Note of Dissent (in Urdu), Gazette of Pakistan Extraordinary, 30 August 1956, pp. 1594-97.
43. General Ayub Khan, the Commander-in-Chief of the armed forces, had taken over the government under Martial Law in October 1958.
44. Muslim Family Laws Ordinance 1961, Gazette of Pakistan, 2 March 1961, PLD 1961, CS, p. 201.
45. The Basic Democracies, President Order No. 18 of 1959, Gazette of Pakistan Extraordinary, 27 October 1959, PLD 1959, CS, p. 367.
46. Punjab Government Notification No. SO (VI)2/74/88, 6 December 1988.
47. Fahimuddin vs. Sabiha Begum and others, PLD 1991, SC 1074.
48. Ghulam Fatima vs. Anwar alias Anwar Begum, 1981, CLC 1651.
49. Head Notes of Cases—Nazar Hussain and others vs. Anwar Begum and others 1991 CLC Note 238 at p. 184.
50. Allahrakha and others vs. Federation of Pakistan and others Shariat Decision 2000 SD 723.
51. PLD 1980, CS p. 89; Gazette of Pakistan, 27 May 1980.

2

FAMILY PRESSURE

A strong patriarchal system, based on a family-oriented society, pervades Pakistan. Marriages within the family and clan are common. The focus is on patrilocal residence and patrilineal descent. The social system is extremely gender stratified. The marriages of both men and women are normally arranged by their families. Such unions usually take place between relations, among communities and *beradaris*. Marriages among cousins are very common.

Genetic Considerations

There is no concern that such marriages may result in deformed, abnormal, or unhealthy offspring. 'Lack of medical facilities, awareness, and cousin marriages are the main cause of abnormal births in the country. We have to break away from the tradition of "intermarriages" in our society to have a healthy new generation. It is forbidden in the West to marry cousins unless certain prescribed medical tests are carried out to rule out hereditary complications.'[1]

The Prophet (PBUH) instructed that genetic traits be considered, in order to avoid genetic problems. He said: 'Choose where you deposit your sperm for the line of descent is conducive.' (Authenticated by Ibn Maja.) Inbreeding is discouraged: it is also common advice (not Hadith). Marry from outside your kin and kith, lest you beget puny children. Caliph Omar told the clan of al-Sa'ib, who concentrated marriages within their clan: 'You have had puny children, you should marry outside the clan.' (Authenticated by Ibrahim al-Harbi.) Despite this, I should emphasize that marriage between cousins is not prohibited in Islam. After all, the Prophet (PBUH) allowed his daughter Fatima to marry his cousin Ali; but this was in a healthy family.[2]

Kinship Union

Estimates from national and regional surveys in Pakistan indicate that around 40 to 60 per cent of all marriages are between close biological relatives with an overwhelming majority of such unions being first cousin marriages....

Among participants who reported to be married to a non-biological relative, a large proportion of marriages were contracted within the same kinship group with only a third of marriages (30 per cent) contracted outside the definable bounds of endogamy.....

Irrespective of the type of marriage, almost all marriages were arranged by parents or the family elders with women having little or no say in the decision-making process. While marriage decision-making processes were acknowledged to be grounded in a complex set of social and economic factors, the most commonly cited reason for the continued strong preference for close kinship unions was the element of relatives being a 'known entity', which greatly facilitated the terms of transaction of such unions and more importantly provided parents with a sense of reassurance regarding the stability of such unions. Many participants across a number of group discussions also cited expectations of 'better treatment of the daughter by the in-laws or from a daughter-in-law who was also a relative' as one of the main reasons for a continued preference for cousin marriages...

In fact, the intense restraint on physical activity of young women during their peak childbearing years was acknowledged to be part of the larger societal mechanism that attempts to actively control women's sexuality....

It is important to emphasize that the added complexity of multiple relationships for women in close kinship unions results in their interests being further compromised.... Thus within the larger oppressive societal structures, kinship marriages tend to reinforce the subjugation of younger women.[3]

Restraints on Women

There is no doubt that young girls, who have been trained to respect their elders, paternal and maternal uncles and aunts, would respect and obey them even more when they become father-in-law and mother-in-law by marriage. Freedom or self-assertion becomes difficult for these young women.

In feudal families the daughters are married to a paternal cousin to prevent distribution of lands outside the family by inheritance. At times, a daughter is married to a cousin much younger than her, a complete mismatch. In such marriages the husband later marries a woman of his choice and lives with her and the children, ignoring his cousin wife. She is often left alone and childless in the village. Even Pakistan's former Prime Minister, Zulfiqar Ali Bhutto, was married at a young age to a cousin much older than him. She remained childless.

> Islam entitled women to inherit property and the only way to keep the land within the family was through marriage. Such a 'business' marriage had been arranged between my father (Zulfiqar Ali Bhutto) and his cousin Amir when he was only twelve and she eight or nine years older. He had resisted until my grandfather tempted him with a cricket set from England. After their marriage, she had returned to live with her family and my father had returned to school, leaving him with a lasting impression of the inequity, especially as far as women were concerned, of forced, family marriages.[4]

Where there is no possibility of marriage within the family, the daughter is guided or cajoled into the custom of *haq-bakshwai*, marriage with the Quran, denying her all the advantages of matrimony.

Under Muslim Law there is no bar against marriage with a cousin. Muslim societies encourage such a union. Marriage is a family affair. The family reflects on the conditions of life for the wife. She is expected to respect and obey her husband and the elders of his family. In most cases the newlyweds live with the husband's family and the wife has to interact with all the members of the family. In liberal families in urban areas the husband and wife and their children live separately in a nuclear setup.

Bars to Marriage

When certain relationships either by blood or marriage exist between men and women, these are considered impediments to their marrying. On grounds of consanguinity certain classes of women are prohibited to a man and likewise certain men are prohibited to a woman. These classes are parents or grandparents, children or grandchildren, sisters and brothers, aunts and uncles, nephews and nieces.

In certain circumstances, fosterage (suckling) can result in prohibition for purposes of marriage. Affinity established by valid lawful coition, and also by zina (illicit relations) can result in prohibition for purposes of marriage. A man is prohibited from marrying his wife's mother, or his wife's daughter, or the wife of his father, or the wife of his son. A man is not permitted to have at the same time two wives who are so related to each other by consanguinity, affinity, or fosterage, that if either of them had been a male, they could not have lawfully intermarried, as for instance two sisters, or aunt and niece. According to some exponents of Shia Law, a man may marry his wife's aunt but he can marry his wife's niece only with the permission of his wife.[5]

Nikah

A man and a woman are tied together in the marriage bond by nikah. For the young wife this is the most important aspect of her life. If she has a good, compatible, earning, and loving husband with considerate in-laws, most of life's problems are smoothed. But when the in-laws are mean and harsh or if the husband is cruel or inconsiderate and addicted to any of the vices, or is interested in other women, or is constantly unemployed, the burdens of life multiply. The untrained, uneducated, unemployed young wife, without parental support or means of her own, is dependent for her every happiness on her husband and his family. Having no training to earn a living and without autonomy, she has to accept his guiding her every movement, even down to visiting friends and relatives. Most wives are docile. They accept violence by the husband as their fate, because they have no place to go or they do not wish to be parted from their children.

Muslim marriage is a contract whereby mutual rights and obligations between the husband and the wife can be defined, which are lawful in accordance with Muslim Law. In Islam every Muslim of sound mind who has attained puberty may enter matrimony. A minor or a person of unsound mind can only be married by a guardian. The free consent of the parties to the marriage is an essential part of the marriage contract. Each of these statements needs elaboration.

Free Consent

Consent of the parties to the marriage is an important aspect of the marriage contract. Men and women who have reached the age of puberty, normally presumed at the age of 15, are both *sui juris* for marriage. The *nikahnama* requires the signature of the bridegroom or his vakil (attorney) and the signature of the bride as well as that of her vakil, if any, to signify the exercise of freedom of choice by the parties to the contract of marriage. Emphasis has been placed on the free consent of the bride by requiring her signature on the marriage contract even where she has appointed a vakil. This is an added protection against misrepresentation of the bride's interests, in view of the near dependent social and economic status of young girls entering marriage.

Ordinarily marriages are arranged by the parents or guardians of both the female and male. The extent of the freedom of choice available to the parties to the marriage depends on the family. In a modern family setup, it is possible for the male or female to independently choose their own marriage partners. In some families the parents may consult their son or daughter for consent. At the other extreme the parents choose the partner for their son or daughter, and the acceptance of such an arrangement is taken for granted. Needless to say, the male has far more freedom in the choice of a marriage partner than the female, who is much more cloistered and dependent on her parents. In certain cases pressure is exerted by the parents, forcing their daughter into an unwanted wedlock.

Consent is a necessary condition for a valid marriage. A *sui juris* woman can contract nikah of her own will in law. In cases where the girl expressly states that she was not a consenting party to the nikah and circumstances prove her contention, the alleged marriage may be declared as not valid.

Proprietary Control

There is a strong sense of ownership of the daughter, which exposes her to complete control by her family. The daughter is expected to obey every order of her parents, especially her father. The sons are expected to provide for and care for their parents in their old age. The daughter is brought up for marriage, leaving her parents' home for her husband's family and serving them. The money and care expended on her upbringing is at times considered recoverable, resulting in the custom of bride price in some communities. A young daughter may be sold in marriage. Another damaging custom jeopardizing the rights of women is *watta-satta*, or exchange marriages. A young daughter may be given in marriage in exchange for receiving from the bridegroom's family a young girl in marriage for her brother or even her father! Women have become commodities, being sold for money, obligations, or honour in the name of marriage.

Islam does not subscribe to or encourage these evil practices subjugating women. Under Islamic Law women are free to marry of their own choice and their consent is important.

Effect of the Media

Young men and women, even in rural areas, have been exposed to television and radio. Love has been dramatized and affects their thinking. Research has also emphasized the impact of love stories in poetry. In a recent book depicting the images of women in poetry by Shah Abdul Latif Bhittai, saint and mystic of Sindh, the positive portrayal of Sassi, Marvi, Laila, and Moomal, all heroines of love stories, have been highlighted.[6]

Literature and the mass media have conditioned young men and women to revere love, and driven by natural desires, cases of so-called runaway marriages, without the consent of the parents, are increasingly reported in the press. Journalists have become vocal for the rights of women.

The promulgation of the Zina Ordinance acted as a catalyst to make women aware of their rights. It also resulted in a number of cases of harassment and prosecution of men and women marrying of their own choice.

Police Harassment

There has been a tendency for the police to harass and question couples living together on suspicion that they are not married to each other. The police have been known to pursue couples and cause panic, especially at the instigation of a rival party. In a recent case decided by the High Court, it was held that where the petitioner being *sui juris* of 20 years contracted a valid marriage with a person of her own choice even without her father's consent, the couple must not be harassed by the police officer. The couple were entitled to live together and enjoy their marital life. Neither the police nor any other state agency has the authority to interfere in the marital life of a couple where husband and wife are *sui juris* and they have contracted the marriage with their own free consent. The Court emphasized that it is the duty of the police or other state agency to protect marriage as enjoined by Article 35 of the Constitution. The police were directed not to cause any harassment to the couple or other members of the husband's family, and anybody feeling aggrieved by such a marriage could approach the proper court, but the police have no business to interfere in matrimonial disputes.[7]

Case Law

It has been consistently held by courts that under Muslim Law, a female, irrespective of her age, after the attainment of puberty (presumed to be at 15 years) is fully entitled to enter into a marriage and the marriage is valid. There are several rulings of superior courts to this effect, particularly in cases where the girl has married without the consent or against the wishes of the father or guardian. The Federal Shariat Court in a criminal case held that a woman is *sui juris* to marry of her own choice and does not require the presence or consent of her father or guardian.[8]

Several cases decided by superior courts unequivocally upheld the right of a woman to marry of her own free will. To quote one case, Mst Shameem had married Bashir Ahmed. On a complaint of abduction by her mother Mst Bakshi, the police tracked down Mst Shameem and handed her over to Ibrahim, the husband of Mst Bakshi (who she had married after the death of her first husband, father of Shameem).

Mst Bakshi, the appellant, challenged the judgment of the High Court. The Supreme Court allowed Mst Shameem the liberty to go where she will holding that: 'It is abundantly clear from the statement of the girl that she, of her free will, married Bashir and wants to live with him, but is unwilling to go back to her mother or her mother's second husband Ibrahim.'[9] The Court accepted the right of the young girl, having attained puberty, to marry of her own free will without the shackles of the consent of the *wali* (guardian or father of the girl).

Questioning Marriage

There has been a tendency by courts to question the validity of marriages performed without the consent of the parents, especially where the registration of marriage is not proved and the girl is in her early teens.

In the case of Saima, the runaway bride who was sixteen years old, the Court opined that Saima had failed to establish that she was *sui juris* capable of taking independent decisions. The Court accepted the contention that one may be legally entitled to be given over in marriage but still may be incapable of taking independent decisions. Considering the circumstances that she was lured to marry a person who was not only physically handicapped but also had married thrice before and had been having an affair with her when she was still a student of the eighth standard, the Court did not accept her right to marry of her free will and refused to recognize the marriage, especially as the nikah was not registered. The Court held that:

> Islam gives the right to all individuals to act according to their will but not under the influence of fear or temptations. An act like nikah is not possible without parents/*wali*, or vakil, or reliable witnesses. The circumstances under which the nikah of Saima with Abid Ali was performed, particularly the non-production of the nikah *khawan*, cast a serious doubt on its genuineness....
>
> In the present application under section 491, CrPC I think I should not hold any detailed inquiry or record any conclusive finding because these proceedings are generally of a summary character. The Family Court will be the proper forum to decide the question of legality/validity of the marriage. For the present I think I can safely proceed on the tentative view that Saima was incapable of understanding the nature and effect of the transactions made by her nor had the capacity to manage her affairs independently....
>
> In the result, I accept the petition and restore the custody of Saima to her father. The parties feeling aggrieved may have recourse to the Family Court or any other court of competent jurisdiction for the redress of their grievances. Necessary police assistance may be provided to Syed Farman Ali for the safe custody of his daughter to his house.[10]

The Court thus forced a young girl, who in law is allowed to marry of her own choice, to go to her parents' house instead of with her husband.

Besides, in a recent decision of the High Court of Lahore, it has been held that the permission of the *wali* is essential for the validity of the marriage, even of an adult girl.[11] This has come as a shock to many people, especially Muslim women, who have for centuries believed that Islam has granted them rights as a fair and just religion and has ended their subjugation. The free consent of a woman for marriage in Islam has always been accepted in theory, though not always practised.

There was a strong reaction against the judgment. A large number of non-governmental organizations combined to consider the trend of misapplying Islam by limiting the rights of women, and increasing the legal constraints on them. Traditions and customs controlling women's sexuality are pitched against the needs of women to assert themselves. The increasing number of cases of marriages without parental approval to an extent indicate that there is a change in female attitudes and at least some women are raising their heads and refusing to be controlled.

Consent of *Wali*

The judgment can have an adverse effect on the situation of women in Pakistan. The ground reality is that women are already subjugated. If women have no freedom in marriage, the practice of selling girls, especially young women, will multiply. Society will degenerate. The institution of marriage, which is the keystone of women's lives, will become a commercial proposition with a price to be paid for the consent of the *wali*.

The verses of the Quran do not support the contention for the consent of the *wali*. For instance:

> *When you divorce women, and they fulfil*
> *the [Iddat], do not prevent them from*
> *marrying their (former) husband....* (2:232)

This verse clearly indicates that a woman is free to marry without interference from any person, even to remarry her former husband, within the precepts of the Holy Quran.

Though another Quranic verse as quoted in the above judgment provides:

and give not your daughter in marriage to
Al-Mushrikan till they believe in Allah. (2:221)

Yousuf Ali translated it as follows:

Do not marry
Unbelieving women (idolaters),
Until they believe;
A slave woman who believes
Is better than an unbelieving woman,
Even though she allure you.
Nor marry (your girls)
To unbelievers until
They believe. (2:221)

This is a recommendation against marrying unbelievers, but to attach and attribute to this verse the meaning that a woman cannot marry without the consent of the *wali* is completely fallacious.

There is an obligation to enter into marriage as a religious duty. To quote the Quranic verse:

And marry those among you who are single. (24:32)

Requiring the permission of the *wali* as essential for a valid nikah will deter many young and older women from marriage where the *wali* is not discernible, or not available, or not willing to allow the marriage of the woman with a person of her choice. There is a verse in the Quran, which states that,

except for these, all others are lawful, provided
you seek (them in marriage) with gifts from
your property, Desiring chastity, not lust. (4:24)

Apart from women within the prohibited degrees and married women, a man is allowed to marry any other willing woman. The only criterion is ethical, i.e. 'chastity'. There is no requirement for the consent of the *wali*. Requiring the permission of the *wali* not only curtails the Quranic rights of the female but also that of the male.

In the next verse the Quran refers to marriage with slaves and here clearly states:

Wed them with the leave of their owners. (4:25)

Requiring the consent of the *wali* equates women in Pakistan with slaves, which is an insult.

There are several books on Muslim Law by eminent scholars where there is no mention of consent of the *wali* as being essential for a valid nikah. There were several judgments of our High Courts where the rights of a *sui juris* adult woman to marry in accordance with her free will has been supported and such marriages have been held valid.

Justice (retired) Aftab Hussain (former Chief Justice of the Federal Shariat Court) opines:

Views differ on the question whether the marriage of an adult girl requires her consent only or the consent of her *wali* or guardian also. Among the Hanafis and the Shias, the capacity of an adult woman to contract her marriage is absolute. The Shia Law says that 'In the marriage of a discreet female (Rashida or adult) no guardian is required.' Hedaya says that 'A woman who is an adult, and of sound mind, may be married by virtue of her own consent, although the contract may not have been acceded to by her guardians, and this whether she be a virgin or *sayyaba*.' (*Sayyaba* is a woman who had previously been married and lived with her husband)....

Among the Shafeis and the Malikis (and not Hanafis and Shias) although the consent of the adult virgin is as essential as among the Hanafis and the Shias to the validity of the contract of marriage entered into on her behalf, she cannot contract herself in marriage without the intervention of the *wali* (guardian). The presence of the *wali* or guardian is essentially necessary to give validity to her contract...[12]

'The marriage of a free and adult woman (contracted) without (the interference of) a guardian is valid, even though the match be unequal, and though the guardian may make an objection with respect to the latter. By the mention of "a free and adult woman", it is intended that marriages of minors, lunatics, and slaves are not valid; for, it is agreed by all, that guardians are necessary for the validity of their marriages.'[13]

'Every Muslim of sound mind and having attained majority is competent to enter into a contract of marriage without the intervention of a guardian. In the event of a female contracting marriage with a socially unequal person (*ghayr kufu*) or for inequitable dower, her guardian, however, is entitled to get the marriage contract annulled through a competent court of law (proposed section 10).'[14]

Women and men in Pakistan will suffer much more from the un-Islamic Zina Ordinance if women are denied the freedom to marry of their own free will. What alternatives will be available to them but to remain single or commit suicide?

To require the consent of the *wali* for valid marriage by an adult woman would be a gross violation of the basic human rights of a woman to marry according to her free will. As some women are coming forward to assert their rights, limiting their rights by not allowing them to marry according to their choice without the consent of the *wali* will deny Pakistani women their basic human rights.

The question then arises as to who is the *wali*, especially in circumstances where the natural guardian father is dead. In the case of a widow or divorcee, will she need to go to her son, whom she bore, for his consent to remarry? This will be a return to the pre-Islamic era where the sons inherited their mothers. Are women to remain under the dominion of a male from birth to death?

There is a procedure under the Constitution of the Islamic Republic of Pakistan 1973, empowering the Federal Shariat Court to declare a law repugnant to the Quran and Sunnah as void. Can a single judge of the Lahore High Court take upon himself this function? It has been clearly set down in section 5 of the MFLO that every marriage solemnized under Muslim Law shall be registered in accordance to the provisions of the Ordinance, which includes a standard form of *nikahnama/marriage* contract. Significantly, nowhere in the entire *nikahnama* is there a mention of *wali* though there is mention of a vakil (attorney). It is debatable that so long as the MFLO 1961, section 5,[15] remains valid law in Pakistan, whether a single judge of the High Court can pronounce a marriage validly entered into under the law as void.

The so-called revival of Islam has not led to progress and protection for women as the liberals expected. On the contrary it has confined and limited women's lives.

Reinterpretations of the Quran by liberals are being overturned and conservatism has set in. This is also evident not only in the questionable Islamization of laws by President General Ziaul Haq, but also through the law enforcing agencies' actions or refusal to act. Recent decisions of the superior courts are a manifestation of the forces of conservatism applying Islamic laws limiting the rights of women. The issue of 'Consent of *Wali*' is a case in point.

Case Law

The single judge of the Lahore High Court holding that the consent of the *wali* is essential for a valid marriage referred to above, noted:

> In both the cases, although there is a slight difference in the ages of the two petitioners, namely, Mst Ayesha and Mst Shabina, Ayesha being slightly over 13 years of age, whereas Shabina is alleged to be 19 years, nevertheless there is a common ground taken by both the learned counsel for the petitioners that both are *sui juris* and are entitled to marry as per their sweet will. This is a civil contract pure and simple and any man or woman who is a major (attained puberty) and is *sui juris* is competent to enter into a contract of marriage....

On the other hand, it is contended by the learned counsel for the respondents that this is not a purely civil contract in which offer and acceptance coupled with consideration is sufficient to constitute the contract. This is an institution and an Islamic institution, which has background and detailed history and if every girl attaining puberty is allowed to run away and enter into a trap of a clever person, the fabric of the family system would stand destroyed and there will be complete anarchy in society. The writ petition, according to the learned counsel for the respondents, is baseless and deserves forthwith dismissal and the police should be allowed to investigate the matter fairly and properly, and take it to its logical conclusion....

The meaning and scope of the marriage and its nature as visualized by the courts has, to a great extent, been responsible for this tornado of sexual rebellion in the country. As referred to earlier, no attempt till today appears to have been made to reinterpret the matter in the light of the original and major sources of Islam, i.e. Quran and Sunnah. The Hon'ble Supreme Court had very clearly held in Khurshid Bibi's case (PLD 1967 SC 97) that fundamental laws of Islam are contained in the Quran and this is the primary source of law of Muslims. Next comes the Sunnah of the Holy Prophet (PBUH) and thereafter in the sequence is *ijtehad* and *ijma*.[16]

After discussing authorities, the Court opined:

Now let us examine the conditions for a valid marriage in the light of Holy Quran and Sunnah together with the views of the great jurists of Islam....

The jurists have mentioned a number of conditions for a valid marriage but there is a consensus about the following conditions that if either of them does not exist, no proper marriage takes place and in the absence of the first two conditions, namely, the consent of *wali* and the consent of the parties to nikah, a marriage, if contracted, would be *batil*, i.e. wholly void. The principal conditions are as follows:

1. Consent of *wali* or guardian.
2. Consent of the proposed husband and wife if they have attained puberty and subsequent *Ejab-o-Qabool* by them.
3. Payment of dower, and
4. Presence of two male witnesses or one male and two female witnesses....

As for the consent of the *wali*, no marriage except the marriages of the Holy Prophet (PBUH) is valid without permission of the *wali* of the woman proposed to be married....

It would thus be clear that a man and a woman are quite equal to each other in their origin, their abode as well as in their place of return, and are as such entitled to similar and equal rights. Islam gave her the right to life, to honour, and to property like men. Men and women are also equal in their rights to realize their material needs in the world including similar rights to hold property and dispose of it, as they should wish. They are free to mortgage their property, to give it in lease, or bequeath it, sell or buy it or exploit it for his or her own benefit. The Quran says:

> Unto the men belongeth a share of that which parents and near kindred leave, and unto the women a share of that which parents and near kindred leave. (4:7)

and again

> Unto men a fortune from that which they have earned, and unto women a fortune from that which they have earned (4:32).[17]

.... If the consent of *wali* is required for marriage, the consent of the bride or bridegroom is equally essential and no marriage is valid without these two consents, whereas in the West the only emphasis is on the consent of the couple which is being married and not that of their parents....

What we conclude from the aforesaid discussion is that the marriage contracted by both the petitioners in these cases is wholly void being without the consent of their *walis* and as such the cases have been rightly registered. The police would be at liberty to investigate the cases and to take them to their logical conclusions. There is no merit in the writ petitions which are hereby dismissed.[18]

Different Decision

Another case on the same question, whether a marriage nikah without the permission of the *wali* is valid, was referred to a bench of three judges of the Lahore High Court for decision. The facts were as follows:
The Court recorded:

> The father of the girl raised, *inter alia*, the following questions:
> i. Whether the parents have a right to be obeyed and their right of obedience is judicially enforceable.
> ii. Whether marriage in Islam is a civil contract.
> iii. Whether or not the permission of the *wali* is one of the main conditions of a valid nikah.[19]

It was argued by the petitioners before the Court that a virgin girl stepping out of her house without the consent of the parents can be asked to go back. Reliance was placed on the Holy Quran, and several authorities in support.

The arguments added that children are under an obligation to obey their parents. It was argued that marriage in Islam is not a civil contract and is one of the *ibadat* and, at best, may be called a social contract (compact), that the dower is not a consideration for marriage, that even acceptance by the spouses will not make the marriage a simple contract. It was argued that nikah without the consent of the *wali*/father is not valid. The learned judges made reference to the prevailing conditions in Western countries, particularly noting that there are 33 per cent single mothers in the UK and the divorce rate is increasing and that America witnessed a sharp rise in illegitimacy, the latest figures being 33 per cent.

> It was added that it has wrongly been attributed to Imam Abu Hanifa that nikah without the consent of the *wali* is valid. It was explained that Imam Abu Hanifa had not written any book himself and his views were not recorded in the authentic book written by his pupils or contemporaries.... It was submitted that it is a matter of common knowledge that runaway marriages are not solemnized

in accordance with the principles of Islam. There is even no proper nikah because no nikah *khawan* is prepared to perform the nikah ceremony, no registrar is prepared to register nikah, no person is willing to witness the same and show his participation because they are all afraid of being involved in a case under Offence of Zina (Enforcement of Hudood) Ordinance 1979....

It was argued that it is clear from verse 2:232 that the *wali* was restrained from not standing in the way of a woman remarrying her previous husband. This clearly was an exception to the rule that the *wali* is to arrange for the marriage of his dependent females. There is a complete unity of views (*ijma*) of Sahaba Kiram (RZA) on this point. [20]

The respondent, Ms Asma Jehangir, in reply before the Court countered the contentions of the petitioner and relied on a number of authorities, especially case law. She contended that the superior courts have normally permitted the girl *sui juris* to have her own way. She explained that a different view was taken in some cases, but this was mostly on account of the girl being a minor or there being no *nikahnama* or more than one *nikahnama*.

It was maintained that normally the courts have allowed a female detenue to have her own way. This is the rule. It was argued that restraint on movements of females against their will is unconstitutional and would result in violation of Articles 10, 11, 14, 15, 20, and 25 of the Constitution. She submitted that the fundamental rights should not be violated.

One of the judges on the bench, Mr Justice Ihsan-ul-Haq Chaudhry noted:

In fact the commands of Almighty God with reference to marriage are to the women and not to the men. We have already recorded that there cannot be a marriage without the consent of the female. A marriage forced on her is not a valid marriage in accordance with the injunctions of Islam....

In my humble opinion this not only was in line with the command of the Holy Quran but also supported the above Hadith that a woman cannot marry herself. It is a matter of common knowledge that this mode is in vogue in the Muslim society including this Sub-Continent till today.... We have recorded our views on the point with reference to the Holy Quran, Ahadith, *Ijma,* and in the historical perspective. The admitted position is that there is a difference of opinion on the point amongst *A'imma* and *Faqihs.* Assuming that there is no Quranic verse or Hadith or *Ijma* on this point then this Court may form its own opinion....

Section 3 of the Shariat Act 1991, Shariat is the supreme law of the country.... It is, therefore, held that Mst Saima Waheed and Arshad were not validly married....

It is made clear that the rule as to participation of the *wali* in the marriage would have no application to the marriages solemnized in the past except those which are the subject matter of this and other connected petitions. [21]

Justice Khalil-ur-Rehman Ramday, the second judge on the bench held:

The one crucial question, amongst others, which is common in all these petitions is as to whether such a nikah marriage, surreptitiously contracted, by a male or a female of his or her own accord and otherwise than through (a *wali,* a guardian, or an elder) was or was not valid in terms of the injunctions of Islam?.... Islam hastened to recognize a female as an independent legal entity, vested with all legal rights....[22]

After considering several authorities he held that:

This brings me to the conclusions that I draw from all that has been discussed by me above and the same are as follows:
a) invalidating a marriage entails rather serious and even penal consequences not only for the wife and the husband but even for the innocent children born out of such a union. Such a declaration could, therefore, not be given unless material was available which was of an unimpeachable character admitting of no doubt. The authenticity of the Ahadith relied upon for the purpose is not incontrovertible. Therefore, it could not be said that the marriages in question were invalid and I hold accordingly;
b) the consent of the man and the woman who are getting married is an indispensable condition for the validity of a marriage and

the *wali* has no right to grant such a consent on behalf of the woman without her approval;

c) Islam abhors establishment of liaisons between men and women and courtships, pre-marital relationship, secret friendships, and secret marriages are forbidden in Islam....

I would further recommend that the Legislature also consider the advisability of making such-like immoral relationships and secret marriages etc., a penal offence....[23]

The judge held that the marriage in question contracted without the consent of the *wali* is valid.

Justice Malik Muhammad Qayyum, the third judge on the bench, did not agree with the finding of Justice Ihsan-ul-Haq Chaudhry and held that 'I have despite my best efforts not been able to discover any principle on the basis of which it can be held that nikah of *sui juris* Muslim girl without consent of her *wali* would be invalid.'[24]

It was thus held by a majority judgment of two judges 'that the marriage in question contracted without the consent of the *wali* is not invalid'.[25]

The judgments have been reproduced in detail as they indicate present-day viewpoints. The proposition advanced is that it is highly immoral for a girl to choose her own partner even though admitting that Islam allows a woman the freedom to marry the man of her choice without the consent of any *wali*.

At present, the question of a girl marrying without the consent of the family is being debated in several quarters. Such marriages though allowed in Islam, result in complaints of zina (adultery/fornication) by the parents of the girl and also result in the serious crime of *karo kari* (honour killings), which are increasing daily.

Appeals have been filed before the Supreme Court against the judgment of a single judge holding that the consent of the *wali* is essential and against the full bench judgment that consent of the *wali* is not necessary for a valid nikah marriage. The Supreme Court has granted leave to appeal in both cases.[26]

The judges in the above High Court case have recommended reforms. PAWLA Legal Aid Centre is often faced with the dilemma of very young girls entering into nikah marriage without the knowledge or consent of their parents. Recently, there was a case of a girl of twelve, claiming to be married to a man four times her age and pregnant by him. The mother had filed the complaint of zina. The police had arrested the girl and held her at the police station. The man had disappeared.

The police are prosecuting the girl for zina on the grounds that she was not validly married, thus she was sent to jail. It will take a long time to get the case dismissed. The girl did not want to be bailed out as her husband is also in jail and she did not want to go back to her mother, as she feared being sold in marriage to another man. PAWLA is defending the case of the girl and her husband.

Age of Marriage

Connected with the issue of parental consent for the marriage of a young girl is the question of establishing the appropriate age at which a girl should be free to marry.

Under the Majority Act of 1875,[27] a person ceases to be a minor on the completion of 18 years. Section 2 of the Act, however, makes an exception in matters relating to marriage, dower, adoption, and divorce, where personal law takes precedence. Thus, for the purpose of marriage where the parties are Muslim, the rule of Muslim Law must apply, according to which any person who has attained puberty is entitled to act in the matter of marriage.

Under the Child Marriage Restraint Act of 1929[28] as amended by section 12 of the Muslim Family Laws Ordinance 1961, the minimum age for marriage for females is 16 years and for males 18 years. Under the Act a female under the age of 16 years is defined as a 'child' and it is an offence to marry her. A marriage contracted after the attainment of puberty and before the age of 16 years for females and 18 years for males, is valid under Muslim Law. The Child Marriage Restraint Act does not make such a marriage invalid or void.

The Act prescribes punishment for the male above the age of 18 years marrying a child (that is a female below the age of 16 years), for the person who performs, conducts, or directs any child marriage, and for the person in charge of the minor. The female who enters into a child marriage is not liable to any punishment under the Act.

The Child Marriage Restraint Act was enacted in 1929, to restrain the solemnization of child marriage. Originally, under the Act a child was defined as a female below the age of 14 years, and male below the age of 18 years. Subsequently, under the Muslim Family Laws Ordinance 1961, this was amended so that a female below the age of 16 years is defined as a child.

There are defects in the Child Marriage Restraint Act, as section 9 provides that 'No court shall take cognizance of any offence under this Act except on a complaint made by the Union Council, or if there is no Union Council in the area, by such authority as the provincial government may prescribe....'

In most cases immediate action is needed to stop a child marriage and there is little possibility of invoking the Union Council or the provincial authority to take action under the Act.

Section 12 has empowered the court to issue an injunction prohibiting marriage in contravention of this Act, where the court is satisfied, from information laid before it through a complaint or otherwise, that a child marriage is being arranged. No doubt the clause 'through a complaint or otherwise' has widened the scope. However, subsection 2 requires that a notice has to be issued before granting any injunction. This weakens the section for granting injunctions. It is well known that serving notice to the party complained against is not an easy process and the respondents often refuse to receive the notice.

The law should be amended so as to allow the complaint to be made by any aggrieved or concerned person and to permit *ad-interim* injunctions against the person intending to perform child marriage or the parents and guardians, without notice to the respondent.

There is need for another reform. It is recommended that a girl should be of a minimum age of 18 years to enter into a valid marriage, after which she is free to enter into marriage of her free will. A marriage before the age of 18 years without the consent of the parents should not be recognized as valid. This will go a long way to protect the girl child from forcible or persuasive sex and other abuses and meet the parents' concerns in most cases. It will prevent nefarious men from enticing the girl child for marriage, especially with ulterior motives.

The Act has not had the effect of being an immediate deterrent to child marriage. Gradually, by the force of circumstances such as education, awareness, and changes in customs, the Act has been instrumental in defining norms for the minimum age of marriage.

Rising Age of Marriage

The following table shows the percentage of married males and females at different ages in Pakistan.

AGE	MARRIED FEMALES (%)	MARRIED MALES (%)
15-19	18.2	03.5
20-24	65.7	29.3
25-29	90.0	66.5
30-34	96.8	88.1
35-39	98.4	95.1
40-44	98.2	97.1
45-49	98.5	98.0

Source: Pakistan Demographic Survey, 1997. Federal Bureau of Statistics Division. Published by the Manager of Publications, Government of Pakistan, Karachi, September 2000, p. 31.

According to the above table, nearly 82 per cent females in the age group 15-19 were single in 1997 as compared to 25 per cent in the 1961 population census. This indicates more than a threefold increase in thirty-six years in the percentage of unmarried females between the age of 15 to 19 years.

'Comparing the proportion of never-married females by age from various data sources, it is evident that the age at marriage is rising. For instance, the proportions of never-married females in the age group of 15-19 years increased about 2 per cent in 1997 as compared to 1995. The percentage of never-married females in the age group of 20-24 years also increased by 4 per cent for the same period. When compared with the 1961 census, the corresponding proportions of these age groups showed a remarkable increase.'[29]

The accuracy of these figures is debatable. Many respondents, especially among married females, claimed to be older than they were.

There are customary social pressures on families for protecting the chastity of women, which force them to marry their daughters young. In a number of cases parents arrange their daughter's marriage before the age of 16 years. There is a feeling in many families that the daughter is a liability and a responsibility, and parents are inclined to find suitable matches for their daughters and arrange marriages even before she has attained the age of 16 years. Even though the age of marriage is continuously rising, it cannot be said that the Child Marriage Restraint Act is closely adhered to by one and all. In rural communities marriages do take place before the girl reaches the minimum prescribed 16 years. In most families, especially in urban areas the age of marriage of females and males is usually above the prescribed minimum of 16 years and 18 years.

Demographic studies indicate that there is a rise in the age at marriage of both males and females. This suggests healthy social changes in the attitudes of families towards the marriage of their daughters, and means the fuller development of girls both physically and mentally before they enter matrimony. The trend towards later marriages can be harnessed to educate and train young girls and can lead to their personal development and more meaningful economic contribution towards family and society.

NOTES

1. 'Cousin-marriages main cause of abnormal births', *Dawn*, 15 November 2001, p. 21, quoted from the statement of Chief Executive on Science and Technology, Dr Abdul Qadeer Khan, at a Seminar on Awareness in Society for the Needs of Special Children.
2. Abdel Rahim Omran, *Family Planning in the Legacy of Islam*, pp. 22 and 23, published by Routledge, a division of Routledge, Chapman and Hall, Inc., 29 West, 35th Street, New York, NY 10001, 1992.
3. Dr Rafat Hussain, 'The Effect of Marriage Preferences on Women's Autonomy: A Case Study,' p. 15. Presented at the Conference on Pakistan's Population Issues in the 21st Century, 24-26 October 2000, Karachi, Pakistan. Organized by Population Council and Aga Khan University.
4. Benazir Bhutto, *Daughter of the East*, p. 28. Hamish Hamilton Limited published by the Penguin Group, 27 Wrights Lane, London W8 5TZ, England, 1988.
5. Neil B.E. Baillie, *A Digest of Muhammadan Law*, Premier Book, Lahore, Fourth Impression 1963, p. 23.
6. Dr Fahmida Hussain translated by Dr Amjad Siraj Memon, *The Images of Women*, published by Shah Abdul Latif Bhittai Chair, University of Karachi 2001.
7. Nazira Bibi vs. SHO, PLD 1996, Lahore 709 (b).
8. Mohammad Imtiaz and others vs. the State, PLD 1981, FSC 308.
9. Mst Bakshi vs. Bashir Ahmed and others, PLD 1970, SC 323, p. 324.
10. Syed Farman Ali vs. Abid Ali and others, PLD 1995, Lahore 364, pp. 373, 375, 376.
11. Mst Ayesha Ijaz vs. SHO, 1997, MLD 641.
12. Justice Aftab Hussain (former Chief Justice of the FSC), *Status of Women in Islam*. Published by Law Publishing Company, Kachery Road, Lahore, Pakistan, 1987, pp. 455 and 456.
13. S.C. Sircar, *Al-Sharia'a (Sunni and Imamiyah Code)* Vol. I, p. 320, deducted from: Fatwa-i-Alamgiri, Fatwa-i-Sirahiyyah, Sharifiyyah, Sirajiyyah, Durr-ul-Mukhtar, Hidaya, Shary-ul-Vikayah, Jami'ur Ramuz, Sharaya-ul-Islam, Rouzat-ul-Ahkam, Mufatih, Irshad, and Tahrir-ul-Ahkam. Published by Law Publishing Company, Kachery Road, Lahore, Pakistan.
14. Dr Tanzil-ur-Rehman, *A Code of Muslim Personal Law* (Proposed). Published by Law Publishing Company, Kachery Road, Lahore, Pakistan, 1987.
15. Muslim Family Laws Ordinance 1961, PLD 1961, CS, Gazette of Pakistan, 2 March 1961.
16. Ayesha Ijaz vs. SHO, MLD 1997, pp. 641, 655 and 656.

17. Ibid, at p. 660.
18. Ibid., pp. 670-72.
19. Hafiz Abdul Waheed vs. Miss Asma Jehangir, PLD 1997, Lahore 301.
20. Ibid., pp. 318 and 319.
21. Ibid., p. 351.
22. Ibid.
23. Ibid., pp. 380 and 381.
24. Ibid.
25. Ibid., p. 384.
26. Muhammad Iqbal vs. SHO, Batala Colony, Faisalabad and others, 1997, SCMR 987.
27. The Pakistan Code, Vol. II, p. 224.
28. The Pakistan Code, Vol. VIII 1966, p. 430.
29. Ibid., p. 32.

3

DIVORCE

In today's world, the Quranic verses are not only misinterpreted by Muslim countries, including Pakistan, but are being destroyed, denying women their Quranic human rights. Technological advances are being misused to further hamper women's rights. Recently, the Muslim community in Dubai, Singapore, and Malaysia has been faced with the problem of the wife receiving a Short Message Service (SMS) on the phone with the words, 'You are divorced'. In Pakistan we are often faced with similar unilateral talaq by courier, telephone, fax, or e-mail. This is immoral and un-Islamic. When the *nikahnama* has to be with the consent of both parties and is in the nature of a contract creating mutual rights and obligations, how can the contract of marriage be dissolved unilaterally by the husband?

The Fatal Pronouncement

In Pakistan there were three different forms of divorce, which were accepted in law, in practice, and by the majority of ulema. The first type of talaq is Talaq-i-Bidat, which is a single pronouncement of talaq three times consecutively, 'talaq, talaq, talaq,' resulting in dissolution of marriage. This form is commonly adopted by Hanafi Sunni Muslims. The other form is Talaq-i-Ahsan, in which the husband pronounces one talaq during a *tuhr*, or period between menstruation, during which cohabitation has not taken place between the parties and then abstains from cohabitation during the *iddat*, after which dissolution of marriage takes place. The third form, Talaq-i-

Hasan, is effected when the husband pronounces talaq during a *tuhr* in which he has not had sexual relations with his wife and then repeats the talaq during the next two *tuhrs*. The Shias recognize only the two latter types of talaq, which are the approved forms of talaq, also known as Talaq-us-Sunnat.

Misinterpretations of Islam have made it possible for a husband to unilaterally pronounce talaq, talaq, talaq and what was commonly accepted as a valid talaq/divorce ensued. Home, husband, and children were all lost to the wife by one fatal pronouncement and she could well end up on the streets, unprotected. In many cases, the husband usually does not fulfil his obligations and comply with the wife's needs or recognize her rights to dower, dowry, maintenance, her property in his control, or the custody of the children. For these rights the wife has to knock on the doors of law courts and it can take time for redressal.

The Quranic provision for reconciliation did not exist in law. It was not accepted, it was not countenanced. The ineffective Muslim Family Laws Ordinance 1961 has tried to bring into operation the need for a conciliation council.

The common misconception is that Islam gives the Muslim husband the right of pronouncing talaq, talaq, talaq without any reason, preconditions, impediments, limitations, and without complying with his manifold obligations in Islam. This is in contradiction to the Holy Quran.

The Quran provides:

> *When ye divorce*
> *Women, and they fulfil*
> *The term of their (iddat),*
> *Either take them back*
> *On equitable terms*
> *Or set them free*
> *On equitable terms;*
> *But do not take them back*
> *To injure them, (or) to take*
> *Undue advantage...* (2:231)

The repeated emphasis in the verse on 'equitable terms' is a definite limitation on the misunderstood unilateral, unlimited right of the man to pronounce talaq without considering the justification of his act, or the repercussions on the wife and children by the pronouncement of talaq. The Islamic concept of *Adl,* signifying equity, which has been repeated several times in the Holy Quran in Surah Nisa dealing with women, has been negated.

For again the Quran says:

> *...if ye fear a breach*
> *Between them twain,*
> *Appoint (two) arbiters,*
> *One from his family,*
> *And the other from hers;*
> *If they wish for peace,*
> *God will cause*
> *Their reconciliation;*
> *For God hath full knowledge,*
> *And is acquainted*
> *With all things.* (4:35)

Accordingly, if there has to be a divorce, both parties, the husband and wife, through their representatives have to be involved in the process. This verse clearly envisages that where a breach or dissolution is feared, the process of conciliation between the parties must be set in motion for settling the dispute. In many advanced countries, sociologists and family counsellors are advocating alternative forums for the resolution of disputes.

It is suggested that a law should be introduced making it obligatory for the husband to comply with his Islamic obligations and liabilities of paying Huq Mehar, maintenance, return of dowry and custody of minors and satisfy the court on this behalf before the talaq being given by the husband becomes effective. The Pakistan Law Commission has not considered changing the current practice of the husband's talaq to the wife without reason and without complying with the husband's liability in law and in Islam, of paying Huq Mehar, returning dowry, paying maintenance, giving custody of the children to the wife, and arranging for their support.

On the contrary the all-male Commission had proposed the Family Courts (Amendment) Ordinance 2001, wherein it recommended making it compulsory that the wife seeking dissolution of marriage shall also claim in the plaint her dower, dowry, personal property, maintenance, custody of children, or visitation rights to avoid multiplicity of suits.[1]

This procedure if legislated will become a burden on the wife and will complicate and multiply the issues before the court and delay the divorce proceedings initiated by the wife. The time taken for the court to grant a divorce to a woman would increase fourfold. Often the husband does not contest a divorce suit filed by the wife, but if all the above issues were to be included he would definitely contest the suit. Moreover, in cases where the wife had custody of the children she would have been unable to ask for a divorce, even if she needed one and was entitled to one, as she would be afraid of losing her children. The harassed wife will be faced with impediments and delays while seeking the dissolution of her marriage. The Pakistan Women Lawyers' Association (PAWLA) had sent a strong protest to the Law Commission. The government accepted this and as a result the conditions recommended by the Family Courts (Amendment) Ordinance were not made compulsory. Therefore, while the wife could include in the plaint for dissolution of marriage any other claims, she was also free to take them up later as required. PAWLA also recommended that the husband when divorcing his wife must pay her mehar, return her dowry articles, pay her maintenance, give her custody of minor children as required under the law, and arrange for the payment of their maintenance. It further recommended that the husband's presently accepted unilateral right to divorce his wife without any reason be curtailed. Besides, the man who pronounces talaq through no fault of the wife should also be required to pay compensation to the wife. This will be in keeping with the spirit of Islam, as the Quran commands: 'Set them free on equitable terms'. There has been no positive response from the Pakistan Law Commission or the government.

The Prophet (PBUH) has said that the most hated thing in his eyes is talaq. This clearly denotes, in accordance with the Quranic verses quoted above, that there is no unilateral right by the husband to pronounce talaq without valid reason or justification. The talaq should not become effective without the process of reconciliation as set down in the above verses and without the husband complying with his obligations.

Unfortunately in Pakistan, not only has religion been politicized, but also pseudo-religious misinterpretations are put forward to exploit and perpetuate un-Islamic laws, practices, and norms. Today we have feudal Islam, a clergy dictated, sect interpreted Islam, not Quranic Islam.

> *And women shall have rights*
> *Similar to the rights*
> *Against them, according*
> *To what is equitable.* (2:228)

It follows from the above-quoted Quranic verse that women have equal rights with men, yet this is not the policy of the law in Pakistan. In the so-called Islamic Republic of Pakistan the human rights granted to women by the Quran are circumvented and denied.

In Pakistan today, a male who wishes to divorce his wife has only to pronounce 'talaq, talaq, talaq' and submit a notice to the Chairman of the local council, under the Muslim Family Laws Ordinance 1961. If no reconciliation takes place within a period of ninety days the divorce becomes final. The woman, however, does not have a similar right. Even when she wishes to dissolve her marriage by khula (dissolution of marriage at the instance of the wife, where she forgoes benefits received or receivable in consideration of the marriage) she is required to file a suit for dissolution of marriage.

Talaq, Talaq, Talaq

Often, the husband regrets his hasty action and is keen to reverse it and take his wife back. The ulema belonging to the Hanafi sect issued a fatwa declaring that the marriage stands dissolved by the pronouncement of three talaqs consecutively. As there is a strong opinion that the Quran provides for reconciliation and as the MFLO 1961 provides for notice to the Chairman and a reconciliation period of ninety days, there is a continuing controversy.

The question arises as to the effect of three talaqs pronounced consecutively to the wife. Can the talaq be revoked? Certain verses from the Holy Quran are relevant:

> *When ye divorce*
> *Women, and they fulfil*
> *The term of their (iddat)*
> *Either take them back*
> *On equitable terms*
> *Or set them free*
> *On equitable terms;*
> *But do not take them back*
> *To injure them, (or) to take*
> *Undue advantage;*
> *If any one does that,*
> *He wrongs his own soul.*
> *Do not treat God's signs*
> *As a jest,*
> *But solemnly rehearse.* (2:231)

The first line of verse 231 is significant as it states 'When ye divorce women, and they fulfil the term of their (*iddat*) either take them back on equitable terms or set them free on equitable terms,' which means that the divorce as a final break in the husband and wife relationship is at abeyance even after the pronouncement of talaq. All through the period of *iddat* the husband can recall his pronouncement of talaq and he can withdraw the talaq right up to the last day of *iddat*. Nowhere is it stated in this verse that the talaq pronounced thrice simultaneously results in an irrevocable termination of the marriage. Thus, a talaq pronounced thrice at one sitting is subject to the same condition of being revocable.

> The termination of the marriage bond is a most serious matter for family and social life. And every lawful device is approved which can equitably bring back those who have lived together provided only there is mutual love and they can live on honourable terms with each other. If these conditions are fulfilled, it is not right for outsiders to prevent or hinder reunion. They may be swayed by property or other considerations. This verse was occasioned by an actual case that was referred to the Holy Apostle (PBUH) in his lifetime.[2]

Surah 2:228 is important as it is addressed to divorced women and prescribed the period of *iddat* and clearly states:

> *...And their husbands*
> *Have the better right*
> *To take them back...* (2:228)

This clearly indicates that, in accordance with the Holy Quran, the husband has the right to withdraw the talaq pronounced by him and he is entitled to take his wife back....

> Islam tries to maintain the married state as far as possible, especially where children are concerned, but it is against the restriction of the liberty of men and women in such vitally important matters as love and family life. It will check hasty action as far as possible, and leave the door to reconciliation open at many stages. Even after divorce a suggestion of reconciliation is made, subject to certain precautions (mentioned in the following verse) against thoughtless action.
>
> A period of waiting (*iddat*) for three monthly courses is prescribed in order to see if the marriage conditionally dissolved is likely to result in issue. But this is not necessary where the divorced woman is a virgin; Q xxxiii. 49. It is definitely declared that women and men shall have similar rights against each other.[3]

Verse 35 of Surah Nisa states that if a breach is feared between the husband and the wife two arbiters are to be appointed by each of them, and if they wish for peace God will cause their reconciliation. Taking this into consideration, it becomes evident that the Holy Quran is all for continuance of marriage and reconciliation between husband and wife and is in favour of attempts to stop a marriage from being dissolved.

> *Divorce is only*
> *Permissible twice: after that*
> *The parties should either hold*
> *Together on equitable terms*
> *Or separate in kindness....* (2:229)

This verse must be read with the previous verse. It cannot be construed separately. It means that a man who divorces his wife twice—that is on two separate occasions and the divorce becomes final twice—cannot remarry her. It cannot be deduced from this verse that if a man pronounces 'talaq, talaq, talaq' consecutively on one occasion that single pronouncement amounts to three divorces and becomes irrevocable. Such an interpretation is erroneous and not supported by the verses of the Holy Quran with reference to the process of reconciliation. To misread the word 'twice' to mean simultaneous pronouncement on one occasion would be giving it the wrong connotation.

Dr Meerh Nasani in his famous book, *History of Muslim Law*, has recounted events, which unequivocally support the view that during the period of the Holy Prophet (PBUH) the injunctions of the Holy Quran which correspond with Talaq-i-Ahsan and Talaq-i-Hasan were strictly followed and the pronouncement of three talaqs at a single sitting was regarded as only one pronouncement.

It is reported that the Prophet (PBUH) was told of a Muslim who pronounced three divorces against his wife at the same time whereupon the Prophet (PBUH) stood up in anger and exclaimed that the man was making a plaything of the Book of Allah (Ahmed B Ali Al Nasa 1 Sunam, Delhi nd. vii p. 98). It is clear that it was not permissible or acceptable to the Holy Prophet (PBUH) that a husband pronounces three talaqs at one sitting as a valid form of divorce.

The pronouncement of three talaqs at one sitting has always been called Talaq-i-Bidat by jurists. Talaq-i-Bidat means 'undesirable innovation'. The very name condemns it as un-Islamic.

Those who consider that a divorce pronounced three times in succession and in one session, or written down on one piece of paper counts as three divorces rely on a ruling by Calipha Hazrat Umar al-Khattab who, as a ruler of the Islamic state, enforced that piece of regulation. Hazrat Umar meant it as a punishment befitting the misbehaviour of people who precipitate the irrevocability of divorce by divorcing their wives three times in succession. It has unfortunately become an accepted mode of talaq by Muslims who do not comprehend that it violates both the Holy Quran and the Hadith.

According to authentic Hadith reported by Abdullah Ibn Abbas:

> Rukhsan Ibn Abbas divorced his wife three times at the same place and then he was full of grief for having done so.
> Allah's Messenger (PBUH) asked him, 'How did you divorce her?'
> Rukhsan said, 'I have divorced her thrice.'
> The Prophet (PBUH) asked him, 'In one session?'
> He answered yes. The Prophet said 'That is one divorce and you may return to her if you wish.' He revoked the divorce and remarried her.

K.N. Ahmed in his book *Muslim Law of Divorce* discusses the question of triple pronouncement at length. He states that 'there is great controversy regarding the effect of triple pronouncement of divorce at one and the same time.... Abu Hanifa has stated that the three pronouncements shall amount to three separate divorces so that they shall result in a *Mughallazah* or final divorce.'[4]

The view of Imam Abu Hanifa and Hanafi jurists must be read in light of the fact that Imam Abu Hanifa was of the opinion that if there is no urgent need for release from the marriage tie, the divorce is *haram* (forbidden). (Ibn Abidin Al Shammi, Radd al Mukhtar, Cairo 1318 AH.) Muslim jurists have held different views regarding divorce in Islam. According to some, divorce is prohibited but it is permissible in case of necessity. It is stated in Radd al Mukhtar dealing with Hanafi Law that no doubt divorce is forbidden, but it becomes permitted (*mubah*) for certain reasons. Most Muslim jurists while discussing talaq say that talaq being itself a pernicious and disapproved procedure, it is only the urgency of release that can give it sanction.

Therefore, when considering the effect of pronouncement of three talaqs at one sitting under Hanafi Law, the first thing that needs to be considered is whether the pronouncement of talaq was *mubah* (permissible) due to an urgent need for the release of the marriage tie or whether the pronouncement of talaq in itself becomes *haram* (forbidden). If the husband realizes his mistake and wishes to resile from his act, forbidden under Islam and Hanafi Muslim Law, and withdraws the talaq pronounced thrice at one sitting, there is nothing in religion or Hanafi Law to disallow him to do so, especially in view of the fact that the Holy Quran, which is the primary source of Muslim Law, gives him the right to do so.

Islam has permitted the dissolution of marriage in case of necessity, but dissolution has been strongly disapproved of and discouraged. A divorce in the proper form, laid down in the Quran, becomes final and absolute only after the observance of *iddat* and so ample time is given to the husband to think over the matter coolly and to retrieve his action if he so decides. The main idea in the procedure for divorce, as laid down by Islam, is to give the parties an opportunity for reconciliation. If the three pronouncements are treated as a *Mughallazah* divorce, then no opportunity is given to the spouse or the husband to retrieve a hasty divorce. This rule was introduced long after the time of the Prophet (PBUH) and it renders ineffective the measure provided in the Quran against hasty action thereby depriving people of a chance to change their minds, retrieve their mistakes, and retain their wives. The object of the Caliph Umar in treating it as a *Mughallazah* divorce was clearly to stop people from treating the matter of divorce in a light and non-serious way. It must have suited the needs of his own time, but the practice in modern times has resulted in a great deal of harm.[5]

The reforms of Muhammad (PBUH) marked a new departure in the history of Eastern legislation. He restrained the power of divorce possessed by husbands, he gave to the woman the right of obtaining a separation on reasonable grounds, and towards the end of his life he went as far as practically to forbid its exercise by men without the intervention of arbiters or a judge. He pronounced talaq to be the most detestable before Almighty God of all permitted things, for it prevented conjugal happiness and interfered with the proper bringing up of children. The permission, therefore, in the Quran, though it gave a certain countenance to the old customs, has to be read in light of the Lawgiver's own words. When it is borne in mind how intimately law and religion are connected in the Islamic system, it will be easy to understand the bearings of the words on the institution of divorce.[6]

The author of the *Multeka* (Ibrahim Halebi) says: 'The law gives the man primarily the power of dissolving the marriage, if the wife by her bad character, renders married life unhappy, but in the absence of serious reasons, no Muslim can justify a divorce either in the eyes of religion or in the law. If he abandons his wife or puts her away for simple caprice, he draws upon himself the divine anger, for the curse of God, said the Prophet, rests on him who repudiates his wife capriciously.'[7]

Islam has been misinterpreted to allow a husband to unilaterally pronounce divorce by talaq on his wife without any justification, without any fault of the wife, without caring for her welfare and for the children. The injunction in the Holy Quran for *Adl* is completely ignored by the man-made law of divorce allowing unbridled right to a Muslim husband to divorce his wife.

Misinterpretation of the Holy Quran and Sunnah made it possible in Muslim Law for a man to pronounce 'talaq, talaq, talaq' at a single sitting without any reason, and what was accepted as a valid divorce ensued. The Quranic provisions for recalling the talaq during the period of *iddat* was completely ignored.

The above authorities and discussion make it clear that a Muslim husband has the right and the power to withdraw three talaqs simultaneously pronounced. The Holy Quran and the Hadith both allow and encourage the practice of this right. Unfortunately, in Pakistan unilateral divorce by the husband without any fault of the wife and even Talaq-i-Bidat is accepted as a valid divorce.

Muslim Law as Applicable in Pakistan

The Muslim Family Laws Ordinance 1961 endeavours to incorporate the procedures for reconciliation before divorce to a limited extent in line with the Quran. It provides for an Arbitration Council, with a Chairman and two arbitrators, one on behalf of the husband and one on behalf of the wife, but only for the purpose of reconciliation. The husband's so-called Islamic unilateral right to divorce his wife remains intact, except that the procedures of notice of divorce for purposes of reconciliation have to be adhered to.

Section 7 of the Ordinance requires that:

a) Any man who wishes to divorce his wife shall, as soon as may be, after the pronouncement of talaq in any form whatsoever, give the Chairman notice in writing of having done so, and shall supply a copy thereof to the wife.

   Whoever contravenes this provision shall be punishable with simple imprisonment for a term which may extend to one year or with fine up to Rs 5000, or with both.

b) A talaq shall not become effective, unless revoked earlier, until the expiration of ninety days on which notice is delivered to the Chairman.

c) The husband can revoke the talaq before it becomes effective, that is before the expiry of the ninety-day period. The revocation of talaq can be express or otherwise.

d) If the wife is pregnant at the time talaq is pronounced, the talaq shall not be until the ninety-day period from the date of delivery of the notice of talaq, or the pregnancy, whichever is later, ends.

e) Nothing shall debar a wife whose marriage was terminated by talaq from remarrying the same husband without an intervening marriage with a third person, unless such termination has become effective for the third time.

f) The Chairman is required within thirty days of receipt of a notice of pronouncement of talaq, to constitute an Arbitration Council for the purpose of bringing about reconciliation between the parties, and the Arbitration Council shall take all necessary steps to bring about such reconciliation.[8]

The Ordinance lays down the procedure to be adopted by the husband after the pronouncement of talaq. It is obligatory for the husband to give notice of the pronouncement of talaq to the Chairman and a copy thereof to the wife, and the talaq does not become effective before the expiry of ninety days from the day the notice of pronouncement of talaq is received by the Chairman.

Soon after the promulgation of the Muslim Family Laws Ordinance 1961, the first important case decided by the Supreme Court, which aroused a great deal of public interest and also interpreted the Ordinance was the case of Ali Nawaz Gardezi vs. Lt.-Col. Muhammad Yusuf.

The Supreme Court held:

> ... The talaq pronounced to be ineffective for a period of ninety days from the date of notice under section (1) is delivered to the Chairman and this period is to be utilized for the attempt at reconciliation.[9]

In recent times, especially in criminal cases under the Zina Ordinance, there have been different opinions by the High Court on this issue with no unanimity. The Supreme Court in 1994 has set aside the Karachi High Court judgment that section 7 of the MFLO 1961 is in violation of Islamic injunctions, which is discussed later. Therefore, the MFLO is a valid and effective law in Pakistan.

A more recent judgment on the subject was passed in 2000 by the Federal Shariat Court. Deciding several petitions challenging the provisions of the MFLO 1961, the Court held that:

> It may also be of benefit to express our firm view that the period of *iddat* is to commence from the date of pronouncement of talaq and not from the day of delivery of notice to the Chairman as the talaq takes effect from the date of pronouncement of talaq by the husband. Now it may well be that the husband may not give notice of talaq as required by subsection 1 of section 7 with ill-intention for a long time, and thus, by virtue of subsection 3 keep the woman in suspended animation and cause her torture by keeping her bound, although according to the Quranic injunction she would stand released of the bond and under no obligation towards him. This will certainly be a cruelty to the woman by an unscrupulous husband if she marries after the expiry of *iddat* as enjoined by the Holy Quran but before the expiry of the period prescribed by subsection 3 (ibid). Such a situation of uncertainty entailing peril to a party should not be allowed to continue....
>
> Section 7 of the Muslim Family Laws Ordinance 1961 as a whole cannot be declared as violative of the injunctions of Islam. However, the provisions contained in subsection 3 and subsection 5 of the said section 7 cannot be maintained. Resultantly we declare that subsection 3 and subsection 5 of section 7 of Muslim Family Laws Ordinance 1961 are repugnant to the injunctions of Islam and it is directed that the President of the Islamic Republic of Pakistan shall take steps to amend the law so as to bring the above provisions into conformity with the injunctions of Islam. The above provisions of subsection 3 and subsection 5 which have been held to be repugnant to the injunctions of Islam shall cease to have effect on the 31st day of March 2000.[10]

This means that section 7 of the Ordinance becomes redundant. If the period is to start from the date of the pronouncement of talaq by the husband, irrespective of the date of notice to the Chairman, it will become possible for the husband to completely disregard the requirement under the MFLO for notice of talaq and a copy thereof to the wife. Especially as despite the above-quoted dictum of the Gardezi case that a divorce does not become effective before the expiry of ninety days from the date of notice to the Chairman, there has been subsequent case law holding that the talaq becomes effective notwithstanding notice to the Chairman.

It is common practice for most Sunni *Alims* except the *Ahle-Hadis* to give fatwa that a triple pronouncement of talaq by the husband immediately becomes effective and cannot be withdrawn by him. Thus, in a number of cases where the husband realizes his mistake and in the interests of the children and family he wishes to withdraw the talaq he is precluded from doing so. The judgment of the Shariat Court has in effect controverted these fatwas by stating that *iddat* starts from the date of pronouncement of talaq and not from the date of notice to the Chairman. It is clearly implied that the talaq may be withdrawn within ninety days of the pronouncement by the husband.

An appeal has been filed against the afore-noted judgment. The directions of the Federal Shariat Court are automatically at abeyance till a decision on the issue is made by the Shariat Bench of the Supreme Court.

Shia Law of Divorce

In Shia Law talaq has to be pronounced three times separately during three *tuhrs* in the set form of *sega*, in the presence of two reliable witnesses. Several High Court rulings and a recent Supreme Court ruling have endorsed this view. 'Marriage cannot be dissolved unless in the presence of two witnesses of "known probity" in a set form of Arabic words. The Shias insist on the presence of two male witnesses of approved probity at the pronouncement, which must be in proper form and in Arabic terms, if possible, and there must be intention to dissolve the union....'[11]

In the recent case the Court quoted several authorities including Saksena in his book on Muslim Law, p. 113, which states that:

Under the Shia Law, talaq in writing or by signs is not allowed, unless the husband is unable to pronounce the formula of divorce and unless the document is written or the signs made with the intention of talaq and in the presence of two male witnesses... As regards the presence of two witnesses at the time of talaq... I find myself in agreement with the learned counsel for the respondent that the divorce was not pronounced in the presence of two witnesses as required under the Shia Law... In view of the above, I am of the view that no valid talaq as required by the Shia Law was pronounced by the petitioner.[12]

The Supreme Court in appeal has endorsed the finding and it was held: 'No valid talaq as required by the Shia Law was pronounced by the petitioner... Therefore all the courts have held that the talaq pronounced by respondent was not in accordance with *Fiqah Jafria* and was invalid.'[13]

Talaq by Non-Pakistani Muslim Husband

It is interesting to note that the MFLO 1961 applies to all Muslim citizens of Pakistan wherever they may be. In a recent case it has been held that proceedings under section 7 of the Muslim Family Laws Ordinance 1961 could only be invoked by a man who was a Muslim citizen of Pakistan. As the husband was a citizen of the USA, he was not entitled to initiate proceedings against his wife under the provisions of section 7, Muslim Family Laws Ordinance 1961.[14]

It has been held by the courts that a Muslim husband enjoys unfettered powers to pronounce talaq. The fact that the husband happens to be an American citizen or for that matter a citizen of any other country would make no difference to his right to pronounce talaq. In another case, both parties were Sunnis (Hanafi Law) who married in Pakistan, and migrated to the USA. The husband acquired US nationality, and later returned to Pakistan and pronounced talaq in Pakistan and sent notice to the Chairman. The court held that:

Even if it was presumed that the Arbitration Council had no jurisdiction to entertain notice of talaq given by the respondent under provisions of section 7, Muslim Family Laws Ordinance 1961, the right of talaq vested in the husband under Shariat had not been taken away from any Muslim, irrespective of the country to which he belonged.

Despite the restrictions contained in the Muslim Family Laws Ordinance 1961, the husband's right of talaq would prevail as given to him under Quranic injunctions. Divorce pronounced by the respondent had, thus, taken effect under Islamic injunctions even if notice to the Arbitration Council intimating such talaq or subsequent proceedings taken in that regard and the certificate issued by the Arbitration Council endorsing effectiveness of talaq, were ignored.

In this case the marriage was solemnized in accordance with the provisions of MFLO 1961. Originally both parties were Pakistani citizens and thereafter only the husband had acquired citizenship of the USA.[15]

This is the opinion of courts in Pakistan. To what extent the concept of a Muslim husband's unilateral right to pronounce talaq is acceptable outside Pakistan depends on the person's nationality, domicile, and the law in that country.

Talaq to Christian Wife

The Supreme Court has considered the question of the validity of talaq pronounced by a Muslim husband to a Christian wife, following the procedures set down in section 7 of the Ordinance. The appellant, Marina, a Spanish Christian, was married to a Pakistani Muslim barrister under the British Marriage Act 1949, in London. A son was born. Divorce was communicated to the wife on her coming to Pakistan in connection with maintenance proceedings initiated by her in London. Notice of talaq was served to the wife under section 7 of the Ordinance.

The Supreme Court by a majority judgment held that:

Under the rules of Private International Law, the *lex loci celebrationis* as such has nothing to do with the question of divorce which is a matter solely for the law that happens to be the *lex domicili* of the parties, at the time of the suit. This may very well be different from the law that governed the solemnization of the marriage....

So far as the Muslim husband is concerned, the Muslim Personal Law on the subject of marriage would clearly be applicable to him. In the absence of special custom or usage to the contrary, according to section 3 of the Punjab Laws Act 1872, the law applicable to a Muslim would be the Muslim Personal Law. Again, the Family Laws Ordinance 1961 applies to all Muslim citizens of Pakistan wherever they may be. If a Muslim husband is married to a Christian woman in a form recognized by Muslim Law, or to a non-citizen Muslim woman, there is no reason why the provisions of section 7 of this Ordinance should not apply, if he wants to divorce his wife by talaq...

The right of the Muslim husband to grant a divorce to his wife in respect of the marriage recognized by Muslim Law, does not appear to have been taken away by any statute current in Pakistan.

In the circumstances, I have reached the conclusion that the talaq given by the respondent has become effective.[16]

It has been decided by the Supreme Court that a Pakistani Muslim husband can divorce his Christian wife by talaq by adopting the procedure set down under section 7 of the Muslim Family Laws Ordinance 1961.

Divorce by Wife

Muslim family life was deeply influenced by Hindu laws and concepts during the pre-partition period in India. Divorce by the wife was unknown to Hindu Law and Indian customs. Ingrained in Hindu religious thought was the 'Sati', symbolic of the end of the woman's life on the death of her husband. Marriage was considered a lifelong union to continue even in the afterlife, permanent and indissoluble.

Orthodox Muslim thought, divesting itself of Quranic concepts of equal rights for women, fell easy prey to customs prevalent in society, and interpretations denying Muslim women the right of divorce gained credence. Law became the handmaiden of custom in refusing women the right of divorce. For Muslim women, barring a few exceptions, knowledge of Islam was confined to the reciting of the Holy Quran in Arabic, which gave them spiritual solace, but did not enlighten them concerning their rights in Islamic Law. The real concept of marriage and divorce as enunciated by Islam was bypassed. Biased interpretations by the orthodox were accepted by the Muslim masses and the law courts. Such an unnatural situation could not continue indefinitely and voices rose in protest. Social reformers, lawyers, researchers, and forward looking learned ulema gave opinions contrary to the hitherto accepted concept that Islam does not permit a woman to obtain divorce.

Stigma to divorce by the wife is deep-rooted, stemming as it does from years of custom, traditions, and law. Even today, there is a stigma attached to divorce, which makes it difficult for a wife to demand a divorce from her husband either out of court or through legal processes. This stigma is understandable when one recalls that until the late 1930s, Muslim women's right to dissolution of marriage was denied in law and it was only recognized and applied by the statute of 1939.

There was a misconception that Muslim women had no rights to divorce through courts under Hanafi Law. Muslim women, in order to get free from an unwanted marriage, converted to another religion. In British India, courts held that apostasy of Islam, by either party to the marriage, operated as a complete and immediate dissolution of the marriage. Thus apostasy by a married Muslim woman automatically dissolved her marriage. She was entitled to marry again according to the personal law of her new faith.[17]

The Bill for Dissolution of Muslim Marriages Act in its objects and reasons referred to the unspeakable misery experienced by innumerable Muslim women in British India by the lack of provision in the Hanafi Code of Muslim Law (as interpreted by British Indian courts) enabling a Muslim married woman to obtain a decree from the court dissolving her marriage in case the husband neglects to maintain her, or absconds leaving her unprovided for, and under certain other circumstances. Legislation was considered necessary to recognize and to enforce the principles of Maliki Law in order to relieve the sufferings of Muslim women.[18]

The Dissolution of Muslim Marriages Act of 1939[19] brought sweeping changes in law.

Apostasy of Islam by a Muslim wife married under Muslim Law no longer dissolves the marriage, but a number of grounds for dissolution of marriage are specified therein.

Section 4 of the Act deals with apostasy of Islam and provides that the renunciation of Islam by a married Muslim woman or her conversion to a faith other than Islam shall not by itself operate to dissolve her marriage. The Act also provided that after such renunciation or conversion, the woman shall be entitled to obtain a decree for the dissolution of her marriage on any of the grounds mentioned in section 2. It was further provided that the provisions of this section shall not apply to a woman converted to Islam from some other faith who re-embraces her former faith.

The Act has not altered the law in respect of the effect on the marriage of apostasy by a Muslim husband married to a Muslim woman. Under Muslim Law, a Muslim female can enter a valid marriage only with a Muslim male, and not with a male belonging to any other religion. Marriage contracted between a Muslim woman and a *kitabia* (male) would be unlawful *abinitio* from the date of the contract of marriage.[20] Where a Muslim husband converts to Christianity his marriage with a Muslim wife is automatically dissolved and becomes void.[21] Muslim Law continues to hold that the marriage of a Muslim male with a Muslim female shall stand dissolved on his apostasy. It would, however, be advisable for the wife to seek a declaration to this effect through the courts.

Section 2 of the Act has specified a number of grounds on which a woman married under Muslim Law can sue for divorce.

The Act continues to be applied practically in its original form except for amendments brought in the Act by the Muslim Family Laws Ordinance 1961, which provided an additional ground for dissolution of marriage, namely that the husband has taken an additional wife in contravention of the provisions of the Ordinance; and that the option of puberty can be exercised where a girl has been given in marriage by her father or guardian before she attained the age of 16 years, whereas formerly this was 15 years.

Grounds for Dissolution of Marriage

The Dissolution of Muslim Marriages Act 1939[22] entitles a woman married under Muslim Law to obtain a decree for the dissolution of her marriage for a number of reasons. The following grounds are specified:

i. That the whereabouts of the husband have not been known for a period of four years:

However, the decree for dissolution of marriage does not become effective for a period of six months from the date of such decree, and if the husband appears either in person or through an authorized agent within that period and satisfies the court that he is prepared to perform his conjugal duties, the court shall set aside the decree.

In a suit for dissolution of marriage on the ground that the whereabouts of the husband have not been known for a minimum period of four years, it is required that the names and addresses of the persons who would have been the heirs of the husband under Muslim Law if he had died on the date of the filing of the plaint shall be stated in the plaint; and notice of the suit shall be served to such persons, who shall have the right to be heard. And the paternal uncle and brother of the husband, if any, shall be party even if he or they are not heirs.

ii. That the husband has neglected or has failed to provide for her maintenance for a period of two years:

Under Muslim Law it is the obligation of the husband to maintain his wife, and where for a minimum period of two years, the husband either neglects to maintain his wife or fails to maintain his wife, she becomes entitled to dissolution of marriage. The fact that the husband is unable to provide maintenance to his wife would not be a good defence. In suits where non-maintenance is a ground for divorce, the question asked is whether the wife is wilfully and without reasonable cause living apart from her husband. In cases where the wife voluntarily and without reason or the fault of the husband leaves her marital abode and refuses to return, in spite of requests from the husband, the ground of non-maintenance for two years for purposes of divorce is not acceptable to the court. On the other hand, if the wife leaves the marital abode due to cruelty or other unbearable circumstances, the husband is liable to maintain her even while she lives apart, and non-maintenance for a minimum of two years is sufficient ground for dissolution of marriage.

ii-a That the husband has taken an additional wife in contravention of the provisions of the Muslim Family Laws Ordinance 1961:

The Ordinance (as discussed earlier) provides that permission be obtained from the relevant authority before a man enters into a subsequent marriage during the subsistence of his earlier marriage or marriages. If the husband enters into another marriage without obtaining the permission to do so, the wife becomes entitled to sue for dissolution of marriage.[23]

iii. That the husband has been sentenced to imprisonment for a period of seven years or upwards:

However, no decree for dissolution of marriage can be passed unless the sentence for imprisonment for seven years or longer has become final, that is to say it has gone through all the legal procedures of appeals and confirmation by the superior courts.

iv. That the husband has failed to perform, without reasonable
      cause, his marital obligations for a period of three years:
There is no definition in the Act as to what the husband's
'marital obligations' towards the wife are. The non-performance
of the marital obligation of maintenance has been specified
separately as a ground for divorce. This can be taken as a wide,
residue clause and includes all those obligations, which a
husband undertakes towards his wife as a result of the
marriage/nikah. Some of the marital obligations are for the
husband to live with the wife or at least to visit her, to share the
bed with his wife, to allow her to conceive a child, to treat her
with care and consideration. Where the husband fails to perform
these and other marital obligations without reasonable cause,
the wife would be entitled to sue for divorce.

> It is incumbent upon a Muslim husband to treat his wife or wives
> with *Husnn-e-Muasirat*, which means such kindly behaviour as is
> recognized as good by all. Thus it is laid down in the Holy Quran,
> *We ashiru hunna bbil maaroof* that is, and behave with them (your
> wives) in such a manner as is accepted as good and kind by all.
>   The Holy Prophet (PBUH) put great stress on meting out kind
> treatment to wives and in his farewell address at the *Hajjatul-Wida*
> (last Haj) he said, 'O my people, you have certain rights over your
> wives and so have your wives over you. They are the trust of Allah
> in your hands, so you must treat them with all kindness.' But a
> breach of this marital obligation does not constitute a cause for the
> dissolution of a marriage under this clause. It may, however, bring
> a case under the operation of clause VIII (a) if it results in making
> the wife's life miserable.[24]

As treating a wife with good and kindly behaviour is accepted
as a marital obligation of the husband, there seems little reason
to deny the wife the remedy prescribed by law for the failure to
perform this marital obligation by the husband without
reasonable cause.

   If the husband refuses to extend the care and consideration to
which the wife is entitled or fails to perform any of his marital
obligations, the wife becomes entitled to dissolution of marriage.

The non-performance of marital obligations without reasonable cause, for a period of three years, can be pressed as a ground for dissolution of marriage, and it will be for the court to decide in the circumstances of each case, whether the husband has failed to perform his marital obligations without reasonable cause.

v. That the husband was impotent at the time of marriage and continues to be so:

Before passing a decree, the court shall, on application by the husband, make an order requiring the husband to satisfy the court within the period of one year from the date of such order that he has ceased to be impotent, and if the husband so satisfies the court within such period no decree shall be passed on the said ground.

This provision of impotency is limited to impotency of the husband from the time of marriage, and does not take into consideration impotency which may occur subsequently. Besides, the court is bound to give one year's time on the husband's application to prove that he has ceased to be impotent.

vi. That the husband has been insane for a period of two years or is suffering from leprosy or a virulent venereal disease:

A wife is entitled to dissolution of marriage if the husband is insane for a period of two years or is suffering from leprosy or a virulent venereal disease. The second clause is without the condition of two years and if the husband is in fact suffering from leprosy or a virulent venereal disease the court should grant a decree for dissolution of marriage.

vii. That she, having been given in marriage by her father or other guardian before she attained the age of 16 years, repudiated the marriage before she attained the age of 18 years, provided that the marriage has not been consummated:

This right does not accrue when a girl enters the marriage contract of her own accord, which she is permitted to do under Muslim Law. Where the girl is given in marriage by her father or other guardian before she is 16 she can repudiate her marriage before attaining the age of 18 years, provided the marriage has not been consummated. This right is known as the option of puberty akin to *Khairul Baloogh* under Muslim Law. The repudiation of marriage may be oral or can be inferred from conduct. With regard to consummation of marriage it has been held that consummation is in the nature of ratification of the contract and ratification of a contract must be made by free consent of the parties. A wife who had not attained the age of puberty, normally presumed at 15 years, cannot be said to be competent to give her consent to the marriage. Consequently, if consummation takes place before puberty, it would not disentitle the wife to exercise this right. Consummation, if it takes place forcibly, against the wishes of the wife, even if she has attained puberty may not debar the wife from exercising the option of puberty.

There is judicial opinion to the effect that a decree of court is not essential to dissolve the marriage, but on the exercise of the option of puberty, the marriage *ipso facto* stands dissolved. However, it would be advisable for the wife, having exercised the option of puberty, to obtain a declaration that the marriage stands dissolved, and also to comply with the provisions of the Muslim Family Laws Ordinance 1961.

viii. That the husband treats her with cruelty, that is to say:
a) Habitually assaults her or makes her life miserable by cruelty of conduct even if such conduct does not amount to physical ill-treatment:
A single instance of assault by an otherwise loving husband would not constitute cruelty; the entire circumstances have to be considered. Mental cruelty is also a ground for divorce. This can be in the form of continuous use of abusive or insulting language, persistence in sexual malpractices, or

inconsiderate behaviour causing mental anguish and misery to the wife, which amounts to mental cruelty.

b) Associates with women of ill repute or leads an infamous life:

Where the husband visits prostitutes or leads an infamous life, it amounts to cruelty to the wife.

c) Attempts to force her to lead an immoral life:

The husband cannot force any kind of immoral living on the wife, if he endeavours to do so it amounts to cruelty.

d) Disposes of her property or prevents her from exercising her legal rights over it:

Marriage does not give the husband any right over the property of his wife. A married woman is free to deal with her property in any legal manner she desires. If the husband disposes of his wife's property without her consent or prevents her from exercising her legal right over it, not only can she sue him in court for redress, but such action is considered cruelty.

e) Obstructs her in the observance of her religious profession or practice:

No husband can prevent his wife from observing or professing her religion and if he does so it is cruelty, a good ground for divorce.

f) If he has more wives than one, does not treat her equitably in accordance with the injunctions of the Quran:

Islam lays great stress on according equitable treatment to co-wives by the husband. Some writers believe that equity under the Quranic rules implies equality in love and affection, and that such equality being impossible in the weakness of human nature, the Quranic permission virtually amounts to a prohibition of plurality of wives. However, the Sunni concept is that equity means equality in maintenance and lodgings and many writers also specify sharing of time with the co-wives as essential to equity.

ix. On any other ground recognized as valid for the dissolution of marriage under Muslim Law:

After defining the grounds available to a wife to sue her husband for divorce the Act has endorsed any other grounds recognized by Muslim Law without defining or enumerating them, as valid grounds for divorce. An instance is the false imputation of un-chastity or a false charge of adultery against the wife, based on the concept of *Lian* in Muslim Law. It has been held by the High Court that in a case where dissolution is claimed on the grounds that the husband has accused his wife of adultery, 'the case of the wife should be that the charge against her is not true, but she is not bound to prove the falsity of the charge. It is for the husband to show that the charge is true if that be his case. So a dissolution is to be based on a charge of adultery which is denied and which is not proved.'[25]

Under Muslim Law the husband can retract the charge of adultery against his wife. Two judicial views have been taken as to whether the plea of retraction is available to the husband in proceedings for dissolution of marriage. According to one view, in order that retraction should be valid, three conditions are necessary: (1) the husband must admit that he made a charge against his wife for adultery (2) he must admit that the charge was false, and (3) he must make the retraction before the end of the trial. Such a retraction permits the husband to successfully resist the wife's suit for dissolution. The other view is that the plea of retraction of a false charge of adultery is no more available in as much as the Act, which is complete and self-sufficient, nowhere prescribes that in case the dissolution is sought on the ground of a false charge of adultery against the wife its effect can be nullified if the husband retracts the charge.

Ila and *Zihar*

Other grounds include *Ila* and *Zihar*. *Ila* takes effect when the husband swears that he would not have intercourse with his wife for a minimum period of four months, but desires to re-establish the marital relationship with his wife before the expiry of four months, he cannot do so without incurring a penalty.

Zihar occurs when a man compares his wife to some physical sexual part of his mother or any other female relation within prohibited degrees. Sexual intercourse is prohibited between the spouses till the husband does penance. If he does not do penance the wife can ask the court to dissolve the marriage. *Zihar* was one of the ways in which pre-Islamic, unenlightened Arabs used to deprive their wives of sexual enjoyment and tie them down in misery. Islam freed the wife and discouraged the practice by making it clear that a wife does not become the mother or other female relation by the idle foolish talk of a person. While a penalty has been imposed on the husband who has expressed *Zihar* but wants to retain the wife, the wife has been empowered to force the husband to either divorce her or re-establish matrimonial ties on payment of the prescribed penalty. This type of divorce is practically unknown in present times.

Inequality

Kufu technically means equality in marriage. Muslim jurists hold the view that equality between the spouses is essential to promote the objects of marriage. Some writers are of the view that Muslim Law allows the dissolution of marriage on the basis of inequality in marriage. The wife may file a suit for dissolution of marriage on the ground of inequality in marriage. It will be for the court to define the degree and extent of inequality between the spouses and surrounding circumstances to determine whether the inequality and circumstances are such as to entitle the wife to a dissolution of her marriage.

Talaq-i-Tafwiz

The husband can at the time of marriage, or at any time during the marriage, delegate to the wife his right to pronounce talaq. The delegation of the right can be unconditional or there may be conditions attached to it, which are valid under Muslim Law.

The wife having the right of Talaq-i-Tafwiz can exercise the right and dissolve the marriage tie in the same manner as the husband can. Significantly, the right of the wife to be delegated the right of Talaq-i-Tafwiz by the husband has been recognized and included under clause 18 of the standard form of *nikahnama*. Clause 18 questions whether the husband has delegated the right of Talaq-i-Tafwiz, and if so, under what conditions.

Mubarat

Muslim Law recognizes divorce by consent of both the parties to the marriage contract. The husband and wife can mutually agree to the dissolution of their marriage, and such a divorce is known as *mubarat*. The difference between khula and *mubarat* is that if the desire for the divorce is solely from the wife's side and if the husband accepts the offer, khula is effected without going to court. If the husband refuses to grant khula the court can grant khula to the wife. In *mubarat*, intervention by the court or qazi is not required to dissolve the marriage and it is not necessary that dissolution of the marriage be initiated by the wife alone. It may be initiated by the husband, or by both the husband and the wife.

Khula

One of the grounds recognized under Muslim Law for the dissolution of marriage is khula. It is the most common ground pressed in petitions for dissolution of marriage by the wife. Khula is usually pleaded as an alternative ground for dissolution of marriage and in a large number of cases, decree for dissolution of marriage is passed. The word khula literally means to remove or put off and signifies the removal of the matrimonial bond. The wife can sue for khula as the primary ground or alternative ground on the premises that she has irreconcilable differences with the husband and it is not possible for her to live with him as his wife. The wife is required to forgo her Huq Mehar and return to the husband benefits she has received from him at the time of marriage.

In pre-partition India, khula was only accepted as a ground for divorce by the British Indian courts when the husband agreed to the dissolution of marriage by khula. In a case decided by the Privy Council it was held that on the grounds of khula a court cannot grant dissolution of marriage on the petition of the wife where the husband does not consent.

Case Law

The law has undergone considerable change thereafter. The first case bringing in changes in the concept of khula was of Bilqis Fatima,[26] in which it was argued before the High Court that khula is the right of the wife, that the wife can at any time come to court and demand a divorce on grounds of khula and seek the return of any benefits she may have received from her husband.

The question referred to the full bench was whether under Muslim Law the wife is entitled to khula as of right. The full bench relied upon instances wherein the Holy Prophet enforced the right of khula:

> In the first incident, his (Sabit's) wife Jamila came to the Prophet (PBUH) and stated her complaint in the following words: 'Oh Prophet of God. Nothing can bring me and him together. When I raised my veil, he was coming from the front with some men. I saw that he was out of them the shortest and ugliest. I swear by God I do not hate him because of any defect in him, religious or moral, but I hate ugliness. I swear by God that if it was not for fear of God I would have spat at his face when he came to me. Oh Prophet of God, you see how handsome I am, and Sabit is an ugly person. I do not blame his religion or his morals but I fear heresy in Islam.'
>
> On hearing this the Prophet of God said to Jamila: 'Are you prepared to return the garden that he gave you?' She said: 'Yes, oh Prophet of God, and even more.' The Holy Prophet said: 'No more,

but you return the garden that he gave you,' and then the Holy
Prophet said to Sabit: 'Take the garden and divorce her.'

The Court held:

> Let me review the argument in brief and state my conclusions. The
> only proper interpretation of the verse relating to khula is that
> khula depends on the door of the judge and not on the will of the
> husband. This is the implication of the words 'if you fear' being
> addressed to a judge, or the head of the State. The judge ought to
> grant khula if he finds that they will not observe the limits of
> God.[27]

In a leading case decided by the Supreme Court of Pakistan,
Khurshid Bibi versus Baboo Mohammad Amin,[28] the Court
endorsed the view taken by the Lahore High Court in Bilqis
Fatima's case and further clarified the law on the subject.

Special leave was granted by the Supreme Court to consider
the question whether the courts below were right in holding that
the case was not governed by the principles laid down in Mst
Bilqis Fatima's case (discussed earlier). The Supreme Court
quoted the views of Allama Ibn-e-Rushud in the Urdu translation
of Badayat-ul-Mujtahid: 'And the philosophy of khula is this,
that khula is provided for the woman, in opposition to the right
of divorce vested in the man. Thus if trouble arises from the
side of the woman, the man is given the power to divorce her,
and, when injury is received from the man's side, the woman is
given the right to obtain khula.'

The Supreme Court held:

> The husband is given the right to divorce his wife, though, of
> course, arbitrary divorces are discountenanced. There is a saying of
> the Prophet (PBUH) to the effect that the most detestable of lawful
> things in Allah's view is divorce. (Abu Daud . . . .) Similarly, the
> wife is given the right to ask for khula in cases of extreme
> incompatibility though the warning is conveyed by Ahadith against
> too free exercise of this privilege, one of which says that women
> asking for khula will be deprived of the fragrance of paradise

(Trimizi). The warning both to man and woman in this regard is obviously placed on the moral rather than the legal plane and is not destructive of their legal rights.

The Quran also declares: 'Women have rights against men, similar to those that men have against them.' It would be surprising if the Quran did not provide for the separation of the spouses, at the instance of the wife, in any circumstances.

The Quran expressly says that the husband should either retain the wife, according to well-recognized custom (*Imsak-un-bil-ma'roof*) or release her with grace (*Tasreehun-bi-ihsan*). The word of God enjoined the husband not to cling to the woman, in order to cause her injury. Another Hadith declares *Lazarar-wa-lazarar-fil-Islam*, 'Let no harm be done, nor harm be suffered in Islam.' In certain circumstances, therefore, if the husband proves recalcitrant and does not agree to release the woman from the marital bond, the qazi may well intervene to give redress and enforce the Quranic injunction.

The Supreme Court observed:

This difference arises owing to the fact that two situations are contemplated by the writers. One is where khula takes place as a result of the mutual consent of the spouses, which is technically called *mubarat*. In such a case it appears that no reference to the qazi is necessary. But where the husband disputes the right of the wife to obtain separation by khula, it is obvious that some third party has to decide the matter and, consequently, the dispute will have to be adjudicated upon by the qazi with or without assistance of the Hakams. Any other interpretation of the Quranic verse regarding khula would deprive it of all efficacy as a charter granted to the wife. It is significant that according to the Quran, she can 'ransom herself' or 'get her release' and it is plain that these words connote an independent right in her.

The Supreme Court relied on the Hadith:

There is a Hadith of the Prophet concerning Barairah, who was married to a slave named Mughis. She did not live with her husband who followed her disconsolate and weeping, in public. The Prophet advised her to go back to her husband. She asked, 'Is this an order?'

The Prophet said that it was merely a recommendation. She then declined to go back to her husband, saying, 'I have no need of him.' This shows that a woman cannot be compelled, if she has a fixed aversion to her husband, to live with him.

The Supreme Court allowed the appeal and concluded that 'the person in authority, including the qazi, can order separation by khula even if the husband is not agreeable to that course. Of course the Quranic condition must be satisfied that it is no longer possible for the husband and the wife to live together in harmony and in conformity with their obligations.'

For the restitution by the wife to the husband in lieu of khula the Supreme Court held:

Though, according to the Hedaya, it is abominable on the part of the husband to have more than the dower itself in case of separation by khula, yet if he insists, it is legally permissible for him to demand something more than the dower, and to the extent that he might have been out of pocket in respect of gifts given to the wife on marriage, he may, in law, demand restitution. This would necessitate an enquiry into the facts and the final decision as to what compensation must be paid by the wife for her relief must rest with the court. I would, therefore, allow the appeal and send back the case to the trial judge, with the direction that the parties may be permitted to lead evidence as to what gifts, if any, and of what value, were given by the husband to the wife on the occasion of the marriage, so that if the husband wants to take more than the dower, the condition may be imposed on the wife to pay the additional sum expended by the husband on her, to the grant of khula.[29]

In the context of the above-quoted juristic concepts, khula in Islamic Law is the right of the wife to dissolve her marriage without assigning any reasons. She has to forgo or return what she is to receive or received from the husband on the marriage as presents or Huq Mehar. Khula is a right of the wife similar to that of the husband to dissolve the marriage by pronouncement of talaq without assigning any reasons. The right of the wife to khula, as presently implemented, is considerably restricted and hedged in by the fact that she has to go to court to seek khula, and the court will only grant khula where the conscience of the court is satisfied that it is not possible for husband and wife to live within the limits ordained by God. The court has also to consider and decide, when required by the husband, the question of restitution of the property to the husband by the wife on khula.

In view of the Quranic verses relating to the rights of divorce by the wife, and the interpretations by learned jurists of khula being the right of the wife to seek divorce on the same basis as the right of talaq by the husband, in equity the same procedures should be made applicable for a husband to divorce his wife by talaq as for a wife to divorce her husband by khula. The husband should also be required to seek redress through the court for the enforcement of his right of talaq, and the court should only grant him permission to divorce his wife by talaq where the conscience of the court is satisfied that the limits ordained by God will not be observed, that is, in their relations towards one another, the spouses will not obey God.

Notice Under Muslim Family Laws Ordinance

Section 8 of the Ordinance lays down that where the right of divorce has been duly delegated to the wife and she wishes to exercise it, or where any of the parties to a marriage wishes to dissolve the marriage otherwise than by talaq, the provisions of section 7 of the Ordinance shall, *mutatis mutandis* and so far as applicable, apply. This means that where the wife dissolves the marriage in any manner, or the marriage is dissolved at the instance of the wife, even where the dissolution is by a decree of the court, the wife is required to give notice to the Chairman (authority designated) in writing of having done so and supply a copy thereof to the husband. The dissolution of the marriage, unless revoked earlier, expressly or otherwise, shall not become effective until the expiration of ninety days from the day on which notice of the dissolution of marriage is delivered to the Chairman. The Chairman is required, within thirty days of the receipt of the notice, to constitute an Arbitration Council for the purpose of bringing about a reconciliation between the parties. Besides, if the wife is pregnant, the dissolution of the marriage shall not be effective until the expiration of ninety days or the period of pregnancy, whichever is later, ends.

Formerly, by the doctrine of *halala*, on the divorce becoming effective and final, there existed a bar on the woman remarrying her ex-husband. The bar could only be removed by the woman marrying another person, consummation of that marriage, and dissolution thereof. Under the Ordinance this rule has been modified and the parties may remarry without any intervening marriage by the wife to another person unless the divorce has become effective for the third time under the Ordinance. According to a judicial view, *halala* is not obligatory in case of khula. The marrying of another husband is a condition that has been imposed only in the case of a talaq and not in that of khula.

Iddat or Waiting Period

On the dissolution of marriage by the death of the husband or by divorce, the wife is required to observe *iddat*. After the death of the husband, the wife is required to observe four months and ten days' *iddat* and on the dissolution of marriage three months' *iddat*. During the period of *iddat* the woman cannot enter into a valid marriage contract with any person, except remarriage with her husband. The real philosophy of *iddat* is to ascertain whether a woman is pregnant by her husband. Where the wife is in the family way, the divorce pronounced does not take effect till she is delivered of the child, or ceases to be pregnant. Islam lays stress on the paternity of the child and its legitimacy.

Recent Trends

There is a trend to move backwards. Previous judgments of superior courts which have given rights to Muslim women in Pakistan are being questioned. The wife's right to khula without the husband's consent was agitated in a petition for leave to appeal before the Supreme Court. It was contended that a Muslim judge (qazi) can grant a suit for dissolution of marriage only on the grounds of insanity of the husband, failure to provide maintenance, impotency, or if the whereabouts of the husband were not traceable resulting in presumption of his death. It was further argued that incompatibility of temperament, dislike, or even hatred by the wife is not a valid ground for khula in Islamic Law. Relying on a book and an article wherein it was observed that khula can only be effected with mutual consent of the spouses, an attempt was made to limit the right of the wife to khula only with the consent of the husband.

The Supreme Court rejected the argument and reiterated 'that the controversy stands concluded by the judgment of this court in the case of Mst Khurshid Bibi vs. Baboo Mohammad, and other cases wherein it has been held that a person in authority including the qazi, can order separation by khula even if the husband is not agreeable to that cause.'[30]

In another case the question agitated was whether the khula decree would become effective from the date when it was passed finally by the court or whether it would attain finality when the khula amount fixed by the court had been paid to the husband by the wife. In this case the Family Court allowed dissolution of marriage by khula subject to return of ornaments, or Rs 40,000—the price of the ornaments—to the husband. The wife had admitted that she was given ornaments worth Rs 40,000. The Court held that the decree of khula had become effective from the date when it was passed by the Trial Court as no appeal had been filed against it and the Court did not agree with the contention that the decree for divorce shall attain finality only when the khula amount fixed by the trial court is paid by the wife.[31]

This is similar to when the pronouncement of 'talaq, talaq, talaq' (divorce) by the husband to his wife becomes effective even without payment of dower (Huq Mehar) by the husband to the wife, for which she has to approach the courts if he refuses to pay.

An important question often disputed in cases involving khula is: What are the benefits received by the wife, which are to be returned by the wife to the husband? Dower, if it has not been paid, has to be forgone by the wife. Where it is proved that she has received the Huq Mehar, is it to be returned to the husband?

In a recent case the court held that 'dowry not being Zar-i-khula could not be declined to the wife for a decree based on khula. It is laid down in Muhabbat Hussain's case (1992 MLD 1294) that the husband is entitled to return of ornaments which were given by him to the wife at the time of marriage.... In the present case the husband having not proved taking away of the ornaments and dowry by the petitioner (wife) is not entitled to them....'

The High Court further held that the recovery of benefits being a civil liability the husband can institute a separate suit for their recovery if so advised and the claim of the husband was rejected in divorce proceedings (see p. 15).[32]

NOTES

1. Pakistan Law Commission, Annual Report 2001, p. 28, Government of Pakistan, Pakistan Law Commission, Supreme Court Building, Constitution Avenue, Islamabad.
2. Abdullah Yusuf Ali, *The Holy Quran: Text, Translation and Commentary*, note 265, p. 92.
3. Ibid., note 254, p. 90.
4. K.N. Ahmed, *Muslim Law of Divorce*, pp. 85-7, published by The Islamic Research Institute, Islamabad.
5. Ibid., p. 89.
6. Syed Ameer Ali (Brought up-to-date by Raja Said Akbar Khan), *Mohammedan Law*, p. 432. Published by All Pakistan Legal Decisions, Nabha Road, Lahore, 1965.
7. Ibid.
8. Muslim Family Laws Ordinance 1961, Gazette Pakistan, 2 March 1961.
9. Syed Ali Nawaz Gardezi vs. Lt.-Col. Muhammad Yusuf, PLD 1963, SC 51, pp. 72, 74, and 80.
10. Allah Rakha and others vs. Federation of Pakistan and others, Shariat Decision 2000, SD 723, pp. 780 and 781.
11. Qamar Raza vs. Tahira Begum, PLD 1988, Karachi, p. 169.

12. Ibid., p. 237.
13. Federation of Pakistan vs. Tahira Begum 1994 SCMR 1740, pp. 1744, 1745.
14. Saima Rasheed vs. Imran Riaz Imami 1993 CLC 1331 Lahore at p. 1334 (A).
15. 1998 Monthly Law Digest, 2108.
16. Marina Jatoi vs. Nuruddin Jatoi, PLD 1967 SC 580, at pp. 599, 602, and 607.
17. Mst Zainab Bibi and others vs. Bilquis Bibi and others, PLD 1981, SC 56 at p. 73.
18. Gazette of India, 1939, Part V, p. 154.
19. The Pakistan Code, Volume IX, p. 716.
20. Mohammad Ishaq Yakoob vs. Umaro Charli and Others, CLC 1987, 410, p. 411.
21. Sardar Mohammad vs. Mst Mariyam Bibi, AIR 1936, Lahore 666.
22. Ante 19, The Pakistan Code, Volume IX.
23. See Polygamy, chapter 1, p. 33.
24. K.N. Ahmed, 'A Commentary on the Dissolution of Muslim Marriages Act', Legal Publications, 77 Garden West, Karachi, 1955.
25. All Pakistan Legal Decisions, 1957, Lahore 998, p. 1008.
26. Bilqis Fatima vs. Najmul Ikram Qureshi, All Pakistan Legal Decisions 1959, Lahore 566, pp. 573, 574, 575, 582, 593.
27. Ibid.
28. Mst Khurshid Bibi vs. Baboo Mohammad Amin, PLD 1967, SC 97, pp. 112, 114, 117, 119, 121.
29. Ibid.
30. Mohammad Rafiq vs. Mst Kaneez Fatima, SCMR 2000, pp. 1563, 1566, and 1567.
31. Mst Nahida Safdar vs. Muneer Anwar 2000, SD 560, p. 565.
32. Bushra Bibi vs. Judge, Family Court, Bahawalpur and Two others, PLD 2000, 95, pp. 99 and 100.

4

DOMESTIC VIOLENCE

Even though you have tied the chains of domesticity,
shame and modesty around my feet,
even after you have paralyzed me,
this fear will not leave you,
and even though I cannot walk,
I can still think.[1]

Physical, psychological, and sexual abuse in the home spells misery for an astounding number of women. Why are men more violent than women? Is it biological? Is it the structure of the male physique and brain? Is it cultural? Is it tradition or is it just the stronger sex dominating the weaker sex? Why are women the weaker sex?

The difference in the physique and reactions of men and women have been recognized. Men are more violent than women. Humans and chimpanzees are the only two mammals living in patrilineal male bonded communities, out of about 4000 mammal species. Some biologists consider that the die is cast even before birth—in response to hormones released by the ovaries and testes, male and female brains develop differently in utero. Yet most men are not violent and some women are. Environment and relationships in infancy make a difference.

Studies over the last twenty years have shown that the kind of attachment an infant makes to his mother during the first two years of life will affect his or her relationship to others. The mother who meets and responds to her infant's need is far less likely to raise an aggressive, antagonistic child than the angry, controlling, severely troubled mother would. Psychiatric, neurological, neuropsychological, and family evaluations have revealed that the mixture of brain dysfunction, paranoid misperceptions, and a history of having been raised in a violent, abusive household make a lethal cocktail....

Sure, we human females are less physically violent than our male counterparts, but we have our own ways of perpetuating violence. Like it or not, at this stage in evolution, we bear the major burden of raising our young. How we treat them during the earliest years of their lives strongly influences the structure and functioning of their brains, the security of their attachments, and the quality of their emotions, thoughts, and behaviours—in other words, whether or not they become violent.[2]

In Pakistan the mother often has no control over the environment. Poverty, ill health, illiteracy, less physical strength, and domination by males make it impossible for the mother to give her infant a healthy, secure, and peaceful environment to keep her babies from growing up to be violent individuals.

Global Violence

No country or society is free from domestic violence. Millions of women suffer domestic violence all around the world. Even in developed countries, for example in the United States and the United Kingdom, the number of battered wives is exceedingly high. The home, which should be a haven of peace and security, is not safe. 'Women and girls face terror from physical, psychological, sexual, and economic abuse.... Studies estimate that between 20 to 60 per cent of women worldwide have experienced physical violence at the hands of an intimate partner or family member.... It cuts across boundaries of culture, class, education, income, ethnicity, and age.'[3]

Violence against women is a global issue. It goes back to the stone age. Historically, the physical weakness of women, the childbearing function, and the economic dependence of women all combined to assign to men the role of protectors and providers of women, evolving a superior status of the male over the female, and a culture of violence against women. As a result women have suffered the trauma of hurt and pain. Even though the stone age and the atomic age face different challenges, and the present-day needs of time and life have changed, gender-based violence continues, often unreported. The progress of science and technology, the invention of the computer, nuclear power, accelerated population growth, faster travel, world linkages, the discovery of the biochemistry of the living cell, and particularly the extensive use of the electronic media spreading awareness have all combined to limit the role of physical strength. Yet, women have not been freed from the traditional chains of subjugation. Though some women become scientists, astronauts, lawyers, doctors, and bankers, most women are subservient to men.

Simple physical strength does not control life today. Knowledge and science rule the world. Women are as capable of moving the gear of destruction or development as men are. Despite this, millions of women around the world suffer from discrimination and violence because of their gender.

The movement for gender equality is gaining strength. A number of movements have recognized the need to redress the plight of women. 'Gender violence is a daily—and often deadly—fact of life for women and girls around the world. It not only devastates lives and destroys their potential, but also undermines the development and progress of all nations, especially towards equality and the possibility of women to exercise full citizenship. Gender violence involves incalculable and irreversible costs, both human and financial.'[4]

Domestic violence against women is most hurtful and depressing. It is difficult to portray the pain a woman feels when her husband, the so-called life-companion, provider, lover, inflicts mental or physical force to cause injury, or her father/brother violates her.

Domestic Violence—Pakistani Perspective

Domestic violence is the abuse meted out to women within the family and the home. It ranges from abuse to torture, which is physical, mental, sexual, psychological, and emotional. Violence against women has reached crisis levels in Pakistan. It is an obstacle and deterrent to development.

Domestic violence in Pakistan is deemed to be a private matter and as something that does not belong in the courts. Women are usually ignorant of the fact that violence is a crime. Where the aggressor is a close relative, few women come forward to report the abuse to the police. Often they are threatened into being silent. Social taboos and lack of family support for shelter leaves women no alternative but to bear their lot.

In Pakistan, violence within the home is inflicted in various ways, including mental torture, by denying women food, often by threat of divorce or by taking another wife, separating the woman from her infants, forced marriages, exchange marriages, or selling women in marriage, especially to much older men. Violence may include physical assault, force, verbal abuse, ravaging, burning and sexual abuse, rape, and forced prostitution. It is not only the husband who inflicts violence in the home, often in extended families, the wife is violated by her in-laws. The girl child or the woman may be subjected to incest and rape in her own home, and even forced to keep her lips sealed. Women can suffer violence in the home from the men of the family, father, brother, husband, uncles, cousins, and at times from the women of the family, mother-in-law, sisters-in-law, mother, and sisters.

Murders

In marital disputes the woman can be killed as she is regarded as the property of her husband. In a number of cases women are killed in their marital homes and the murder is never reported.

The violence may even extend to murder of women over petty domestic disputes. Occasionally, cases are reported in the press of murder of the wife by the husband as a result of domestic differences and marital disharmony. In an incident in Mangora (Northern Area Swat), a woman was allegedly gunned down over a domestic dispute by her husband, who escaped. In another case Bibi Zadagai, wife of Amir Nawaz, stated in the First Information Report (FIR) that she had developed domestic differences with her husband and came away to her father's house. Her husband along with his friend entered the house of her father and began firing indiscriminately. Her father died on the spot while she was injured, but her husband and his friend escaped. In a third case reported on the same day, in Sukkur in the province of Sindh, three armed men barged into the house of Ghulam Haider Khoso and kidnapped his wife and two daughters. The kidnapping was said to be motivated by a matrimonial dispute.[5] In another incident, Muhammad Ishaq had a quarrel with his wife over a petty issue. Ishaq attacked his wife with an axe.[6] At times men kill their wives over petty domestic issues.

There has been an alarming increase in the crime rate in Pakistan. Even where the woman has the support of her family and returns to her father's home, she is pursued. There have been cases where the husband follows his wife, and on her refusal to accompany him to the marital home, murders her. This is another way of tormenting the wife, as, if she escapes to her parents' house, her family is also terrorized.

Brutality

Brutality towards women surpasses cruelty towards animals. It is said that in rural areas a man values his livestock more than his wife. There is a growing trend of increasing atrocities against women. The newspapers, particularly *Dawn*, render a great service to the women of Pakistan by continuously reporting crimes. A large number of cases of honour killings are reported in *Dawn*. This creates awareness among the people and politicians, of the prevalent violence against women. Often, lesser violence remains suppressed within the woman's heart.

Studies on Violence

A study was conducted in 1998 on violence against women, through four cross-sectional surveys in the Punjab province of Pakistan, to determine the magnitude of domestic violence, to analyze the dynamics of domestic violence, and explain the situation. Thirty per cent of rural women and 17 per cent of urban women, i.e. one-fifth of the respondents, reported physical abuse by their husbands. Three-fifths of women reported having had arguments with their husbands a month before the interview. The most frequently mentioned reasons for the arguments were: (1) money (2) children-related issues, and (3) aggressiveness of the husband.

Interspousal arguing was the most significant predictor of wife abuse. Religiosity emerged as an important predictor of domestic violence. Abuse doubled if the wife was not so religious. According to the researcher, religion presumably emphasized women's subordination to men and encouraged them to readily accept given conditions, thereby reducing the chance of interspousal disagreement and conflict.

In summary, it was concluded that domestic violence against women (VAW) is an important health and welfare issue for women in Pakistan. Substantial proportions of women from all survey sites reported physical abuse by their husbands, and these figures are expected to be underestimates. The highest prevalence of wife abuse was reported from peri-urban areas of metropolitan Lahore, probably due to social stress produced by emerging gender destabilization.[7]

Another descriptive study using a mix of quantitative and qualitative research methods was conducted in Karachi.

One hundred and eight cases of VAW were studied. An attempt was made to learn what provokes violence, why women are so vulnerable, how they respond, what is the impact of violence on children, and why men resort to violence. One reason for violence was incompatibility of the partners. This emerged as a key issue in the case studies. In arranged marriages, where the preferences of the parties are not taken into consideration, differences in expectations of marriage cause frustration, leading to arguments and even violence. Early marriages with lack of maturity and great disparity in the ages of couples also tend to make the partners incompatible....

Surprisingly contrary to popular expectations, neither the preference for a male offspring nor the number of children in the family emerged as a major determinant of violence in the study.... Again, the use of alcohol and drugs 'was not the sole reason' for violence either, but it definitely exacerbated it... It was established that what usually triggered violence was economic stress, unemployment, lack of resources to meet a sudden increase in financial demands due to illness. Interference by the in-laws often made matters worse...

The abuse suffered by women ranged from mild to severe. Slapping, pulling of hair, pushing or shoving, grabbing, hitting with an object such as a stick, a cane or anything near at hand... more than half of the women reported such assaults. Almost one-third suffered more severe forms of violence such as kicking, punching, suffocating, intentional burns, or hitting that resulted in fracture or injury to a vital organ e.g. eye injury or ruptured eardrum....

All women encountered verbal assault—the use of bad and abusive language, threats, name-calling, shouting and putting down remarks about physical appearance, ability as a mother or homemaker, etc.... suspected or actual infidelity and social isolation of the victim....

Half the women suffered some type of economic control—withholding of money or refusal to meet household expenses, control on women's wages or assets.... Economic abuse suffered by a few even included stealing valuable assets like personal jewellery or land....

In an overall situation, 12 per cent of women reported some form of sexual abuse—such as forced prostitution. This was nearly always accompanied by other forms of violence.... In fact, violence emerged as a continuum, first verbal abuse, escalating into anger, exploding into physical assault.

Women's response to the abuse was to initially suffer in silence or cry and talk to friends or mothers. Seldom do women retaliate or beat the cycle of violence because of traditional cultural male dominance, the low status of women in Pakistan, desire to protect their children who need a father, financial insecurity, lack of emotional support and access to legal help.... Only one-fourth initiated some legal action—such as separation, divorce, or measures for return of property....

The long-term effect is that a woman's self-confidence and self-esteem is shaken.... Nine women even made suicide attempts—taking tranquillizers or insecticide.... Over time, women become emotionally exhausted and fatalistic, blaming their *kismet*.[8]

PAWLA's Experience

At the PAWLA Legal Aid Centres, head office, and outreach centres, which deal with one thousand new clients a year, every day there are women complaining of domestic violence. Wife abuse is the major marital problem from which women suffer; practically every woman who comes for redress complains of beating by the husband or mental torture.

The women who come to the centre are poor and often have young children. When PAWLA officials ask them the reason for the beatings it is often because the husband suspects her character or there are disputes about money. In cases where the wife is earning and the husband, who may be a drug addict, demands money, she is mercilessly beaten up if she refuses. In other cases where the husband is not properly supporting the family and the wife asks for money, she is beaten up. Sometimes, the reason can be something like, 'when he came home the food was not ready', or 'he did not like the food I cooked'. A mother-in-law's complaints can result in the wife being thrashed. Demands for money and goods from the wife's parents, which are not met, often result in the wife being beaten up.

In cases where the woman has children, PAWLA often sends a simple notice to the husband and/or his family to come to the centre for mediation, without making any adverse allegations. If the wife wants to go back to her marital home and the husband is prepared to offer reasonable terms and bond or guarantees against violence the couple may be reconciled. In at least 50 per cent of such cases the women come back, violated. If the marriage cannot continue, the separation or divorce may take place with terms and conditions for financial settlements and custody of children worked out with the consent of the parties without going to court. Where disputes cannot be settled a case is filed in court, usually for dissolution of marriage, and to sort out maintenance of wife and children.

When dealing with cases of mediation and reconciliation PAWLA often observes that the same man who was mercilessly beating his wife is prepared to come to terms once he is made to realize that the poor defenceless wife now has legal support and he can be taken to court. The husband usually denies that he was beating his wife or takes the plea that she misbehaved and insinuations against the woman's character are often made.

From January 2000 to May 2001, 708 women filed complaints, which were registered at the PAWLA head office Legal Aid Centre.[9] In 245 cases, that is 34.6 per cent of cases, excessive unbearable violence was reported. These complaints included physical violence such as banging the woman's head against a wall resulting in brain injury; battering; miscarriage due to physical abuse; severe beatings breaking the teeth of the wife or breaking the finger; mental and physical torture by the in-laws; battering by substance-abuser husband; physical abuse on suspicion of loose character; accusing the woman of being possessed by spirits; locking up the wife in the house; forcibly taking away small babies from the mother; torture for non-fulfilment of dowry demands; burning; acid throwing; causing burns with cigarettes; an impotent husband accusing the wife of sterility; unnatural sexual demands; electric shocks; polygamy; physical violence if the wife asks for maintenance or questions the husband's action; rape by the brother-in-law, or friends of the husband; change of religion; *watta-satta*, that is exchange marriages, in which the daughter is forced to marry an old man in exchange for a young girl for her father; forced prostitution;

forced marriages; trying to sell the wife; the mother being threatened over her property by the adult children; refusal to give a share of the deceased father's property to the sister; and other threats.

Redress

Women victims of violence who approach the PAWLA Legal Aid Centres usually come with the purpose of escaping the unbearable violence inflicted on them. They want to be rid of the husband. Often they have been living with the husband and bearing the insults and violence as part of life. The women rarely consider going to the police and filing a complaint. In a number of cases if it is suggested to the women to file a complaint with the police, they recoil from the idea. Punishing a husband who is guilty of domestic violence is not on the cards of Pakistani women, except in cases of extensive injury or death of the women.

The legal redress the women seek from violence is dissolution of marriage from the husbands. In khula, which means dissolution of marriage at the instance of the wife, the woman asserts that she has hatred for her husband and it is not possible for her to live with him as his wife within the limits ordained by God and she returns to him the benefits such as dower and jewellery received by her from the husband. For poor women there is little property given to the woman and the dower has rarely been paid, so this is not an issue. Khula is the right of the wife, which the court must grant. Khula is the common form of divorce filed for women, it is quick and does not need extensive evidence and proof.

Many of the women who approached PAWLA faced the common problem of not receiving maintenance money from their husbands. In fact these women were subjected to physical and mental torture when they made demands for their maintenance.

Polygamy is legally valid in Pakistan, as a result of which a number of women are put through endless suffering. Men in Pakistan do not consider it necessary to inform their existing wife/wives or seek their permission before remarrying as required by law. The punishments for violating the law relating to polygamy are lenient and the fine amount is a negligible sum of money. Thus, women consider it a waste of time to seek redress for their grievances by invoking the provisions of law. In other cases, the existing wife/wives are thrown out of the house on the arrival of a new wife in the marital home.[10]

Weakness of Women

The phenomenon of wife abuse is not confined to low-income families. In my practice of law, I have come across several well-to-do and educated young and middle-aged women bitterly complaining of being severely thrashed by their husbands. I have known doctors, lawyers, executives, and businessmen who have beaten up their wives. An unbelievable case was where both husband and wife were well-known doctors, and from time to time the husband would beat up the wife. In this case the son brought his mother to me for redress, but his mother did not return to file for divorce. She was afraid of creating a public scandal. I have always been astounded as to how women can put up with physical violence day after day and return to the same man!

In one case, a woman came to me for divorce after thirty years of marriage, which was strange. She told me of the terrible beatings her husband showered on her from time to time. She said, 'I had five children and no place to go to. Now my sons and daughters are married, I am nearly 50 years old. I can support myself and want a peaceful life. I do not need a husband and so don't have to take his thrashings any more.' Children are a woman's weakness. In many well-to-do homes the wife and the children get so used to luxurious living that they don't wish to leave. Children, especially grown sons, do become a protection against the father thrashing their mother.

Islam Wrongly Interpreted

> *...As to those women*
> *On whose part ye fear*
> *Disloyalty and ill-conduct,*
> *Admonish them (first)*
> *(Next), refuse to share their beds,*
> *(And last) beat them (lightly);*
> *But if they return to obedience,*
> *Seek not against them*
> *Means (of annoyance).* (4:34)

Sadly, many persons consider that it is the husband's right to beat his wife in Islam. This false notion is based on the controversially misinterpreted verse 4:34.

Despite the wrong translation, Yusuf Ali comments:

> In case of family disputes four steps are mentioned, to be taken in that order: (1) perhaps verbal advice or admonition may be sufficient; (2) if not, sexual relations may be suspended; (3) if this is not sufficient, some slight physical correction may be administered; but Imam Shafi'i considers this inadvisable, though permissible, and all authorities are unanimous in deprecating any sort of cruelty, even of the nagging kind, as mentioned in the next clause; (4) if all this fails, a family council is recommended in 4:35 below.

One mother-in-law, when confronted at the PAWLA Legal Aid Centres with the inhuman beatings meted out by herself and her son to his wife, coolly turned round and said that Islam allows a husband to beat his wife. This misconception is rampant. The real meaning and purpose of the verse is not comprehended. It is time and again misquoted and presented as giving the husband the right to beat his innocent and weak wife. There is no such connotation in the verse.

Even traditional translators accept that it is mentioned in the Quran that a man may lightly beat his wife only when there is disloyalty and misconduct and only as a last resort, after all attempts at communicating and understanding have failed.

Besides there are several different meanings of the Arabic word used in the Quran. *Wadribuhunna* is translated by traditionalists as beat those (rebellious) women. In Arabic the root word *daraba'ala* signifies male/female camels having sexual intercourse.

Ahmed Ali in *Al-Quran Contemporary Translation* renders the following translation:

Men are the guardians of women as God
Has favoured some with more than others, and because
They spend of their wealth (to provide for them).
So women who are virtuous are obedient to God
And guard the hidden
As God has guarded it.
As for women you feel are unyielding
Talk to them suasively;
Then leave them alone in bed (without molesting them)
And have intercourse with them (when they are willing).
If they open out to you, do not seek
An excuse for blaming them.
Surely God is sublime and majestic. (4:34)[11]

He comments that the Arabic word *qanitat* only means devoted or obedient to God, and does not lend itself to any other meaning. For the three words *fa'izu, wahjaru,* and *wadribu* in the original, translated here as 'talk to them suasively,' 'leave them alone (in bed—*fi'l-madaje)*', and 'have intercourse', respectively, see Raghib, *Lisan al-' 'Arab,* and Zamakhshari.

If this meaning is accepted, the Quran does not give permission to beat the wife but to have intercourse with the wife when she is willing. The interpretation of the Quran since the earliest times had been done entirely by men, in a male-dominated patriarchal culture, which has adversely affected the rights of women. It is difficult to accept that the Quran would give the husband the right to beat his wife without spelling out a similar right to the wife.

The Quran has subsequently stressed (according to the changing times and circumstances in Arabia) that men should be kind to their wives and give them their due respect. The obscurantist mullahs, however, have given a very distorted view and interpretation of the issue and hence domestic violence is deemed excusable under this pretext. Shariat is not rigid at all. In fact, the word 'Shariat' in Arabic means a path through running water for people and animals to drink in safety. Hence, if the dignity of women is to be maintained and social justice be done, then the true Islamic spirit should be followed, which treats women with consideration and protects them from domestic violence.

Burn Cases

Cases of women burnt by stoves or acid are continuously reported in the press. The question creeps into the mind, was it deliberate, designed to kill, or an accident? A lot of research and discussion has taken place in neighbouring India. Several cases of bride burning have been discovered and complaints followed up. A special law has been enacted to deal with such cases in India. There have been limited studies in Pakistan, but they all indicate the prevalence of this heinous form of domestic violence.

PAWLA has dealt with two significant cases of women with severe burns. In one case the woman, Hamida, was admitted to the Civil Hospital in Hyderabad for treatment of burns caused by acid thrown at her by her husband. A complaint was filed and the husband was jailed. The woman was being treated in a hospital, her parents were looking after her, the doctors were cooperative, but the finances were very tight. PAWLA helped sustain them with moral and legal support and to some extent with financial support. Private donors also contributed and the Human Rights Cell of the Government of Pakistan provided Rs 20,000 for Hamida's treatment and rehabilitation. But over time the financial help dried up. The couple's six children were in serious financial difficulty. They were known to be begging on the streets with no provider. How long could they manage without proper funding?

The other case was of a woman with serious burns in a hospital in Karachi. When PAWLA workers spoke to her and her family, it became clear that the woman had deliberately been burnt by her husband. The police report filed showed it as an accident. The victim at one point of time wanted to change her statement to the truth. The in-laws were present and threatened her that if she put the blame on her husband he would be picked up by the police and put in jail indefinitely. Her family made it clear that they would not take care of the seven children, who would be on the streets. PAWLA was not in a position to give any guarantee for the support of the children. The mother's weakness and her love for her children forced her to hide the truth. She died the next day.

Another heart-rending case is of the daughter-in-law of a politician, millionaire zamindar well known through the revealing autobiographical novel *My Feudal Lord*,[12] written by his ex-wife, disclosing compulsive wife beating and terror.

As reported in the press his son by his first wife, Bilal Khar, married Fakhra, father unknown. She had to leave her 4-year-old son with her mother. She was not accepted as a legitimate daughter-in-law by the family. Bilal, who was a heavy drinker, started beating Fakhra within two months of the marriage, followed by two years of pain and misery. In April 2000, Fakhra decided to leave Bilal and returned to her mother's house. Bilal went there and asked for her, and when she went to the door he threw a container full of strong acid on Fakhra's face. She collapsed screaming. He left with his accomplice. Fakhra's neck, face, chest, and arm were extensively burnt, her lips were fused together, one eye was severely damaged. She spent three nightmarish years in the Civil Hospital at Karachi.

Her aunt, Shahida Malik, registered the FIR against Bilal with the Napier Road Police Station. On receiving a threat from Bilal to kill Fakhra's son Noman, the family agreed not to pursue the FIR, as even the police were reluctant to follow up the complaint, the accused being from a prominent political party.

The doctors were helpless. Fakhra suffered skin disfigurement, her eye needed major surgery, her right hand was crippled, her neck was immobile. She was in great physical and mental agony. Conscious of the burden she had brought to her poor family, she decided to return to Bilal, who was feeling deeply sorry for what he had done in a fit of rage. They lived in Karachi for a few months, but Bilal was unpredictable. He took Fakhra to Tehmina Durrani, his stepmother, in Lahore. She promised to help Fakhra and organized the money required for reconstructive and eye surgery in Italy. Bilal refused to allow this and forced Fakhra to go to his father's farm. She became fearful for her life and sent a message to Tehmina, who had her brought back.

In order to obtain travel documents Fakhra needed an identity card, which was not possible because she did not know who her father was. Fearing adverse reporting by the international press, the authorities thwarted her attempts especially as Pakistan was already being blamed for human rights violations against women. Fakhra was offered treatment in Islamabad by the government which was not successful. Tehmina held a press conference and revealed the case to the press. Fakhra is just one of several women who suffer.[13] 'After a long and painful ordeal, and hideously disfigured by her powerful husband in an acid attack she was finally provided with travel documents to proceed abroad for treatment.'[14]

Stove Burn Murders

According to a research report by the Progressive Women's Association (PWA), in 'Choola Death' cases, the area of the body burnt always exceeds 30 per cent and can be as much as 60, 70, or 90 per cent. Medical experts state that the areas likely to be burnt in a genuine stove accident are the arms, legs, and abdomen. Strikingly, this is not the case for victims of stove burnings, whose genitalia are often burnt. The nature of injuries, the position of the victim in the family (she is usually a daughter-in-law, or a daughter to be married), and the frequency with which these 'accidents' occur provide circumstantial evidence of a grim pattern; that these women are burnt not by accident, but are victims of deliberate murder.[15]

Police Indifference

Ironically, in our country, the response of the police to domestic violence is deplorable. Instead of working effectively to eliminate violence against women, they put obstacles in the way of the victim's right to seek justice. Corruption and gender bias reign supreme amongst underpaid police officials. Most of them do not consider wife beating a crime or even wrong.

Though the wife may complain against domestic violence the police are usually not inclined to entertain what they term as husband-wife disputes. In a complaint filed before the police, requesting the police to call the offending husband to the police station, the Station Head Officer (SHO) emphatically refused on the ground that this was not a cognizable offence and the police could not summon the husband even for the purpose of questioning or investigation.

In the experience of PAWLA, it is more effective to send such complaints through the Citizen Police Liaison Committee (CPLC), which is a statutory body working from headquarters at the Governor House, Karachi and other sub-offices. As they have some power the parties are more receptive and the injured woman can get redress.

In a case forwarded to the CPLC by PAWLA, the woman appeared severely beaten, and fearing further violence and kidnapping, needed protection. The police initially refused to register the case. Following the intervention of CPLC the case was registered, investigated, and the husband was put in jail. Finally the case was settled by divorce and return of jewellery. The woman when questioned at the PAWLA office said all she wanted was to be left in peace with her children. She was not prepared to go through the lengthy, often disturbing and terrifying process of a criminal trial especially as her husband was a rich and influential person.

Before the police can start their probe and file a First Information Report, a medical report is required from a government hospital medical officer. The woman has to be examined for injuries. The examination of a woman is required to be done by a female medical officer, yet in several places a female medical officer is not available.

In a recent case handled by PAWLA and other NGOs, there were no female medical officers and the male medical officer examined the woman with all her clothes on. He did not see the injuries on her concealed body. His report was defective and non-committal. The police were reluctant to file the FIR, and only after much insistence was the report filed.

Detention and Custodial Rape

Illegal detentions by police are commonplace. In a habeas corpus petition, the High Court considered a complaint that some women and CIA police had broken into their house and picked up Afroz and Husna, wives of Muhammad Sharif and Shahid Ali, and kept them in illegal detention. The Sindh High Court officials raided the women's police station and found Afroz and Husna with three children in illegal detention. The SHO was asked to appear in court with the detainees.[16]

It has also been noted that women are subjected to custodial sex and rape. When a woman is in police custody, a near relative, the mother, father, or aunt is often seen sitting outside the police lockup, to protect the detenue against custodial rape.

In view of the increasing cases of custodial rape there is a directive by the government that no woman shall be kept in a police lockup overnight, and that no woman should be arrested after daylight except in cases of dacoity or murder. It was made mandatory for a woman officer to be present at the time of the arrest of a woman and during her interrogation.

This directive is not adhered to in all cases. The law requires that an accused be produced before a magistrate for remand within twenty-four hours. In complaints under the Zina Ordinance the accused women are looked down upon as being of loose character and in some cases the police keep them in detention to take undue advantage.

From time to time reports appear in the newspaper of complaints of custodial rape. In a case where a woman was produced before a court, arrested in a zina case, she complained that four policemen raped her at the police station.[17]

Facts and Figures

No consolidated figures showing crimes against women are available on an all Pakistan basis, from the Bureau of Police Research, Government of Pakistan.[18]

However, for the province of Sindh more detailed reports are available on violence against women. The report shows:

VIOLENCE AGAINST WOMEN IN SINDH PROVINCE[19]

S. No.	Heads	1998	1999	2000	2001
01	Murder of Women	312	305	325	351
02	Beating by the Husband	23	28	34	26
03	Beating of Women by Male other than Husband	107	80	113	108
04	Zina/ *Zina-bil-jabr*	134	135	180	184
05	*Karo Kari*	183	183	196	102
06	Burning	25	40	37	28
07	Sexual Assault	32	32	49	42
08	Abduction of Women	615	606	654	640
09	Gang Rape	3	3	2	6
10	Suicide of Women	99	116	161	121
11	Dowry-related Violence	-	-	1	-
12	Forced Prostitution	-	1	-	-
13	Forced Marriage	-	2	4	2
14	Incest	16	11	29	7
15	Trafficking in Women	-	-	-	1

The above table shows that very few cases of beating by the husband are reported to the police. Similarly, a limited number of cases are reported on burning of women, sexual assault, and incest and only a few cases of gang rape and forced marriages. One case of forced prostitution and only one case each on dowry-related violence and trafficking in women appear to be reported. This is not a true picture of violence against women. The police usually refuse to register cases of domestic violence, and as a result violated women often refuse to go to the police to complain about their injuries.

Why the Silence?

The reasons why a large number of wives and victims of violence do not seek punishment for the perpetrators of the crimes, especially close family relations, are manifold. The dependent and inferior legal, social, and economic status of women in law and in practice is a major factor. Other reasons are: no access to conciliatory or legal services; double standards of morality and laws: in cases of wife burning, women dare not complain as it is feared that when the husband is put in jail there is no one to earn; lack of social security; wrong interpretation of religion: due to a lack of knowledge of Islam, women are indoctrinated to believe that it is a husband's right to beat his wife; deteriorating judicial system and delays in court; the police are not usually willing to act in cases of domestic violence; lack of confidence in the police; defective investigation by police; long delays in compiling of medical reports; no specific law against *karo kari*/honour killing; court rulings condoning *karo kari*; Zina Ordinance which discriminates against women; defective rape law: the law can be twisted to make young girls complaining of rape be accused of zina; violence against women for revenge; forced intercourse within marriage is not rape and is not punishable.

The law allows a woman to live separately from her husband in circumstances of cruelty. She can claim maintenance for herself and her children. She may also sue for dissolution of marriage. Neither of these are completely effective remedies against physical violence in the home.

Recent Laws Against Domestic Violence

Formerly there was no specific law or forum for domestic violence. Aggrieved wives seeking redress had to resort to the general law. The Pakistan Penal Code could be invoked. This was an ineffective process in cases of domestic violence. The need for reform of the law was strongly felt. PAWLA had time and again made recommendations to Benazir Bhutto's government and Nawaz Sharif's government for reforms, with no positive response. The pressure for reforms was continued with the military government of President Pervez Musharraf. One of the demands was that the Family Law Courts must be given power to deal with cases of domestic violence.

Recent amendments to the Family Law Courts Act 1964 brought in by the President of Pakistan, General Pervez Musharraf, have been enforced by the Gazette of Pakistan Extraordinary dated 1 October 2002. The most important aspect of this amendment, which can benefit wives and victims of domestic violence, is the extension of the jurisdiction of the Family Courts to offences of domestic violence. In the revised schedule, where one of the spouses is a victim of an offence committed by the other, the Family Court has been empowered to adjudicate complaints.

The Family Court judges have been given powers of Judicial Magistrate First Class under the Criminal Procedure Code 1898, to punish offences under the Penal Code between spouses for acts of abetment and causing or intending to cause hurt, wrongful restraint, or wrongful confinement. These powers if properly utilized will go a long way to reduce domestic violence and deter husbands from hurting or confining their wives. Words, gestures, and acts intending to insult the modesty of a woman are also punishable by the Family Court.

The details of the sections of the Pakistan Penal Code 1860 laying down categories of Islamic crimes and their punishments which the Family Courts can adjudicate between spouses are as follows:

337. Shajjah: (1) Whoever causes on the head or face of any person, any hurt which does not amount to *Itlaf-i-Udw* (i.e. dismembers, amputates, severs any limb or organ of the body) or *Itlaf-i-Salahiyyat-i-Udw* (i.e. permanently impairs or destroys).

337-A. Punishment of Shajjah: Whoever, by doing any act with the intention of thereby causing hurt to any person, or with knowledge that he is likely thereby to cause hurt to any person, causes...

(i) *Shajjah-i-Khafifah* (i.e. without exposing any bone of the victim) to any person, shall be liable to *Daman* (i.e. compensation determined by the court to be paid by the offender to the victim for causing hurt not liable to *Arsh* (i.e. specified compensation in the chapter) and may also be punished with imprisonment of either description for a term which may extend to two years as tazir;

(ii) *Shajjah-i-Mudihah* (i.e. exposing any bone of the victim without causing fracture) to any person, shall, in consultation with the authorized medical officer, be punished with qisas and if the qisas is not executable keeping in view the principles of equality in accordance with the injunctions of Islam, the convict shall be liable to *Arsh*, which shall be 5 per cent of the diyat and may also be punished with imprisonment of either description for a term which may extend to five years as tazir;

(iii) *Shajjah-i-Hashimah* (i.e. fracturing the bone of the victim without dislocating it) to any person, shall be liable to *Arsh* which shall be 10 per cent of the diyat and may also be punished with imprisonment of either description for a term which may extend to ten years as tazir;

(iv) *Shajjah-i-Munaqqilah* (i.e. causing fracture of the bone of the victim and thereby dislocating the bone) to any person, shall be liable to *Arsh* which shall be 15 per cent of the diyat and may also be punished with imprisonment of either description for a term which may extend to ten years as tazir;

(v) *Shajjah-i-Ammah* (i.e. causing fracture of the skull of the victim so that the wound touches the membrane of the brain) to any person, shall be liable to *Arsh* which shall be one-third of the diyat and may also be punished with imprisonment of either description for a term which may extend to ten years as tazir, and

(vi) *Shajjah-i-damighah* (i.e. causing fracture of the skull of the victim and the wound ruptures the membrane of the brain) to any person, shall be liable to *Arsh* which shall be one-half of diyat and may also be punished with imprisonment of either description for a term which may extend to fourteen years as tazir.

337-F. Punishment of *Ghayr-Jaifah*: That is, whoever causes *jurh* (i.e. causes on any part of the body of a person, other than the head or face, a hurt which leaves a mark of the wound) which does not amount to *jaifah* (i.e. *jurh* in which the injury extends to the body cavity of the trunk). Whoever by doing any act with the intention of causing hurt to any person, or with the knowledge that he is likely to cause hurt to any person, causes...

Damiyah (i.e. the skin is ruptured and bleeding occurs) to any person shall be liable to *Daman* and may also be punished with imprisonment of either description for a term which may extend to one year as tazir;

341. Punishment for wrongful restraint: Whoever wrongfully restrains any person, shall be punished with simple imprisonment for a term, which may extend to one month, or with fine, which may extend to Rs 500, or with both.

342. Punishment for wrongful confinement: Whoever wrongfully confines any person, shall be punished with imprisonment of either description for a term which may extend to one year, or with fine which may extend to Rs 1000, or with both.

343. Wrongful confinement for three or more days: Whoever wrongfully confines any person for three days or more, shall be punished with imprisonment of either description for a term which may extend to two years, or with fine, or with both.

344. Wrongful confinement for ten or more days: Whoever wrongfully confines any person for ten days or more, shall be punished with imprisonment of either description for a term which may extend to three years, and shall also be liable to fine.

345. Wrongful confinement of person for whose liberation writ has been issued: Whoever keeps any person in wrongful confinement, knowing that a writ for the liberation of that person has been duly issued, shall be punished with imprisonment of either description for a term which may extend to two years, in addition to any term of imprisonment to which he may be liable under any other section of this chapter.

346. Wrongful confinement in secret: Whoever wrongfully confines any person in such manner as to indicate an intention that the confinement of such person may not be known to any person interested in the person so confined, or to any public servant, or that the place of such confinement may not be known to or discovered by any such person or public servant as hereinbefore mentioned, shall be punished with imprisonment of either description for a term which may extend to two years in addition to any other punishment to which he may be liable for such wrongful confinement.

352. Punishment for assault or criminal force otherwise than on grave provocation: Whoever assaults or uses criminal force to any person otherwise than on grave and sudden provocation given by that person, shall be punished with imprisonment of either description for a term which may extend to three months, or with fine which may extend to Rs 500, or with both.

509. Word, gesture, or act intended to insult the modesty of a woman: Whoever, intending to insult the modesty of any woman, utters any word, makes any sound or gesture, or exhibits any object, intending that such word or sound shall be heard, or that such gesture or object shall be seen by such woman, or intrudes upon the privacy of such woman, shall be punished with simple imprisonment for a term, which may extend to one year, or with fine, or with both.

The latter punishment can be given by any court for an offence by any person. However, by the amendments, the Family Court is empowered to adjudicate the offences only between spouses. The Family Court should have been empowered to deal with such acts against any woman by any person. All the above-quoted sections are already in the Pakistan Penal Code 1860, yet they were seldom utilized by women for domestic violence complaints. Domestic violence was not considered to be a crime. Even courts were unwilling to seriously consider and punish husbands on complaints by their wives. The amendments in the law have clearly spelt out that the above-noted offences by either spouse can be taken to court. Now that the complaints can be filed before the Family Court, it is hoped that battered women will emerge from their shell of silence and suffering to demand protection and redress. The clear possibility of the court ordering punishment by imprisonment and or imposing compensation payable to the wife by an erring cruel husband should restrain domestic violence.

These amendments have been welcomed by PAWLA, though they fall short of the demands. Proper utilizing of the changes and encouraging women to go to court with their grievances and implementation in the true spirit can protect women against domestic violence. The demand remains that the Family Court must be empowered to issue orders for arrest or restraining orders against the husbands to stop them from approaching or hurting their wives.

This may initially be difficult to legislate and enforce. In fifty countries laws have been enacted against domestic violence, giving respite to women. Such laws can act as a deterrent to the husband.

Laws in other countries need to be studied. In cases where the house was the dwelling of two or more persons, there are laws which make provisions as to the husband and wife's respective rights of occupation in situations of conflict. The laws also make provisions for preventing the molestation of one spouse by the other, and make provision for the children to live with the mother or father. In Pakistan in a disputed situation the wife is unceremoniously thrown out of the house or forced to leave the marital home often without her belongings. Concentrated acid is easily available to whoever wants it for whatever purpose, despite government regulations. The easy availability of concentrated acid must be stopped.

There have to be reforms to allow illegitimate children all the facilities they are now denied. Why are they to be punished for acts not committed by them?

The situation in Pakistan is completely different from that in other societies due to poverty. There is no possibility of obtaining or availing of social security to maintain the children in distress. The bread-earner husband has the upper hand. There is no doubt that it is the economic dependency, the physical weakness of the woman, and traditional condoning of wife-beating which allows the male to get away with murder. There is a need for the government to seriously consider supporting the wife and children who have suffered serious violence from a special fund, or *Zakat*, or *Bait-ul-mal*.

Responsibility of the State

State violence and harassment against women is growing. The law and order situation has been allowed to deteriorate, and the police often refuse or are reluctant to take action in cases of violence against women. Custodial violence and illegal detentions by the police, slow dispensation of justice, insufficient and inadequate judicial officers, detrimental and discriminatory laws against women, along with lacunae in the laws, allow perpetrators of crimes to be free from trial and punishment. It is the duty of the State to protect the individual from violence, enforce law and order, and provide an unbiased, efficient judicial system. Failure to do this makes the State responsible for neglect to protect the citizens.

A flawed and delayed medico-legal reporting system, paucity of female doctors, limited apparatus for investigation, and untrained officers make it difficult to collect evidence to convict criminals.

Many laws are detrimental to women. For example, the Zina Ordinance has jeopardized the lives of women. Any woman can be accused of adultery or fornication by a complaint to the police, and taken into custody, as it is a cognizable offence. However, in cases of domestic violence the police often refuse to interfere or take any action if the offence is one of hurt and assault, as these are not cognizable offences and the police dismiss them as internal family disputes. There is even a police station in Karachi where there is a sign saying 'No Family Disputes Entertained'.

Several studies, including those by Human Rights Watch, Amnesty International, and the Human Rights Commission of Pakistan, have reflected that the State machinery does not respond to women's rights to safety and protection and concluded:

> The dismissive official attitudes toward violence against women reflect institutionalized gender bias that pervades the State machinery, including the law enforcement apparatus. Partly as a result of deep-seated and widespread biases against women, the criminal justice system does not operate as an avenue for redress and justice for women victims of violence. Victims who turn to the system confront a discriminatory legal regime, venal and abusive police, untrained medico-legal doctors, incompetent prosecutors, and sceptical judges. The deplorable level of medico-legal services in the country is itself a sign of the government's lack of will to tackle the problem of violence against women. [20]

The justice system is so biased and steeped in difficulties for women victims of crime that they are afraid to approach the police and the courts.

Suicide

Out of a reported 2386 cases of suicide during the year 2001, 723 cases were of suicide by women. Unemployment, poverty, inflation, insecurity, police harassment, failure in love, failure in examinations, divorce, domestic violence, financial problems, childlessness, marriage disputes, and mental illnesses seem to be the main reasons behind the sudden rise in cases of suicide in the country.[21]

According to reports, 2917 cases of physical abuse against women were reported all over Pakistan during the year 2001. These included 1390 cases of murder, 1049 cases of injury, 148 cases of torture, sixty-four cases of stripping, forty-one cases of teasing, and forty-three cases of harassment. It was noted that most of the crimes were reported against married women.

Insulting the enemy by stripping their women relatives is a growing phenomenon, particularly in rural areas. The numbers of reported cases of violence against women have risen astonishingly. The rising figure is due both to an increase in reporting and an increase in crimes against women. However, many cases of abuse of women go unreported and unpunished.[22]

Measures to Eradicate Violence Against Women

Steps need to be taken to eliminate violence in relationships as well as society. The following are some suggestions from PAWLA:

Better Intervention Programmes: Domestic violence is a serious violation of human rights. Though domestic violence is considered a private matter in most homes, the State needs to step in, devise and implement intervention programmes, which should be mandatory in nature.

Crisis Centres: Battered women need quick access to crisis centres for emergency help. The State should provide a number of crisis centres all over the country. These centres should help battered women to get medical help in case of injuries, provide required counselling to help cope with the trauma of domestic violence, assist in filing a report with the police if need be, help arrange for a lawyer in case of litigation, make financial help available to the wife and children during the crisis, and provide economic support for rehabilitation.

Shelter Homes: Since most families refuse to house their female relatives when they are turned out of their marital home or shut the door on women facing abuse at the hands of their in-laws and husbands, aggrieved women have nowhere to go. Shelter homes need to be set up by the State for women victims to take refuge in when their families turn their backs on them. Training and rehabilitation programmes should be held at the shelter homes, which should assist battered women to move from welfare to work.

Violence Against Women: Violence within the home must be made a cognizable offence. This will enable the police to deal with these complaints effectively.

Police Stations for Women: Women in Pakistan hesitate to go to all-male police stations and not without reason, as cases of police violence against women are frequent and go unpunished. Police officials are known to rape women victims of violence in their custody, at times subjecting them to illegal detention and torture. In the face of such horrors, police stations for women may be an answer for women victims who need to file their complaints with the police without fear of getting violated again. Even though there are a few women police stations in the cities of Karachi and Lahore, the women police officers have little training and no know-how in dealing with cases of violence against women. There must be concerted efforts to train women police officers and male police officers (in places where women police stations are not feasible) to deal with cases of violence against women.

Health Care: Domestic violence is a health care problem of epidemic proportions. Medical officers should be encouraged to screen their patients for domestic violence. Lawyers dealing with domestic violence should be provided with health care-based training so that they can assist battered women in seeking medical help. Medical reports are required for filing an FIR with the police. It takes at least a week to get such reports. Reports from all medical doctors must be acceptable for filing FIRs. Female medical doctors must be specially trained and empowered to give medical reports for filing FIRs.

Empowerment of Women: Women who are trapped in poverty are also usually trapped in abuse. The State and NGOs should help battered women to attain economic self-sufficiency. Job training, job placements, and work opportunities should be provided to help women become financially independent.

Tackling Gender Discrimination: Women must be made aware that violence is a crime even if inflicted by the father or husband. Women should be educated to know that gender-motivated violence is a form of sex discrimination and requires civil rights protection. It is equally if not more important to spread legal awareness regarding domestic violence among males and females. Boys should be taught to respect the opposite sex from early childhood. Society should encourage people to confront their male friends, neighbours, relatives, co-workers, or strangers and prevent them from abusing women.

Victim Safety and Offender Accountability: Women who face violent relationships can be in extreme danger. When they separate from their abusive husbands, it may have the effect of heightening the potential for lethal violence from their abusers. Domestic violence can be so severe that it can lead to fatalities, hence, it is essential to ensure safety for vulnerable women.

Role of International Agencies: Pakistan should be checked by international agencies for its poor response to the problem of violence against women, especially for disregarding the CEDAW provisions.

PAWLA's Role in Fighting Domestic Violence: PAWLA provides legal aid to women victims of domestic violence, sexual violence, and all forms of violence. Initially efforts are made for a compromise between the couple out of court but when all efforts fail PAWLA represents cases for women free of cost or for negligible legal fees. PAWLA mostly takes up cases of destitute women free of cost and even pays court expenses.[23]

PAWLA operates in Karachi, but such services should be made available all over Pakistan.

International Intervention

The issue of violence against women as a special, separate problem has only recently found its place on the international human rights agenda. It was not until December 1993 that the UN General Assembly adopted the first international human rights instrument to deal exclusively with the issue, namely the Declaration on the Elimination of Violence Against Women.

Radhika Coomaraswamy was named by the UN Commission on Human Rights in 1994 as the first special rapporteur to investigate the causes and consequences of violence against women around the globe. She contends that State negligence can actually lead to increased violence against women. On the other hand, active government intervention can be a catalyst for reforming the 'historically unequal power relations' between men and women, which lie at the root of the problem.

Coomaraswamy cites many causes for violence against women, including attitudes toward female sexuality, cultural ideologies, which justify the subordinate position of women in society, pornography, and the media's glamorization of violence. Doctrines of privacy and the concept of the sanctity of the family have allowed violence against women to persist. She says: 'Most legal systems make a distinction between the public and private spheres and are reluctant to punish crimes which take place in the home; however, this has begun to change in recent times. The "greater cause" of violence against women may be government inaction. There appears to be a permissive attitude, a tolerance of perpetrators of violence against women, especially when this violence is expressed in the home.'[24]

United Nations Commission on Status of Women

In view of the continuous disregard for women's human rights in most parts of the world and the sorry state of women's lives, the UN Commission on Status of Women was set up in 1946. Apart from safeguarding human rights through UN declarations and conventions, separate declarations and conventions have been adopted for women's human rights. The UN Convention on the Political Rights of Women was adopted in 1952 by the UN General Assembly.[25] The UN Convention on the Nationality of Married Women was adopted in 1957,[26] followed by the Convention on the Consent to Marriage, Minimum Age for Marriage, and Registration of Marriage, which was adopted in 1962.[27]

These efforts by the UN to integrate women in the human rights framework did not substantively change the lives of women, particularly in Third World countries. On the request by twenty-two countries including Afghanistan, Iran, and Pakistan, further consideration by the UN on women's degradation led to international consensus for strengthening human rights for women. The declaration for the Elimination of Discrimination Against Women was adopted by the UN in 1967.[28] It was the forerunner for the United Nations Convention on the Elimination of All Forms of Discrimination Against Women adopted by the UN General Assembly in 1979.[29] This is the all-encompassing United Nations law for the protection of women. It became effective as an international treaty on 3 September 1981 after the twentieth country had ratified it.

On the consistent advocacy and pressure from women's groups and human rights activists, Prime Minister Benazir Bhutto's government signed the Convention and ratified it in March 1996. Reservations were made on clause 29, relating to arbitration. However, a general declaration was made invoking the primacy and sovereignty of the Constitution of the Islamic Republic of Pakistan 1973 as being over and above, overruling all the provisions of the Convention. Even this limited acceptance of the Convention was not supported by the religious lobby.

In view of the Islamic Provisions of the Constitution, especially Article 2A making the Objectives Resolution a substantive part of the Constitution, coupled with the overriding declaration of the supremacy of the Constitution of the Islamic Republic of Pakistan 1973 over the Convention, some of the provisions of the Convention cannot be implemented. These include the differing status of husband and wife within the family, particularly the present law of divorce and custody of children, inheritance, legitimacy and the overall discrimination against illegitimate children, the law of evidence, the law governing nationality, and several other customs and practices. In the private and public sphere, law and practice both give inferior rights and roles to women. These are based on supposedly Islamic customs and laws.

The Islamic tradition is of women as homemakers and men as maintainers, providers, and protectors of women. There is a need to deconstruct the wrong meanings assigned to the Holy Quran and reinterpret the Quranic verses to rediscover the intrinsic purity and justice of Islamic Law, to apply it afresh to present needs, and to clearly distinguish it from historical accretions that have made women subservient. There is a long way to go before the concept of equality or even equity for women can be acknowledged by obscurantist religious leaders, who have assigned to themselves the role of the sole interpreters of Islamic Laws, and by the Government of Pakistan.

Domestic Law

Article 24 of the CEDAW provides that:
'States Parties undertake to adopt all necessary measures at the national level aimed at achieving the full realization of the rights recognized in the present Convention.'

This has not been complied with, no amendments having been made to the Family Laws, Evidence Laws, Inheritance Laws, or Criminal Laws. Except for a small change in the Citizenship Act 1951, no other laws have been amended by statute to bring the law in line with the Convention.

Though a permanent Commission on the Status of Women has been established by the Government of Pakistan, this is only a recommendatory body with no powers to change the law or customs. It was dormant without a chairperson for six months and a chairperson has been appointed only recently.

The reservation of 33 per cent seats for women in the local government under the Devolution Plan of 2000 is an innovative reform by the President of Pakistan, General Pervez Musharraf, which can have far-reaching effects. This move was severely criticized and opposed, but the President was not deterred. Elections were held under the Devolution of Power Plan in June 2001 and 3361 women members were elected as councillors. Two women were later elected as District Nazims (District Mayors).[30] Reserved seats for women have been increased. Now there are sixty reserved seats for women in the National

Assembly and similarly in the Provincial Assemblies. The women are to be elected on the basis of proportional representation. If the political parties select forward-looking, knowledgeable women, they may influence the Assemblies for changes in laws affecting women.

Article 18 of CEDAW provides that:

1. States Parties undertake to submit to the Secretary-General of the United Nations, for consideration by the committee, a report of the legislative, judicial, administrative, or other measures, which they have adopted to give effect to the provisions of the present Convention and on the progress made in this respect:

   a) Within one year after the entry into force for the State concerned; and

   b) Thereafter at least every four years and further whenever the committee so requests.

2. Reports may indicate factors and difficulties affecting the degree of fulfilment of obligations under the present Convention.

These reports are the only mechanism to ensure the enforcement of the Convention. For this purpose a body of twenty-three experts elected by the States Parties, to serve in their individual capacity, which form the committee is to examine the reports. The Pakistan government has so far not submitted the required report though the Convention was ratified five years ago. A report of the follow-up of the Beijing Conference and the Country Report at the UN Conference on Women 2000 was presented.

Addressing the 44th session of the UN Commission on the Status of Women, a representative of the Ministry of Women's Development stated that Pakistan has to set up an independent Permanent Commission on the Status of Women to accelerate national efforts, establish an ombudsperson to cater exclusively to gender issues, and take other necessary administrative actions....

He said some specific steps had already been taken, including reservation of one-third of the seats in legislative assemblies for women from national to local levels, an increase in the quota for women in public sector employment from the existing 10 to 25 per cent, recognition of the reproductive health of women as a human right, significant financial allocations under a poverty alleviation programme for women and children, and visible and effective participation of women in the political process and decision-making....

> We in Pakistan believe that the need for rapid action towards achieving equality between women and men and to end all kinds of discrimination against women is not only a moral and human rights imperative, but also an economic necessity....
>
> We believe that our religion and ideology sets ideas and norms for a social vision concerned with the dignity, security, equality, and full participation.... of women.
>
> There is a need to transform traditional attitudes and cultural barriers which obstructed action against violence and crime affecting women, reform the legal and judicial system to provide quick judicial redress to women, and to measure and quantify the existing role and contribution of women in economic production and consumption levels.[31]

Pious statements promising action by government officials, without any action being taken remain meaningless words. True, 33 per cent of seats have been reserved for women presently at the local government level and elections have been held, bringing women into local government. The downside is that no specific role or function has been assigned to the women. To date the whole scenario is in disarray. No effective steps appear to be taken towards fulfilling the 5 per cent quota for women in the public sector, or the recognition of the reproductive rights of women. Several verbal commitments are made by government functionaries, ranging from the President to Ministers and officials, yet there is hardly any practical, effective follow-up.

The country situation report of the United Nations Commission for Human Rights tabled at the 55th session of the

UNHRC in Geneva, which has been prepared by Special Rapporteur and human rights activist Asma Jehangir, also mentions the alleged extra-judicial, summary, or arbitrary executions of women, who continue to be victims of criminal violence and are killed for harming the family's honour by choosing their own marriage partners. In many cases, the report said, tribal councils held quasi-judicial trials and sentenced women to death.[32]

Conclusion

The question then remains as to how best to proceed with the struggle to achieve equal human rights for women in the Muslim world. Can we and should we continue to proceed to struggle within a framework of Islam, or should we instead attempt to work within a secular framework (which some women advocate out of sheer frustration at the intransigence of 'Islamic revivalists')? The Women's Convention partially can play a useful role, both as a political lever and as a point of reference, when attempting to articulate specific demands by women in Muslim societies.[33]

NOTES

1. Kishwar Naheed, *The Distance of a Shout*, from the poem *Anticlockwise* (translated from Urdu by Rukhsana Ahmad). Edited by Asif Farrukhi, p. 58, Oxford Press, Karachi 2001.
2. Dorothy Otnow Lewis, *The Gentler Sex and the Cycle of Violence,* Radcliffe Quarterly Inquiry, Winter 2001, Radcliffe Institute.
3. Statements, Women's World Forum Against Violence, Queen Sofia Centre for the Study of Violence, Valencia, Spain, 2000.
4. Final Statement—Domestic Violence (unpublished), Women's World Forum Against Violence. Queen Sofia Centre for the Study of Violence, Valencia, Spain, 2000.
5. *Dawn*, 18 May 2001.
6. 'Man kills wife over petty issue', *Dawn*, 13 September 2001.
7. Muhammad Hafeez, 'Magnitude and Dynamics of Domestic Violence Against Women: Evidence from Rural and Urban Sites in Pakistan', presented at the Conference on Pakistan's Population Issues in the 21st

Century, 24-26 October 2000, Karachi, Pakistan, organized by Population Council and Aga Khan University.

8. Maisoon Hussain, 'The Violence Within'. Interview with Dr Asma Fozia Qureshi, Dr. Fauzia Rabbani, and Dr Nargis Rizvi with reference to the study on Domestic Violence, Aga Khan University published in *Dawn*. 'The Review', 17-23 May 2001.

9. 'A Study on Domestic Violence, PAWLA's Experience' by Rashida Mohammed Hussain Patel with inputs from PAWLA's Executive Council members, project and law officers and intern Ms Sonia Mansoor, November 2001, Pakistan Women Lawyers' Association (PAWLA), 710, Kashif Centre, Shahrah-e-Faisal, Karachi.

10. Ibid.

11. See also Chapter on Marriage Laws, pp. 22 and 23.

12. Tehmina Durrani, *My Feudal Lord*, published by Tehmina Durrani, 1991, Pakistan.

13. *The Herald*, July 2001, pp. 45 and 46, printed and published by Ghulam Ali A. Mirza at Pakistan Herald Limited, Dr Ziauddin Ahmed Road, Karachi, Pakistan.

14. Syed Talat Hussain, 'Acid victim finally gets papers for treatment,' *Dawn* 4 July 2001.

15. '223 women died due to burn injuries during the year 2001', Madadgaar's Press Release, 24 January 2002.

16. 'Five found in illegal detention', *Dawn*, 18 May 2001.

17. 'Cops "rape" woman in custody', *Dawn*, 3 November 2000.

18. 'Crimes reported during the year', Bureau of Police Research and Development, Ministry of Interior, Government of Pakistan.

19. 'Violence against women in Sindh province', SO/Crimes, Dy Inspector General of Police, Crimes Branch, Sindh Police, Karachi, 17 January 2002.

20. *Crime or Custom? Violence Against Women*, Oxford University Press, published by arrangement with Human Rights Watch 2001, p. 102.

21. 'Madadgaar's analytical report on the cases of suicide during the year 2001', Press Release, 8 January 2002.

22. '1390 women murdered during the year 2001', Madadgaar's Press Release, 14 January 2002.

23. Ante 9, pp. 14-16.

24. Radhika Coomaraswamy, UN first report on the issue of VAW, news release, 'Government inaction said key factor in VAW' published by US Information Services, Collector's Lane, 8 Abdullah Haroon Road, Karachi.

25. General Assembly Resolution 64 (VII) of 20 December 1952.

26. General Assembly Resolution 1040 (XI) of 29 January 1957.

27. General Assembly Resolution 1763 (XII) of 7 November 1962.

28. General Assembly Resolution 2263 (XXII) of 1967.

29. General Assembly Resolution 34/180, UN Document A/Resolution/34/180, of 1979.
30. 'Milestones in Commitment', *Dawn*, 10 December 2001.
31. 'Pakistan committed to rights of women', *Dawn*, 3 March 2000.
32. Nasir Malik, 'UN report accuses govt of extra-judicial killings', *Dawn*, 12 April 1999.
33. Shaheen Sardar Ali, *A Comparative study of the UNCEDAW, Islamic Law, and the Laws of Pakistan*, p. 141, printed at Shaheen Press, Peshawar, June 1999.

5

MURDER FOR MALE HONOUR

To control the sexuality of women outside marriage, the custom of honour killing has evolved. The boundaries of sex for men and women are defined within marriage. As a woman is considered the property of the male, the father before marriage and husband after marriage, a tradition has evolved to avenge the illicit sexual relations of the daughter, or wife, or sister, as the case may be, by murdering the woman concerned and her paramour. This is permitted or condoned as honour killing by the community and the law in certain places.

Honour killing, that is killing women in the name of honour, occurs in many parts of the world. It is a heinous crime, which is traditionally accepted. These murders take place in Bangladesh, Brazil, Ecuador, Egypt, India, Iran, Iraq, Israel, Italy, Jordan, Lebanon, Palestine, Syria, Mexico, Sudan, Turkey, Uganda, the United Kingdom, Yemen, and particularly Pakistan.

In most countries the punishment for this crime is not the same as for murder. Suspecting or finding a female relative having a sexual relationship with a male outside marriage is considered mitigating circumstances in almost all the countries named above. Often, when there is proof of such a killing only one to three years of imprisonment is awarded by courts. Until recently, even in many of the Western countries, the punishment for honour killing was minimal.

In some countries legislation does not consider such killings as murder, condoning the crime as vindicating family honour. For example, in Jordan statutory law protects the perpetrators. A husband or close relative who kills a woman caught in the act of adultery or suspicion of adultery can be exempted from punishment or be awarded a light sentence for the crime. On the other hand, in India a law was enacted in 1987 to prevent and abolish crimes against women in the name of religion and custom, yet the crimes continue.

'In Pakistan, traditional perceptions of honour severely limit some of the most basic rights of women. Every year hundreds of women of all ages, and in all parts of the country are reported killed in the name of honour. Many cases are unreported. Almost all go unpunished. Nearly 1000 women were killed last year in Pakistan against a world total of 5000 under this head of crime.'[1]

Increasing Crimes

It is heart-rending to read in the Pakistani newspapers every morning stories about the killing and maiming of women. There is a strong upsurge of crimes against women. Only FIRs registered with the police are reported in the press, many more cases remain unreported. On the basis of newspaper reports of the past six months it can be estimated that in the first quarter of the year 2001, at least 100 cases of honour killing have been registered. For example, a newspaper reported: 'Four women fell victims to honour killing in Bhagor village, 40 km from a small town in Punjab. Nasir Ahmed with his accomplice, shot dead his mother-in-law and two sisters-in-law, as he found strangers in the house of his in-laws. A case has been registered.'[2]

Karo Kari–Siya Kari

Honour killing is known as *karo kari* in Sindh, *kala-kali* in Punjab, *tora-tora* in the NWFP, and *siya kari* in Balochistan. *Karo* is the name for the male offender and *kari* is used for the female offender. Both mean black. *Siya, kala,* and *tora* also mean black, denoting the dark colour of the crime being punished.

Karo kari traditionally means the right of the community or the near relatives, husband, father, or brother to kill the female relative and her paramour for an illicit sexual relationship outside marriage. Presently the tradition is misused and murders are justified in cases merely based on suspicion or where the male or female marry or seek a divorce without the consent of the family. The tradition is also misused in murders for ulterior motives.

> Under the laws of this country a man is considered justified in killing a woman of his family if she is involved in *siya kari* (illicit sexual relationship). That is, if a man finds a woman of his family in a compromising position with a stranger he can murder her. The Penal Code places this kind of offence in the category of killing under grave and sudden provocation, i.e. 'culpable homicide not amounting to murder', and in such cases the accused is usually sentenced to imprisonment of a few months only....
>
> In certain areas of Pakistan *siya kari* is used as a defence in cases of intentional murder of an enemy. This is accomplished by separately murdering the enemy and one's own close female relative and then placing their dead bodies together in a compromising position. It is then claimed that they were both killed under grave and sudden provocation and in order to vindicate the family honour....
>
> During my tenure as Judge of the High Court a case came before me where a man had killed his enemy and then fired at his 14-year-old blind daughter with a shotgun. Some of the pellets accidentally injured his buffalo which happened to be nearby. His concern for the safety of the buffalo prevented him from transporting the body of his daughter and placing it next to that of his enemy in time, and it was thus revealed that he had murdered his daughter intentionally in order to dispose of his enemy.[3]

Sadly, by and large honour killing has become an honourable institution in Pakistan. Those who commit murder for vindicating their honour are applauded by their peers. In police custody and in jails, persons undergoing trials for honour killing are often given special treatment and respected for killing for the sake of honour, *ghairat*.

Strong opposition is building up against honour killing. The daily reports in the press, sometimes two or three or four, are creating awareness of the enormity of the problem and its injustice.

Comparatively speaking, the killing of women by men is treated as minor news and finds place in the inside pages, usually with a single-column display. When a woman kills a husband it is headline news on the first page. This depicts not only gender discrimination against women but also the rarity of a woman committing murder.

A recent front page headline glared, 'Woman hacks husband to death'. The wife, Parveen, had allegedly drugged the meal of her husband Saifur Rind and after he fell unconscious, hacked her husband to death and stuffed the pieces of his body into a trunk in Syed Village, Malir, a suburb of Karachi. According to Parveen, the mother of two sons aged seven and five, her husband Saif had been unemployed for several years and had forced her into prostitution.[4]

The question that arises is whether this is an honour killing. Can it be claimed that the woman killed her husband to preserve her personal honour?

The other side of the question also arises. When a man is having extramarital relations is the woman entitled to kill him for honour, or *ghairat*? Or does society and custom only grant the male the privilege of vindicating his honour by murder?

Similarly, another news item read: 'Five die in family feuds.' 'A boy, Gulzar, with his accomplice Shahzada, gunned down his stepmother and father in Par Hoti, Mardan.... It was learnt that the accused was annoyed over the second marriage of his father. One Ayaz Ali shot dead his wife on suspicion of illicit relations with his brother Asad Ali, who was killed one week ago. The father of the girl, Sher Afzal, lodged an FIR with the Rustam Police.'[5]

Yet another news item proclaimed: 'Man kills wife, two die in incidents.'

'A woman was stabbed to death by her husband in Buffer Zone on Wednesday on suspicion that she had developed illicit relations with a man in the locality. The victim, Mir Nigar, 40, was stabbed several times in the abdomen by her husband Daulat Khan, a 50-year-old labourer in a katchi abadi of sector 16-A, in Sir Syed Town. Later, the accused surrendered to the police.'[6]

The underlying reasons for these killings are the concept of ownership of the women by men, customs, religious misinterpretations, defective laws, both statutory, tribal, and customary, taunting by peers, suspicion, marrying or divorcing without the consent of elders, ulterior motives such as quarrels over land, old family enmity, camouflaging common murders as *karo kari*, and the failing judicial system.

Tribal Law

Honour killing is pre-Islamic and not supported by Islam. The traditional custom of honour killing is centuries old. It is part of the tribal culture. It has survived with the patriarchal family system. The tribal system prevails in certain areas of Pakistan, especially the northern border regions and remote areas. In many other areas the tribal law system coexists side by side with State law. Under State law, honour killing is a crime, though a lenient view is taken by courts in awarding punishment. Under the tribal honour system it is not a crime at all, it is a legitimate killing to avenge the violation of honour. There are two different laws and attitudes: *karo kari* is a crime in terms of State law, and a duty under traditional and tribal law. The tribal and traditional culture prevails even in several urban areas.

Jirga

Jirga is a customary judicial system for trial of cases and deciding punishment or reward. It has been a means of resolving tribal criminal conflicts and civil disputes between individuals, families, and tribes. It applies the *Pakhtoonwali*, an all-encompassing code of conduct and of honour.... There are *sarkari jirgas* established under the Frontier Crimes Regulations (FCR) 1901,[7] initiated by the British. The magistrate, the political agent, and his assistant can designate a group of elders to try a criminal or a civil case in the tribal areas.

Apart from the legally formulated *sarkari jirga* there are the *jirgas* which do not have direct government sanction, yet operate in the tribal areas. These community-based *jirgas* are operating in many parts of Pakistan, including Karachi. In certain areas where a particular ethnic population has settled down with their families, they have their own *jirgas*.

The FCR authorizes the settlement of quarrels by the *jirga* that arise out of *zan, zar, zamin* (women, money, and land). It is worth noting that women are included as a subject matter for the *jirga* to decide upon, along with money and land. This reflects the notion that all legal disputes include women, along with money and land, and that a woman is considered part of the man's property, like other property. These are the characteristics of male domination and feudalism, exercising control over women as a matter of honour and prestige. This attitude is not confined to tribal *jirgas*, it is an attitude which finds expression all over Pakistan.

In fact, this crime has its roots in Baloch and Pushtun tribal custom not only in Balochistan, the NWFP, and Upper Sindh, which has a strong Baloch influx, but in Punjab province as well....

They follow their code called *riwaj, mayar,* or *Pakhtoonwali*..... This is an oral constitution whose enforcers are the people..... The honour has been codified in the psyche that guides the tribal societies. The Baloch and the Pushtuns have honour codes, enforced since centuries. According to a local chief, Sultan Ahmed Mugheri, *ghairat* is *izzat* and this comes with money and property. And if *izzat* is violated—then it is justified to kill and die for 'honour'....

More than just a punitive redress of honour, *karo kari* is a ritual that is carried unto death. But in doing so it does not lose the ceremonial aspects of ritual....

Upper Sindh Sindhi tribes like Mehars of Larkana and Ghotki just banish the women to a faraway land. This could be the psychological death of the woman....

Increasingly honour can be redressed by taking money even from the woman accused of being a *kari*. In Tangwani area in Jacobabad the *kari* would be banished and a huge amount of money would be charged from the man co-accused.....The relation between the market and the killings can be gauged from an interesting amendment in the tribal justice of the Mehar tribe. They reduced the fine for the *karo* (black man) to Rs 30,000 so that there is little incentive for men to accuse their wives, banish them, and get a fine in damages for that.[8]

Accordingly, even this crime of passion of honour killing can be negotiated in terms of cash. If the fine is low it may not be sufficient incentive for the husband to pursue the guilty or innocent wife, according to tribal perceptions.

Under tribal law the woman hounded as *kari* can seek refuge with the sardar of the tribe. If the sardar grants her refuge she can be spared the death punishment so long as she serves him, at times as his concubine or slave. On the other hand the tribal law also envisages that the person claiming compensation for illicit sex with his wife or daughter can seek support from the sardar of the tribe. The *jirga* decides the amount of compensation to be paid by the offending male and the sardar of the tribe receives a large percentage. Either way, the sardar wins.

Sindh Situation

According to press reports, there has been a phenomenal rise in cases of *karo kari*, especially in the province of Sindh. The incidents of *karo kari* are usually from upper Sindh as in those areas there are Pathans as well as settlers from Afghanistan, Balochistan, and southern Iran.

These groups have not changed their customs, which is the reason why women are targeted for revenge. These crimes against women are part of a feudal society. There are three main reasons for *karo kari*—revenge, property, and loans. If it is a matter of revenge, the woman of the family is murdered and the blame is put on the enemy claiming that the woman was having an illicit relationship and that her murder is an honour killing. Women are also killed for fear of distribution of property for inheritance.

Sometimes women are killed so that the family can collect monetary compensation for her death...

To get rid of a creditor, he is alleged to be *karo* and killed along with a woman *kari*. However, in Sindh the number of women killed on other accounts every day are more than those killed for *karo kari*. In Shadadkot, a poor woman social worker, Khalda Junejo, was kidnapped by influential people of the area. Apart from the parents of the woman, all the social, political, religious, literary, and activist groups have appealed for her recovery to the local authority and government. Even after three weeks she has not been found and the local officials are silent spectators of the kidnapping. There is no institution which has conducted a field study of the number of women who have been killed as *kari*.[9]

Murder for Marriage

The crime of *karo kari* is not confined to cases of illicit sex alone. The designation of what constitutes honour has widened. Cases in which the daughter of the family marries against the wishes of her parents can result in honour killing. The custom has come to the larger cities like Karachi where immigrant communities have brought in their code of honour. Particular ethnic groups usually live within their chosen areas. Even in cities like Karachi the ethnic groups apply their own tribal laws and practices.

In January 1998, Karachi witnessed riots. Riffat, a young Pathan girl, a student at the University, dared to marry her neighbour, from a Mohajir family, against the wishes of her family and tribe. Her parents charged the husband with kidnapping and zina (adultery) claiming that Riffat was already married to her cousin. Riots broke out in Karachi as opposing ethnic groups accused each other of violating their code of honour, protesting against the authorities and accusing them of inaction. The husband was absolved of all charges by the court but injured by gunshots when he appeared in court. The couple had to go into permanent hiding, seeking asylum in other countries.

In my personal experience, a Pashto-speaking mother came for consultation about the divorce of her erring daughter. The 16-year-old girl, who had spent many years in London, had been brought to Karachi. She fell in love with a young man. They eloped and got married. His parents accepted the marriage. They started living with his parents. The girl's mother was informed of the marriage. She immediately went and brought her daughter home saying she would arrange the customary *rukhsati* ceremony of sending the daughter to the husband's home. Apparently, at home the girl was persuaded or realized that the marriage was wrong and both the girl and the husband were willing to divorce by *mubarat* (mutual agreement).

I agreed to prepare the papers, but required the mother to bring her daughter to me so that I could witness her signature and be sure it was of her free will. When the girl was brought to me I requested the mother to wait outside the room as I wished to talk to the girl alone. The mother immediately brought out a pistol and said if her daughter did not comply she would kill her and her daughter's husband. She explained that the girl's father was out of the country, and if he returned to find this situation, he would kill all of them, including herself. However, with some persuasion the mother went out of the room. The girl was emphatic that she could not live with the man she had married. She recounted to me how she had to sleep on the floor, work like a servant in her in-laws' house, and was not willing to go back. The matter was thus resolved.

In another case a well-known Pathan doctor arranged the marriage of his daughter, who was also a doctor, to the son of a Memon family friend. The son was educated and working in the USA. He came to Karachi and they had the wedding with great pomp and ceremony. The couple went to the USA, but could not get along with each other. The girl left her husband after six months. The parents of the boy had been trying for the last three years for a divorce, but the girl's parents were against it. They would not let their daughter come into the picture, and she was untraceable.

The girl's father categorically stated that in their tribe there is no divorce, if the husband divorces her they would kill him, as it would violate their honour. He insisted that the husband be called to Karachi to take his wife back. The boy's parents were afraid of sending for their son for fear that he would be murdered.

Despite Islam allowing divorce, tradition and custom are so strong that the girl's parents were continuously saying that the daughter's death was preferable to a divorce.

The husband was insistent on a divorce. As it is possible for the husband to unilaterally pronounce divorce, a *talaqnama* (divorce deed) was prepared and along with notice under section 7 of the MFLO,[10] it was sent to the wife through her father and to the relevant authority, Chairman, Vice-President, Cantonment Board. There were numerous threats to the family of the husband. Safety through security guards and police protection had to be sought. Finally, the Chairman, who was required to summon the daughter or her father as her whereabouts were unknown, summoned her father and informed him that under the law, the Chairman had to record the case and the divorce would be final within ninety days. He persuaded the parents to accept a large sum of money as compensation for the expenses they had incurred and the return from the husband of expensive jewellery given at the time of marriage. The boy's father complied, as he was afraid for the life of his son.

Changes in Law Affecting Honour Killing

During the Zia regime, in December 1980 the Draft of Offences Against the Human Body, Qisas and Diyat Ordinance prepared by the Council of Islamic Ideology was published for public comments.[11] The Draft Ordinance was part of the so-called Islamization process. The proposed Ordinance was aimed at bringing the concept of qisas (punishment causing similar hurt or death) and diyat (compensation) into the legal system. About 1500 comments/objections were received by the Islamic Ideology Council. The Draft Ordinance was rejected following the several hundred adverse comments by scholars and a number of non-government organizations.

The women's movement was up in arms and held demonstrations. Their main objection was that the proposed ordinance was anti-female, especially as it proposed that the diyat of a female victim of murder will be half that of the male. The Draft law was scrutinized by various committees. The select committee of the Majlis-e-Shura, by a majority opinion, disagreed with the proposals of the Council of Islamic Ideology.[12] The Majlis-e-Shura was dissolved before the law could be adopted due to the continuing controversies.

In 1989 the Supreme Court Shariat Bench considered the laws relating to Offences Against the Human Body applicable in Pakistan and held that sections 54 and 299 to 328 of the Pakistan Penal Code and certain sections of the Criminal Procedure Code were repugnant to the injunctions of Islam.[13]

The Supreme Court held that:

Under the Anglo-Saxon jurisprudence, Society represented by State, holds a direct control over serious offences concerning person and property. The launching of the prosecution, the withdrawal of the prosecution, reprieve and pardon after conviction, and sentence by the State and its functionaries are all manifestations of this feature. The victims of the crime or his heirs have no say in the matter....

Under the injunctions of Islam this is not so at least in respect of offences against person. In Islam the individual victim or his heirs retain from the beginning to the end entire control over the matter including the crime and the criminal. They may not report it. They may not prosecute the offender. They may abandon prosecution of their free will. They may pardon the criminal at any stage before the execution of the sentence. They may accept monetary or other compensation to purge the crime and the criminal. They may compromise. They may accept qisas from the criminal. The State cannot impede, but must do its best, assist them in achieving their object and in appropriately exercising their rights. To that extent section 345 of the Code of Criminal Procedure is deficient.[14]

To implement the order of the court, the qisas and diyat provisions were added to the law. These changes more or less make the law of Offences Against the Human Body equal to personal grievances and compoundable. The effect has been anti-women in most cases.

Offences Affecting the Human Body

A new chapter has been added in the Pakistan Penal Code (PPC) of 1860, substituting sections 299 to 338-H for the previous sections 299 to 338.

Qatl-i-amd (intentionally causing death) is punishable with qisas (punishment causing similar hurt or death) or by tazir, (imprisonment), which may extend to twenty-five years.

Qatl-i-amd is not liable to qisas in cases where the offender is a minor or insane and when the offender murders his child or grandchild and where the *wali* of the victim is the child or grandchild of the offender. *Walis* are the heirs of the victim according to his personal laws or the government if there are no heirs.

This provision of law to a great extent protects the offender against the death sentence. For instance, in cases where the husband murders his wife who leaves behind a child, as the child is the *wali*, the offender would not be liable to the death penalty.

For easy reference the relevant sections of law—S302, S303, S304, S305, S306, S307, S308, S309, S310, and S311 are given below.

302. Punishment of *qatl-i-amd*. Whoever commits *qatl-i-amd* shall, subject to the provisions of this chapter be—
a) punished with death as qisas;
b) punished with death or imprisonment for life as tazir having regard to the facts and circumstances of the case, if the proof in either of the forms specified in section 304 is not available, or

c) punished with imprisonment of either description for a term, which may extend to twenty-five years, where according to the injunctions of Islam, the punishment of qisas is not applicable.

303. *Qatl* committed under *Ikrah-i-Tam* or *Ikrah-i-Naqis*. Whoever commits *qatl*:

a) Under *Ikrah-i-Tam* shall be punished with imprisonment for a term, which may extend to twenty-five years but shall not be less than ten years and the person causing *Ikrah-i-Tam* shall be punished for the kind of *qatl* committed as a consequence of his *Ikrah-i-Tam,* or

b) Under *Ikrah-i-Naqis* (duress not amounting to *Ikrah-i-Tam*) shall be punished for the kind of *qatl* committed by him and the person causing *Ikrah-i-Naqis* shall be punished with imprisonment for a term which may extend to ten years.
(*Ikrah-i-Tam* as defined, means putting a person, his spouse, or any of his blood relations within prohibited degrees of marriage in fear of instant death, or in fear of permanently impairing any organ of the body, or in fear of instant sodomy, or *zina-bil-jabr*.[15])

304. Proof of *qatl-i-amd* liable to qisas, etc.

(1) Proof of *qatl-i-amd* liable to qisas shall be in any of the following forms, namely:—

(a) the accused makes before a court competent to try the offence a voluntary and true confession of the commission of the offence; or

(b) by the evidence as provided in Article 17 of the *Qanoon-i-Shahadat* 1984 (PO 10 of 1984).

(2) The provisions of subsection 1, shall, *mutatis mutandis*, apply to a hurt liable to qisas.

305. *Wali*. In case of a *qatl*, the *wali* shall be—

(a) the heirs of the victim, according to his personal law; and

(b) the government, if there is no heir.

306. *Qatl-i-amd* not liable to qisas. *Qatl-i-amd* shall not be liable to qisas in the following cases, namely:—

(a) when an offender is minor or insane:

Provided that, where a person liable to qisas associates with himself in the commission of the offence a person not liable to qisas with the intention of saving himself from qisas, he shall not be exempted from qisas.

(b) when an offender causes death of his child or grandchild, how low-so-ever, and

(c) when a *wali* of the victim is a direct descendant, how low-so-ever, of the offender.

307. Cases in which qisas for *qatl-i-amd* shall not be enforced. Qisas for *qatl-i-amd* shall not be enforced in the following cases, namely:—

(a) when the offender dies before the enforcement of qisas;

(b) when any *wali* voluntarily and without duress, to the satisfaction of the court, waives the right of qisas under section 309, or compounds under section 310; and

(c) when the right of qisas devolves on the offender as a result of the death of the *wali* of the victim, or on the person who has no right of qisas against the offender.

308. Punishment in *qatl-i-amd* not liable to qisas, etc.

(1) Where an offender guilty of *qatl-i-amd* is not liable to qisas under section 306 or the qisas is not enforceable under clause (c) of section 307, he shall be liable to diyat:

Provided that, where the offender is minor or insane, diyat shall be payable either from his property or by such person as may be determined by the court.

Provided further that where at the time of committing *qatl-i-amd* the offender being a minor, had attained sufficient maturity, or being insane, had a lucid interval, so as to be able to realize the consequences of his act, he may also be punished with imprisonment of either description for a term which may extend to fourteen years as tazir.

(2) Notwithstanding anything contained in subsection 1, the court having regard to the facts and circumstances of the case in addition to the punishment of diyat, may punish the offender with imprisonment of either description for a term which may extend to fourteen years, as tazir.

309. Waiver (*afw*) of qisas in *qatl-i-amd*.

(1) In the case of *qatl-i-amd* an adult sane *wali* may at any time
and without any compensation, waive his right of qisas:

Provided that the right of qisas shall not be waived—

(a) Where the government is the *wali*, or

(b) Where the right of qisas vests in a minor or insane person.

(2) Where a victim has more than one *wali*, anyone of them may
waive his right of qisas:

Provided that the *wali* who does not waive the right of qisas
shall be entitled to his share of diyat.

(3) Where there is more than one victim, the waiver of the right of
qisas by the *wali* of one victim shall not affect the right of
qisas of the *wali* of the other victim.

(4) Where there is more than one offender, the waiver of the right
of qisas against one offender shall not affect the right of the
qisas against the other offender.

310. Compounding of qisas (*sulh*) in *qatl-i-amd*.

(1) In the case of *qatl-i-amd*, an adult sane *wali*, may, at any time
on accepting *badal-i-sulh*, compound his right of qisas:

Provided that only giving a female in marriage shall not be a
valid *badal-i-sulh*.

(2) Where a *wali* is a minor or insane, the *wali* of such minor or
insane *wali* may compound the right of qisas on behalf of such
minor or insane *wali*.

Provided that the value of *badal-i-sulh* not be less than the
value of diyat.

(3) Where the government is the *wali*, it may compound the right
of qisas.

Provided that the value of *badal-i-sulh* shall not be less than
the value of diyat.

(4) Where the *badal-i-sulh* is not determined or is a property or a
right the value of which cannot be determined in terms of
money under Shariat the right of qisas shall be deemed to have
been compounded and the offender shall be liable to diyat.

(5) *Badal-i-sulh* may be paid or given on demand or on a deferred
date as may be agreed upon between the offender and the *wali*.
('Compounding' here means compromise, adjustment,
forgoing.)

Explanation: In this section *badal-i-sulh* means the mutually agreed compensation according to Shariat to be paid or given by the offender to a *wali* in cash or in kind, or in the form of movable or immovable property.

311. Tazir after waiver or compounding of right of qisas in *qatl-i-amd*. Notwithstanding anything contained in section 309 or section 310, where all the *walis* do not waive or compound the right of qisas or keeping in view the principle of *fasad-fil-arz,* the court may, in its discretion having regard to the facts and circumstances of the cases, punish an offender against whom the right of qisas has been waived or compounded with imprisonment of either description for a term which may extend to fourteen years as tazir.

Explanation: For the purpose of this section, the expression *fasad-fil-arz* shall include the past conduct of the offender as being a previous convict, habitual or professional criminal, and the brutal manner in which the offence is committed.[16]

Evidently in cases where the offender cannot be punished by death as qisas, the offender is liable to diyat (compensation). However, irrespective of the punishment by diyat the courts in view of the facts and circumstances of the case, may punish the offender to up to fourteen years of imprisonment as tazir (S308(1)). This is seldom done in cases where the parties settle the matter.

The adult sane *wali* has a right to waive the right of qisas. Where there are more than one *wali* anyone of them may waive the right of qisas. However, the *wali* who has not waived his right of qisas will be entitled to receive his share of the right of diyat.

Besides, an adult *wali* of sound mind has the right of *sulh* (*badal-i-sulh*) that is, a mutually agreed compensation in cash or kind. There used to be a common practice of giving females in marriage as *badal-i-sulh*. The law has provided that simply giving a female in marriage would not be a valid *badal-i-sulh*. This means that a female can still be given in *badal-i-sulh*, along with other compensation as a *badal-i-sulh*. The law must be amended and giving of a female as compensation should be made a criminal offence by law.

I had a driver named Zaman working with me in Karachi whose brother was murdered in their home village in the Northern Areas. He had a wife and children. One day his wife came crying to me that Zaman's father had settled *badal-i-sulh* with the murderer, by accepting two young girls for marriage in their family. He had married one of the girls to Zaman's brother and intended to marry the other girl to Zaman. I called Zaman and threatened him with dismissal and urged him not to destroy his family life by the marriage. He admitted that he did not want to marry the girl, but he could not say no to his father. His father was very adamant. According to them, the girl had nowhere else to go now, except live as a wife in the family of the *wali* of the victim. Finally the father decided to marry the girl himself. Such is life for the woman!

The above-noted changes in the law were brought about as a consequence of the Supreme Court judgment for Islamization of the Pakistan Penal Code. Among other things it has made it possible to compound the offence of murder. It has also exempted certain persons from being penalized by the death penalty for murder. These changes have encouraged honour killings, which have increased manifold.

The Pakistan Penal Code sections 302 (a), 306 (c), 307, and 308 have been discussed by courts to determine the question whether *qatl-i-amd* (murder) committed by the husband of his wife, leaving behind child or children was liable to qisas (like punishment).[17]

The facts of the case according to the prosecution were as follows:

The petitioner, the accused husband, was married to the deceased four years before the occurrence. His wife gave birth to Mst Amina who was two years of age at the time of the occurrence. On the eventful day, at about 11.00 a.m., she went to the house of her father Faqir Ullah situated in Mohallah Harni Shah, Gali Lasoori Wali, Sharaqpur, to stitch some clothes for her daughter as Eid was approaching. The petitioner came there and started abusing the deceased for visiting her parents. The same day at 9.00 p.m., Faqir Ullah, father of the deceased, accompanied by Muhammad Saeed visited the house of the petitioner to give *Eidi* to his daughter and also to counsel the petitioner.

They found the petitioner and his co-accused, namely Jamil-uz-Zaman and Asif-uz-Zaman, quarrelling with his wife for visiting her parents. Jamil-uz-Zaman and Asif-uz-Zaman, within their view, caught hold of the wife, while Khalil-uz-Zaman, the petitioner husband, fired a shot from a pistol, hitting the left side of her chest resulting in her death on the spot.

The Supreme Court noted that the daughter was a *wali* of the deceased and was also the direct descendant of the offender/ husband. Both the Trial and Appellate Courts were fully aware of this aspect of the case. Yet, the offender had been sentenced to death as qisas under section 302(a) of PPC, whereas provisions of section 306(c) PPC clearly lay down that *qatl-i-amd* committed by the husband of his wife leaving behind child/ children was not liable to qisas. The Court further noted that the law has specifically provided punishment for *qatl-i-amd* not liable to qisas, under section 308 PPC, which does not provide death penalty, so the Trial Court and also the Appellate Court had no lawful authority/jurisdiction/power whatsoever to convict the accused under section 302 PPC or to impose the death penalty on him, and had acted in gross violation of the law. 'The courts derive authority to punish the accused from the statute. If the statute does not provide death penalty for the offence then obviously the court would have no jurisdiction to award the same, and as such, the conviction and sentence of the accused recorded under section 302 PPC was *Coram non-judice...*'[18]

The father of the deceased daughter filed a review against the order. The Supreme Court, in its review petition, held that the offender is absolved from the sentence of death by way of death if the *wali* of the victim is a descendant of the offender.

The Court opined:

We are, however, unable to agree with Mr Muhammad Ismail Qureshi, learned Senior Advocate Supreme Court, that there is no injunction of Quran that absolves an offender from the sentence of death by way of qisas if the *wali* of the victim is a descendant of the offender. We have been able to lay our hands on at least three commentaries on the Islamic Law of Crimes, which support the view adopted by the learned Division Bench of this Court, which had passed the impugned order.....

Due to paucity of time we have not been able to make further research in the matter ourselves. The opposite side had also not assisted us on the subject. Nonetheless, the amendments were introduced in the year 1990 in the Pakistan Penal Code including the provisions of clause (c) of section 306 and clause (a) and (b) of section 304 of the PPC with a view to bringing those provisions in conformity with the injunctions of Islam and Sunnah.

The presumption, therefore, is that the aforementioned provisions are not violative of any Quranic text or the Sunnah of the Prophet (SAW). The second contention is, therefore, devoid of any force.[19]

Sadly the Supreme Court, according to its own statement, did not have time to research the question even though the rights of the minor child were involved. Besides no consideration was given by the learned judges to section 309, which provides that the right of qisas shall not be waived where the government or minor is the *wali*. Evidently the minor daughter was the *wali* in the above case.

The Option of *Lian*

The prosecution's story was that the deceased had been called by Saleh (brother of the present applicant) to his house on some pretext. After a while when a gunshot was heard from the house, the complainant, the wife of the deceased, Mst Laila, and mother-in-law of the deceased Mst Soomri, along with his cousin Bahero rushed to the spot where Saleh was found with a gun in his hand, his brother Khair Muhammad had a gunshot injury to his arm and Sohrab (the applicant) was holding the injured. In their presence Saleh fired twice at his brother Khair Muhammad, who died instantly. It was disclosed by Saleh and Sohrab that the deceased was *karo* (had illicit relations with Mst Zubeda, the wife of Saleh) so he had been murdered. Soon after that both the accused went into the house and killed Mst Zubeda on the basis of allegations against her that she was a *kari* (one who has sexual relations with a person other than her husband). The learned judge held that:

> No doubt if any person finds his wife in objectionable condition he would definitely lose his temper to murder the sinners but if a person has doubts or clues against the immoral activities of his wife then Islam has its own Laws and Rules to meet with such situations, which have to be followed by every believer if he/she has faith in Allah and His Apostles. It does not support effervescence of vengeance by taking the lives of persons but promotes tolerance... In such cases the Islamic Law of *Lian* has been introduced, which has to be applied by the court and not by the individuals.
>
> Resultantly, the petition for bail of the applicant fails and is dismissed in spite of the fact that the learned counsel for the State conceded to the grant of bail.[20]

The Court has implied that no wife should be killed on suspicion or accusation of adultery as Islam has provided the *Lian* procedure for accusing women of adultery by the husband ending in divorce where the woman refutes the allegation four times.

There are a few cases where a distinction has been made between the crime of honour killing wherein the murder is committed by the husband losing his mental balance on actually witnessing his wife having illicit relations, as opposed to killing on mere suspicion. In the above case, the honourable judge has taken a balanced view and refused to grant bail to the accused Sohrab, brother of Saleh the husband.

Compounding the Punishment for Murder

In a series of seminars for police officers, at the one held in Peshawar, Justice Nasir-ul-Malh of the Peshawar High Court said that compared to other homicide cases it was easier to compound the offence under the Qisas and Diyat Laws in honour killing cases, under sections 309 and 310 of the PPC, though the prosecution could still press section 311 for punishment. Advocate Qazi Jamil, the former attorney-general, referred to sections 309 and 310 and stated that under these sections a *wali* could waive or compound his right of qisas. Qazi Jamil recalled the 1999 murder case of Samia Imran in the office of a lawyer in Lahore. In that case, he said, the accused first killed Samia and then compounded the offence as the *wali* in that case was her husband, from whom she was trying to get a divorce, in accordance with case law.[21]

> Police officials at a four-day seminar here have recommended reviewing the Qisas and Diyat Ordinance (PPC sections quoted above) so as to prevent compounding of the offence in cases of honour killing. The seminar proposed: 'The Law should be reviewed regarding compounding of the offence under Qisas and Diyat Ordinance because the next of kin in most of the honour killing cases are actually amongst the conspirators....
> Post-mortem exemption must not be granted in honour killing cases, investigation officers must be given in-service training so as to distinguish between pre-planned murders and honour killing.
> The media should play its role in creating social awareness about the subject; and genuine cases of honour killing should be separated from cases of planned murder.[22]

The press has been consistently depicting the atrocities being committed by society in condoning crimes of honour and clearly underlining the lacunae and injustices in the law and legal system. To date there is not a single case of death penalty being awarded in cases of honour killing and several cases go unreported, are not prosecuted or dismissed as they are not pursued for lack of evidence. If in some cases a few criminals are awarded death or severe penalty the incidence of the offence may decrease. It is essential to review the qisas and diyat provisions in the PPC regarding compounding of the offence, especially as in most honour killing cases the conspirators are the next of kin. Exempting the husband from the death penalty for killing his wife if his child is the *wali* can hardly be termed justice.

Grave and Sudden Provocation

One of the changes introduced in the Pakistan Penal Code was that the exception of 'grave and sudden provocation' was dropped from section 302 of the PPC. In a Supreme Court judgment, it was held that the 'grave and sudden provocation' exception in section 302 is not available in the amended Pakistan Penal Code for reducing the punishment for murder.

This was a case in which the accused had murdered his brother Mushtaq Ahmed and Mst Sheema, on seeing them in an objectionable position. The learned judge granted bail to the accused on the basis of 'grave and sudden provocation' as he had seen the deceased in a compromising position. The Supreme Court cancelled the bail and held that the learned judge in the High Court fell in error in not taking into account the amendment of the relevant law and the latest precedents. 'In this view of the matter, the position is converted into appeal and allowed. The bail granted to the respondent No. 1 is cancelled. He shall be taken into custody to stand his trial.'[23] This is a welcome change in applying the law by judicial activism in a case of honour killing.

However, in another case, the court held a different interpretation and ruled:

The Qisas and Diyat Ordinance has deleted both the provisions of provocation from PPC section 300 exception and section 304 (I) from the Pakistan Penal Code but this does not mean that now zina-related plea of grave and sudden provocation cannot be raised at all and if established cannot serve as a mitigating circumstance for awarding lesser punishment. Such a plea can certainly be taken but the accused doing so shall have to prove it, by producing evidence in accordance with the standard laid down by the Islamic Law that the victims were committing zina liable to death. If the plea is established through such evidence it will serve as a mitigating circumstance for awarding lesser punishment under clause (c) of section 302 PPC.[24]

However, in the above case acquittal of the accused was ordered on the grounds that 'there is no ocular evidence'.[25]

In another case, Abdul Waheed and his co-accused Khalil Ahmad were charged with committing the murder of one Shaukat Nizami. While Khalil Ahmad was acquitted, the learned Trial Court awarded seven years' RI under clause (c) of section 302 PPC to Abdul Waheed on the basis of his statements under sections 340 and 342 CrPC, wherein he had taken the stance that on seeing the deceased committing zina with his sister he had killed him under grave and sudden provocation.

The appeal filed by the State was accepted by the learned Supreme Shariat Appellate Bench and the convict was sentenced to death as qisas under clause (a) of section 302 PPC for the reason that he had not produced the requisite evidence to lend support to his plea. The following is an excerpt from the said judgment:

> The observation made in Gul Hassan's case clearly shows the grave and sudden provocation is not an exception per se and the punishment of qisas, where *qatl-i-amd* is committed under grave and sudden provocation, can be mitigated only if proof of zina is produced, which conforms to the required standard of evidence prescribed under the Islamic injunctions. In other words, *qatl-i-amd* by the husband (or, by inference, by a near relative, as in the instant case) will attract a punishment lesser than qisas only if proof of commission of such zina exists which satisfies the required standard of evidence prescribed under Islamic injunctions.[26]

The rationale is that under Islamic Law, the punishment of qisas death is only applicable if a husband on seeing his wife and her paramour committing zina (which is punishable with death) kills one or both of them and proves the factum of zina by producing the requisite evidence. Where he does not prove zina by the standard laid down by Islamic Law, that is the evidence of four adult truthful male witnesses who have seen the occurrence, he cannot claim the exemption from death punishment.

Under the law grave and sudden provocation was not considered by the courts. Proof for punishment for zina requires 'four adult witnesses'. Where zina is alleged the Islamic criteria of proof of the commission of the crime detailed in section 8 of the Zina Ordinance for *hadd* punishment is required to be produced and only then the penalty of death by qisas is to be excluded and the court may give lesser punishment.

In certain circumstances courts have refused to believe the plea of grave and sudden provocation. In another case the court recorded that the plea of sudden and grave provocation was put forward after a lapse of eight years. The accused surrendered to the police fifteen hours after murdering his wife.

The record did not indicate that the accused informed the police as to the cause of his action. The judicial confession of the accused was recorded six days after his arrest. Even in his confession the accused did not disclose that he saw his wife in a compromising position with the complainant. The accused did not put such a suggestion to prosecution witnesses when they were examined under section 164 CrPC where he was given the opportunity of cross-examination. The accused did not put such a suggestion to witnesses even during the trial. The court held that the accused had come up with the theory of sudden and grave provocation after the death of the complainant when he was not available to deny or reply to the allegation against him. The plea of sudden and grave provocation was discarded.[27]

However, in another case it has been held that:

Prima facie, it appears that the deed was done by Muhammad Faisal, petitioner, in a fit of rage when he had lost control over his senses under sudden and grave provocation.

The question is whether the plea of grave and sudden provocation is still available or not, the answer is to be found in the Quranic injunctions contained in verse 34 of Surah Nisa ordaining that 'Men are in charge of women'. A husband, father, and the brothers are supposed to guard the life and honour of the females, who are inmates of the house and when anyone of them finds a trespasser committing zina with a woman of his family, then murder by him whilst deprived of self-control will not amount to *qatl-i-amd* liable to qisas because the deceased in such a case is not a *masoom-ud-dam*.[28]

The total number of honour killings reported in Pakistan by the Bureau of Research and Development, Ministry of Interior, Government of Pakistan[29] are as follows:

Year	Punjab	Sindh	NWFP	Balochistan	Islamabad	Northern Areas	Total
1995	345	125	49	39	1	7	566
1996	322	143	67	45	0	8	585
1997	354	116	56	32	0	5	563
1998	356	133	48	48	2	13	600
1999	357	138	72	52	3	12	634
Total	1734	655	292	216	6	45	2948

Karo Kari Statistics for the Province of Sindh

The details of *karo kari* cases registered from the year 1980 up to 2000 in the province of Sindh have been compiled by the SO Crimes, Sindh Police.

According to these figures, in the year 1980, 160 cases were registered in which 200 people were murdered, out of these 103 victims were females and 97 were male. The highest ratio is in the year 1999, where 274 cases were registered, in which 340 people were killed, including 206 female and 134 male victims. The year 2000 shows a slight decrease, with 181 female victims and 113 male victims out of a total 294 victims in 232 cases.[30]

Comparatively, not only have the number of registered cases increased but the number of women victims has doubled from 1980 to 2000. This increase of cases of *karo kari* points to the mounting discrimination against women, the growing double standards for assigning blame and punishment on women, and the difficulty for women to flee to avoid being killed.

From the years 1980 to 2000, in 1205 cases of *karo kari* 1222 men were allegedly killed as follows: eleven wives killed their husbands, eighteen brothers killed their siblings, two sons killed their father, one daughter killed her father, 893 distant relatives and 297 non-relatives killed men for *karo kari*.[31] The high number of distant relatives and non-relatives apparently consists of the relatives of the co-accused women in the cases of *karo kari* or people who claim *karo kari* to camouflage other crimes. In a few cases in which brothers have killed brothers, this may well be for land disputes. No father was accused of killing his son. This clearly shows that in the immediate family the father does not consider illicit sex by the son of the family as a crime to be punished to vindicate the family honour. Where the daughter is suspected or accused of adultery, the reaction by the family is quite contrary.

In one thousand nine hundred and sixty-seven cases of *karo kari* from the years 1980 to 2000, one thousand nine hundred and ninety-eight women were reported killed. Of these, 1099 wives were killed by their husbands, fifty-six daughters were killed by their fathers, 189 sisters were killed by their brothers, thirty mothers were killed by their sons, 612 women were killed by distant relatives, and twelve women were killed by non-relatives.[32] The majority of the women were murdered by their husbands.

In 962 cases of *karo kari* from 1980 to 2000, 1073 men and women victims were reported killed.[33]

According to the custom of honour, the immediate relatives of the women, that is the husband, father, and possibly the brother and son, traditionally may be the enraged, aggrieved party. Other relatives such as uncles and non-relations would be completely unjustified. Non-relatives have no business to touch much less kill a woman for so-called honour, except when the killing is by the whole community on the decision of a *jirga*.

In a number of cases it is the extended family relatives and non-relatives who come into the picture and murder the male and the female ostensibly for sex outside marriage, possibly to avenge his having sex with a woman of their family or committing murder for some other motive and involving a woman in order to get away with light punishment.

Slow Disposal of Cases

Disposal of cases is extremely slow in Pakistan. It appears that the State, who is the prosecutor in these cases, does not pursue the cases diligently. The investigation is poor. Equipment and technical expertise for scientific investigation is extremely limited. Unnecessary delay in obtaining reports deters the trial. There is little cooperation from families of the victims in most cases. The family rarely considers *karo kari* a crime. Tragically, the murdered victim is condemned unheard, for alleged unproved illicit sexual relations. The dead cannot defend themselves.

Few Convictions

The following figures depict the delay in handling and disposal of *karo kari* cases:

In the year 2000, 129 cases were registered in which 135 women were killed, but only one case was disposed of during the year 2000, and most probably this was a case from a previous year. In twelve cases investigations were pending and 116 cases were challaned. There were fourteen acquittals, and 102 cases are under trial.[34] These figures may also include cases registered in previous years, but which were prosecuted in the year 2000, when the accused persons were challaned, acquitted, or convicted.

From 1980 to 2000, 962 cases were registered in which 1073 victims, both men and women were killed, 1967 cases were registered in which 1998 women were killed, and 1205 registered cases in which 1222 men were killed.[35]

Accordingly, in the two decades from 1980 to 2000, 4154 cases for the offence of *karo kari* were registered, of which 4060 cases were challaned, and the remaining were dropped.

Out of these 122 cases were disposed of, 139 cases are pending investigation, and in 2106 cases trials are pending in courts. Only 243 accused persons were convicted over a period of two decades and 1704 accused persons were acquitted.[36]

This is a very poor reflection on police performance and the judicial system in awarding punishment to the guilty in cases of the heinous crime of murder. Even where punishment was awarded, though no details are available, the penalty must have been minimal on grounds of the so-called mitigating circumstances of honour!

The cases of *karo kari* reported to the police are much lower than the incidence of the crime. The family is averse to reporting the crime, especially as in most cases it is the husband, father, or brother who are to be accused of the crime.

At times, the family of the wife files the report or the perpetrator of the crime surrenders to the police, as he has no option as the woman is dead and the criminal believes that by confessing to honour killing, he will gain freedom and respect, and his punishment will be minimal.

State as Complainant

Recently, steps have been taken in the province of Sindh to curb the crime of *karo kari*. The police have been alerted and are documenting cases of *karo kari*. Files dating back to 1994 of cases of murder where *karo kari* has been alleged are under review. In the district of Larkana a committee has been set up comprising representatives of the administration and civil society to recommend measures to reduce the crime. In some of the affected districts, local committees made up of elders of the area have been set up to follow cases of *karo kari*. In November 2001 the SHO, that is the head of the police station of the taluka of the city of Larkana, '..... lodged as complainant the first FIR of a *karo kari*-related murder on Monday in light of the newly framed strategy of the district government and police to combat this social evil. An unmarried girl, Shahzadi, aged 14, was killed on the pretext of *karo kari* allegedly by her uncle in village Tharo Luhar in the outskirts of Larkana on Monday. The accused, Moula Bakhsh Luhar, escaped after committing the crime.'[37]

If a complaint is to be filed by the police on behalf of the State it will to some extent reduce incidents of *karo kari* not being recorded at all. Vigilance by the local police and the local people can go a long way towards controlling the crime. Local journalists have to a great extent facilitated the reporting of the crimes through continuous activism.

Reasons for Increase

Honour killing has become a daily affair. There are several reasons for this: diminishing consideration and respect for women; the concept of owning the women of the family, which has become widespread; the Zina Ordinance, which has created an atmosphere of blame and suspicion questioning the chastity of women; inadequate punishments and limited convictions by courts not applying the penalty for murder; legal acceptance of honour killing as mitigating circumstances resulting in trivial punishment; community and families justifying honour killing and non-cooperation of the family in bringing forward evidence; the police bias against women; negative attitude of the police towards gender issues; untrained crime investigators; dearth of equipment and personnel for forensic tests and medico-legal reports to courts; the lacunae in the law; a weak and dilatory judicial system which allows most criminals to go unpunished; and the all-male gender insensitive judiciary. In addition to these factors, the propagators of *karo kari* misinterpret Islam to support honour killing as a religious duty.

The faltering economy of the country may be a possible cause for the increase in crime. It has been observed in many countries that the crime rate rises when the economy is in decline. There is little doubt that in Pakistan the economy is deteriorating, and there is a serious problem of unemployment and rising prices. The status of women has been getting worse.

'For the most part, women bear traditional male control over every aspect of their bodies, speech, and behaviour with stoicism, as part of their *kismet* [fate], but exposure to media, the work of women's rights groups, and a greater degree of mobility have seen the beginnings of awareness of women's rights seep into the secluded world of women.

'But if women begin to assert these rights, however tentatively, they often face more repression and punishment: the curve of honour killing has risen in parallel to the awareness of rights.'[38] This indicates that as women become aware of their rights and try to assert their rights, they are endangered. They do not have the means or social support to stand up for their rights.

The discriminatory and derogatory laws adopted during the Zia regime have not been changed. Inadequate, unjust family laws make wives subservient. The economic and social dependence of women have made them much more vulnerable to sex-related crimes. The code of honour is not applied equally to men and women. The discrimination against a woman follows her to her grave in *karo kari* murders. The *kari* is buried, but the *Fateha* prayer is not allowed for her, whereas the *karo* is buried in the family graveyard and prayer is allowed for him.

The deteriorating anti-women climate is further compounded by pseudoreligious factions, especially those under the spell of the Taliban philosophy of segregation and subordination of women, which is having a negative impact on women.

According to a survey by a group of journalists in Sindh during the first quarter of 2001, out of 87 victims of *karo kari* 62 were women. Men accused of *karo kari* can run away, but women suffer as they have no place to go.

There are only a few shelter homes in large cities, which are virtual prisons. They are called *Dar-ul-Aman* and require a court order before a woman can be admitted or allowed to leave. In some cases, women seeking court protection are sent to prison under section 107 CrPC, which deals with public tranquillity, just to keep them safe from murder or injury, as there is no other place women can be sent.

There is a need for action-oriented research into the causes of the increase in *karo kari* and action plans and projects for social change need to be implemented.

Law Reforms

The President of Pakistan, General Pervez Musharraf, declared at the Convention on Human Rights and Human Dignity that 'The Government of Pakistan vigorously condemns the practice of so-called "honour killings". Such actions do not find any place in our religion or law. Killing in the name of honour is murder, and it will be treated as such.'[39] Such statements do not change the law and the attitude of the courts. There is abundant case law where honour killing has been considered a mitigating circumstance, even where the crime is not committed in a fit of grave and sudden provocation, the courts follow these rulings as binding precedents. It is absolutely necessary that a specific provision is added to the Penal Code stating that killing a woman or a man by an individual, a family, community, or tribe on accusations of sex outside marriage, will not amount to mitigating circumstances for awarding less severe punishment than that for murder. The basis for this is that any accused person is entitled to a fair trial by a court of law and cannot be punished by individuals, the community, or even by *jirgas*.

Besides, compounding the crime of honour killing must not be allowed under the Pakistan Penal Code. The crime is within the family and easily compoundable. The exemptions to the criminal, where the *wali* is his child, or his *wali,* must be abolished.

Repeal or at least amendment of the Zina Ordinance to end discrimination against and degradation of women is essential to restore the dignity of women. Any allegation of illicit sex must be tried by a Family Court, and police arrests should not be made merely on receiving a complaint. Not a single case of honour killing has been sent to the gallows. Justice is not done. Criminals go free with inadequate punishment and often the cases are compounded. The law must change to remedy this situation.

Strategies to End Honour Killing

- Final conviction, awarding severe punishment for honour killing in at least ten cases all over the country, would go a long way in bringing home to the criminals that honour killing is punishable. The threat of punishment can be a deterrent.
- Murder for honour must not be compoundable.
- The acceptance of honour killing as honourable must be attacked by creating awareness.
- Widespread media presentations should show that honour killing is not justifiable and not Islamic.
- Education to counter discrimination against women.
- Ensuring security of women in family life through improved laws.
- Implementation of Penal Laws and an effective judicial system dispensing justice.
- Facilities for shelter homes, counselling, rehabilitation, and support services.
- Training and gender sensitizing of police officers, judges, and related government agencies to bring about a positive response to women's complaints and to address their complaints.
- Religious leaders must come forward publicly to assert that *karo kari* is un-Islamic. Positive viewpoints and fatwas can have a balancing effect on the psyche of the people. The State must go all out through the radio and television to widely present the true Islamic interpretation.
- Research is needed into the causes of increase of *karo kari* and to find ways and means of curbing the evil.
- Improving the economic status of women by providing employment opportunities.
- Education and training of women, to make them self supporting.

- Legal Aid Services must be made available to all women being accused or pursued for the alleged offence of illicit sex.
- Accused women must be supported by material, medical, psychological, and rehabilitation services.

NOTES

1. Chief of Sindh Police, Mr Aftab Nabi, unpublished paper presented at the PAWLA Seminar on Violence Against Women held in November 2000.
2. *Dawn*, 21 May 2001.
3. Justice Javid Iqbal, Judge Supreme Court of Pakistan. 'Crimes Against Women in Pakistan.' Keynote address, APWA Conference, Karachi, 1988. PLD 1988 (4) Journal Section 195, p. 198.
4. 'Woman hacks husband to death', *Dawn*, 21 May 2001.
5. 'Five die in family feuds', *Dawn*, 23 May 2001.
6. 'Man kills wife, two die in incidents', *Dawn*, 24 May 2001.
7. Central Statutes.
8. Syed Viquarun-nissa Hashmi, unpublished paper, Crimes Against Women presented at the PAWLA Seminar on Violence Against Women.
9. Professor Aijaz Qureshi, Chairman, National Rural Support Programme, Chairman, Sindh Non-Government Organizations Federation (SINGOF), Ex-Professor, Jamshoro University. Paper in Urdu presented at the PAWLA Seminar on Violence Against Women, November 2000.
10. The Muslim Family Laws Ordinance 1961, Gazette of Pakistan Extra Ordinance, 19 June 1961 (PLD 1961 Central Statute–275).
11. Draft of Offences Against the Human Body, Qisas and Diyat Ordinance, Council of Islamic Ideology Extra Part III, 13 December 1980, Islamabad, Government of Pakistan.
12. Rashida Patel, *Islamisation of Laws in Pakistan*, Faiza Publishers, Karachi, 1986.
13. See also pp. 190 and 191.
14. Federation of Pakistan vs. Gul Hassan Khan, PLD 1989, SC 633, pp. 640 and 684-85.
15. S209 PPC(g), ibid.
16. Ss 299 to 338F substituted initially by the Criminal Law Amendment Ordinance of 1990 and finally by the Criminal Law Amendment Act (II of 1997, 11 April 1997, PLD 1997 CS), p. 326.
17. Federation of Pakistan vs. Gul Hassan Khan, PLD 1989, SC 633.
18. Khalil-uz-Zaman vs. Supreme Appellate Court, Lahore and Four others, PLD 1994, SC 885, p. 891.

19. Faqir Ullah vs. Khalil-uz-Zaman and Others, SCMR 1999, 2203, p. 2212.
20. Sohrab vs. the State, PLD 1994, Karachi 431.
21. Faqir Ullah vs. Khalil-uz-Zaman and others, SCMR 1999, 2203, p. 2212.
22. 'Review of Qisas Ordinance Suggested', *Dawn*, Peshawar, 24 May 2001.
23. Khurshid Mohammad vs. Aisha Muhammad & the State 1997, SCJ 119, pp. 121, 123(c).
24. Abdul Nabi vs. the State 1997, SD 115, p. 118.
25. Ibid.
26. 1992 PSC Cr. 498.
27. Murtaza Ali Khan vs. the State, PLD 1986, Karachi 121, p. 128.
28. Muhammad Faisal vs. the State 1997 MLD 2527, p. 2528.
29. Letter ref. No. 1/7/2000-SRO, 16 Jan 2002, Government of Pakistan, Ministry of Interior, Bureau of Police Research and Development.
30. 'Cases of *karo kari*, reported victims killed during the year 1980 to 2000 in Sindh province'. Unpublished figures from the DIG, Sindh compiled by SO Crimes, Sindh, D/Dcrime/*Karo Kari*/Victim Men & Women Killed (1980 to 2000).
31. 'Statement showing details of *karo kari* (in which victims were men only) registered in Sindh province during the year 1980 to 2000', ibid.
32. 'Statement showing details of *karo kari* (in which victims were women only) registered in Sindh province during the year 1980 to 2000', ibid.
33. 'Statement showing details of *karo kari* (in which victims were both men and women) registered in Sindh province during the year 1980 to 2000', ibid.
34. Ante 31. Details of *karo kari* (in which victims were women only).
35. Ante 30, 31, 32. Details of *karo kari* (in which victims were men, women and both).
36. Ibid.
37. 'Police file first *karo kari* case as complainant', *Dawn*, 13 November 2001.
38. *Pakistan, Violence Against Women in the Name of Honour*, published by Amnesty International, International Secretariat, 1 Easton Street, London WCIX 0DW, United Kingdom 1999, p. 1.
39. Pakistan Convention on Human Rights and Human Dignity, April 2000 published by the Ministry of Information and Ministry of Law, Justice and Human Rights, Government of Pakistan, Islamabad 2000.

6

POPULATION CONTROL

The world, especially the developing countries and particularly Pakistan, is facing grave danger due to population problems. Though Pakistan started its programme for population control five decades ago, even today the country is plagued by over-population. Nine babies are born every minute. This has denied economic stability and adversely affected the status of women. For a large number of children there is not enough in terms of education, food, nutrition, housing, and health care. Women suffer along with their children. Their health suffers and women have no time or energy to think about developing and caring for themselves.

Presently, Pakistan has a population of 140 million[1] and it is expected to double in twenty-five years. Pakistan's population growth used to be 3.1 per cent, one of the highest in the world. According to the 1998 census figures, it came down to 2.61 per cent, and in the year 2000 the population growth has been further reduced to 2.2 per cent. In Pakistan there are 30 million women in the age group of 13 to 49 years, which is the fertile group. Nearly five million women become pregnant every year.

The crude birth rate per 1000 has come down from 42.7 in 1984-88, to 35.2 in 1996. This is an insufficient decline. The crude death rate has declined from 10.9 during the period 1984 to 1988 to 8.8 in 1996. The sex ratio, according to the 1998 census, was 67,840,000 males and 62,739,000 females.[2] There are five million more men than women. This is a different picture to developed countries, where women outnumber men.

Initiating Population Control

In the 1950s it was the Family Planning Association of Pakistan (FPAP), an NGO, which introduced the concept of organized family planning services. At the government level, family planning was forcefully supported in the 1960s by President Mohammad Ayub Khan. He had taken over the reins of government in 1958 as the Chief Martial Law Administrator, assuming the title of Supreme Commander of the armed forces. The Population Policy was for the first time integrated in Pakistan's Third Five-Year Plan, 1965 to 1970. Ayub Khan's political support for population control was used by religious parties to oppose him. His opponents exploited this measure as being un-Islamic. After Ayub Khan the population control programme underwent changes and lost emphasis due to weakening political support. Not only were the population programmes and policies changed, but the name was also changed to population welfare programme in deference to public opinion. There was little political commitment to the programme and implementation was poor. When the Martial Law regime of General M. Ziaul Haq took control of the country in 1977, the programme for population planning was almost abandoned on the plea of being forbidden by Islam. It was later restarted slowly in the shape of the population welfare integrated programme.

'Ever since its inception in the mid-60s, the population welfare programme has undergone many administrative and programmatic changes. Several approaches were taken, but none were successful, partly because of little demand for family planning, fluctuating political commitment, and inadequacies in design and implementation. The population welfare programme has been very much focused on demographic targets, and has been very family planning oriented.'[3]

One of the main reasons for the government not coming out forcefully in favour of population planning in Pakistan has been the extremist propaganda and pressure from the religious lobby. They spread the misconception that Islam is against family planning. This is contrary to the dictum of the Holy Prophet (PBUH).

One of the strongest impediments to family planning/fertility resolution in Pakistan is the negative attitude and preaching of the obscurantist maulvis and maulanis, backed by politico-religious parties. In many other Muslim countries i.e. Egypt, Turkey, Tunisia, Indonesia, Malaysia, Bangladesh, and Iran, religious scholars have strongly supported family planning on Islamic tenets. The Al-Azhar University was the first to pronounce its support for family planning, though the leaders of the religious uprising in Egypt opposed the Population Conference held in Cairo in 1994.

From the Islamic point of view family planning is acceptable. The following authorities are relied upon:

1. The Quran says
Allah desireth for you ease, He desireth not hardship for you... (2:12).

2. The reference sources of Shariat Law as to permissibility (*halal*) or prohibition (*haram*) are the glorious Quran and the tradition (Sunnah) of His messenger (PBUH)....

A thorough review of the Quran reveals no text (*nuss*) prohibiting the prevention of pregnancy or diminution of the number of children, but there are several traditions of the Prophet that indicate its permissibility. This was accepted by jurists of Islamic Shariat. While there is also Sunnah that can appear to be prohibiting, the majority (*jumhour*) of jurists (*fuqaha*) in the legal schools (*madhahib*) agree with the permissibility of *al-azl* (coitus interruptus) where the husband ejaculates outside his wife's vagina....

From this brief review of jurisprudence, it is evident that *al-azl* for temporary prevention of pregnancy is permissible (*jaiz*). The *sahaba* themselves practised *al-azl* at the time of the Prophet (PBUH). He came to know about it and did not prohibit them according to Jabir's tradition reported in *Muslim*, and while the

Quran was being revealed as reported in *Al-Bukhari*. Thus, prevention of pregnancy is lawful as stated above.

Abortion

'The Hanafi opinion supports abortion provided it is performed within 120 days of conception. During this period the foetus is not believed to be a complete human soul. Early abortion is held to be *makrouh* (disliked but not forbidden) when it lacks valid reasons or justifications.'[4]

3. Fatwa-e-Alamgiri

Al Fatwa *Al-Hindiyya* (published in Egyptian Bolaq in 1740). Fatwa-e-Alamgiri was the joint effort of 500 Muslim scholars. It was the result of the research of 500 jurists of Islam. It says:
'There is no disapprobation in *azl* with the consent of the free woman (wife). It is lawful for a woman to abort the child so long as no part of him has been formed and this does not take place before 120 days, that is, the pregnancy not having completed 120 days.'

4. Though *azl* is commonly understood as coitus interruptus, according to the well-known book *Al-Taj-al Jama Lil-Usulfi* Ahadith Al-Rasul:
'The term *azl* includes the use of medicines for birth control purposes. It also includes the abortion of the foetus into whom life has not so far been breathed as the purpose in all these cases is the same i.e. birth control and Allah knows better.' (Vol. XI p. 245).

5. According to Allama Abu Bakar Jassas, Imam Abu Hanifa derived the validity of birth control from the Holy Quran, Hadith, and practices of the Companions. The legality of family planning in Islam has not been contradicted by any Hanafi jurist.

6. Shah Abdul Aziz, son of Shah Walli Ullah of Delhi, of the later jurists also agreed with the contention that *azl* is lawful on the basis of authentic and well-known traditions of the Holy Prophet. There is no doubt about its legality in Islam, hence in order to control birth it is quite lawful to use any device that can prevent conception.

7. According to the Jafria School, which is followed by Shias in Pakistan, in almost every authentic book, express permission for *azl* is given. Imam Jafar says, 'There is no harm in practising *azl*.' Imam Zain-ul-Abdin also did not see any harm in *azl*.

8. Regarding birth control, there are nine Al-Hadith of the Holy Prophet (PBUH). Eight support the issue. Allama Shaukani in his famous book *Nail al-Autar*, has stated that the Companions used to resort to *azl* during the lifetime of the Holy Prophet (PBUH) while the Holy Quran was being revealed and when the Holy Prophet came to know of this practice, He did not forbid it.

9. A contemporary Islamic scholar, Khalid Ishaq, has stated in his paper on family planning that: 'It is quite clear that the subject of planned parenthood was of active consideration during the times of the Prophet (PBUH). Many of the Prophet's (PBUH) Companions practised it. The Holy Prophet (PBUH) did not prevent them from such practices.'

10.   In a recent article, Professor Rafi ullah Shehab has stated that 'It is unfortunate that they (ulema) never care to study the teachings of Islam on this issue, otherwise they would have known that family planning is one of those issues on which jurists and scholars of all the Muslim sects totally agree.'

Besides, it is an accepted principle of Islamic jurisprudence that what has not been forbidden is allowed. This principle has been endorsed by the Shariat Appellant Court in Pakistan.[5]

Contraception has nowhere been forbidden in the Holy Quran or by the Holy Prophet (PBUH), though there is disturbing juristic opinion opposing fertility regulation or limiting the devices accepted in Islam for birth control.

In particular, Maulana Maudaudi in his book *The Birth Control Movement* has claimed that it is a plot against Islam, it would usher moral malaise, and that women would feel free to join the labour force and abandon their traditional roles. While he frequently cites theologians, the bulk of the Maulana's book is socio-political rather than theological. Furthermore, the Maulana's views provoked a strong reaction to family planning proponents. Wajihuddin Ahmad, a Pakistani colleague of his, makes the point that the Maulana gives little juristic basis for his opposition to the family planning movement.... 'The theological part of the Maulana's book, less than one-tenth of its total, is devoted to theological views. While the Maulana concedes that the Quran has no clear prohibition of contraception, he argues that those who control their births are no less losers than those who slay their children, invoking the Quranic verse.'[6]

The people of Pakistan are deeply religious and the need for support of the ulema for the population control programme cannot be overstated. Unfortunately, amongst the maulvis and maulanis who have been conditioned by orthodox and politically oriented teachings, there is misunderstanding and misconception of the Islamic precepts. The majority of them are consistently preaching opposition to family planning and propagate against it in their sermons.

At one *Milad*, organized on a large scale by a political party for *Eid-e-Milad-un-Nabi*, I was shocked to hear one very convincing maulani misconstruing the Hadith relating to *azl* and stating that the Holy Prophet (PBUH) was against the practice of *azl* and when it was reported to the Holy Prophet (PBUH) that the Companions practised *azl*, He was very angry and turned His face away in disgust. She followed this by telling the women that if they practise any form of family planning they will burn in the fires of hell. She was a good speaker. Most of her listeners were completely convinced against family planning, by the manipulation of the Hadith. Unfortunately, the average Pakistani and particularly the female population are not adequately conversant with the real teachings of Islam, as those who can read the Quran read it in Arabic without any understanding. They believe what they hear at these sermons.

Recently I was invited to speak at a women's meeting of a political-religious party at a conference on problems facing women in Pakistan. I had told the organizers that they might not like what I was going to say as I had a liberal outlook on issues relating to women. On being assured that, 'we are all Muslims and Pakistanis and care for our religion and country, and that we are seeking different points of view', I agreed to speak on the poverty facing Pakistan.

Addressing the audience I pointed out that in countries and societies where women were subjugated, poverty was higher. I emphasized the need for raising the legal status of women in all spheres, especially family life, employment, education, health services, legal status, and targeting family planning as one of the main planks for eliminating the hardships suffered by women.

The next speaker was a lady doctor, who criticized the concept of employment for women. According to her, men today are suffering due to unemployment, but women get employment easily, especially in commercial and industrial units as women do not form labour unions and can be exploited. She also tried to counter my plea for family planning, saying that although Islam does not ban family planning it does not recommend it. She spoke of the harm that can come to women, especially under the current government programme. Young girls, who have studied only up to the eighth standard are given training for three months and become female health workers. They initiate women to family planning by supplying contraceptive pills although they are not qualified to do so. The pill may have an adverse effect on the health of the women.

These instances are cited to illustrate the attitude towards family planning of the women of the religious-political parties, some of whom are highly educated.

Fatalistic attitudes regarding the number of children are also indirectly considered to be religious in origin, and do not support family planning.... Ten per cent of married women offered religion as a reason for never using birth control measures.[7]

Change in Law

Initially, sections 299 to 338 of the Pakistan Penal Code were replaced and amendments were also brought about in the Criminal Procedure Code. With minor changes the amendments were finally adopted by Parliament as an Act in 1997.[8] The Criminal Law (Amendment) Ordinance 1990[9] amended the Pakistan Penal Code of 1860 and the Criminal Procedure Code of 1898. The purpose of the amendment was to bring the laws into conformity with the injunctions of Islam, as laid down in the Holy Quran and Sunnah.

The amendment was required by the judgment of the Supreme Court Shariat Appellate Bench consisting of five judges, including Maulana Taqi Muhammad Usmani and Justice Muhammad Afzal Zullah as its chairman.

The Court considered that in Islam 'the individual victim or his heirs retain from the beginning to the end entire control over the matter including the crime and the criminal. They may not report it. They may not prosecute the offender. They may abandon prosecution of their free will. They may pardon the criminal at any stage before the execution of the sentence. They may accept monetary or other compensation to purge the crime and the criminal. They may compromise. They may accept qisas from the criminal. The State cannot impede, but must do its best to assist them in achieving their object and in appropriately exercising their rights.'[10]

The Court came to the conclusion that certain sections of the Criminal Procedure Code 1898 and the Pakistan Penal Code

1860 are repugnant to the injunctions of the Quran and declared in respect of the Pakistan Penal Code that:

> Sections 299 to 338 of the Pakistan Penal Code 1860, which deal with offences against the human body, are repugnant to the injunctions of Islam as they
>
> a) do not provide for the qisas in cases of *qatl-i-amd* (deliberate murder) and *jurooh-al-amd* (deliberately causing hurt) as is prescribed in the Holy Quran and Sunnah;
>
> b) do not provide for diyat in cases of *Shibh-ul-amd* and *Khata* of both *qatl* (murder) and *jurh* (hurt) as prescribed in the Holy Quran and Sunnah;
>
> c) do not provide for compromise between the parties on agreed compensation when they make *sulh* (compromise) in cases of *qatl* and *jurh*;
>
> d) do not provide that the offender may be pardoned by the victim in cases of *jurh* (injury), and by the heirs of the victim in cases of *qatl* (murder) whereby the court can only award him a sentence of imprisonment by way of tazir which may not extend to imprisonment for life;
>
> e) do not exempt a non-pubescent and an insane offender from the sentence of death in cases of murder; and
>
> f) do not define the different kinds of *qatl* and *jurh* (murder and injury) in accordance with their respective punishments prescribed in the Holy Quran and Sunnah.[11]

The Court also held sections 54 and 109 of the Pakistan Penal Code 1860, and sections 337 to 339, and sections 345, 381, 401, 402-A, and 402-B of the Criminal Procedure Code 1898 as repugnant to Islam.[12] The Court exercised powers under article 203D of the Constitution of the Islamic Republic of Pakistan 1973[13] and held that this decision shall take effect from 23 March 1990 whereby the provisions referred to above, to the extent they have been held to be repugnant to the injunctions of Islam, shall cease to have effect.

In 1991, Criminal Laws were amended by the Criminal Law (First, Second, Third, Fourth Amendment) Ordinances 1991[14] enacted in order to incorporate the decisions of the Supreme Court Shariat Bench.

Section 7 of the above Ordinances[15] and later Act II of 1997 substituted sections 299 to 338 in the Chapter on Offences Against the Human Body of the Pakistan Penal Code 1860, bringing considerable changes in the law by incorporating the concepts of qisas and diyat.

The Supreme Court judgment did not specifically call for change in the law relating to abortion, yet the government in the process of amending the Penal Code in accordance with the directions of the above judgment has broadened the scope of abortion to a great extent.

Under the former repealed law abortion was allowed only to save the life of the woman. Section 312 of the Pakistan Penal Code provided:

312. Whoever voluntarily causes a woman with child to miscarry, shall, if such miscarriage be not caused in good faith for the purpose of saving the life of the woman, be punished with imprisonment of either description for a term which may extend to three years, or with fine, or with both; and, if the woman be quick with child, shall be punished with imprisonment of either description for a term which may extend to seven years, and shall also be liable to fine.
Explanation: A woman who causes herself to miscarry, is within the meaning of this section.[16]

Following the amendment, abortion is allowed in the early stages of pregnancy not only to save the life of the woman, but also for providing necessary treatment to her. This has widened legal permission for carrying out the abortion in the early stages of pregnancy to a great extent. The amended Pakistan Penal Code changing the law on abortions provides as follows:

338. *Isqat-i-haml*:
Whoever causes a woman with child whose organs have not been formed, to miscarry, if such miscarriage is not caused in good faith for the purpose of saving the life of the woman, or providing necessary treatment to her, is said to cause *Isqat-i-haml*.
Explanation: A woman who causes herself to miscarry is within the meaning of this section.

338-A. Punishment for *Isqat-i-haml*:

Whoever causes *Isqat-i-haml* shall be liable to punishment as tazir

a) with imprisonment of either description for a term which may extend to three years, if *Isqat-i-haml* is caused with the consent of the woman; or

b) with imprisonment of either description for a term which may extend to ten years, if *Isqat-i-haml* is caused without the consent of the woman;

Provided that, if as a result of *Isqat-i-haml*, any hurt is caused to the woman or she dies, the convict shall also be liable to the punishment provided for such hurt or death as the case may be.

338-B. *Isqat-i-janin*:

Whoever causes a woman with child, some of whose limbs or organs have been formed, to miscarry, if such miscarriage is not caused in good faith for the purpose of saving the life of the woman, is said to cause *Isqat-i-janin*.

Explanation: A woman who causes herself to miscarry is within the meaning of this section.

338-C. Punishment for *Isqat-i-janin*:

Whoever causes *Isqat-i-janin* shall be liable to

a) one-twentieth of the diyat if the child is born dead;

b) full diyat if the child is born alive but dies as a result of any act of the offender; and

c) imprisonment of either description for a term which may extend to seven years as tazir;

Provided that, if there is more than one child in the womb of the woman, the offender shall be liable to separate diyat or tazir, as the cases may be, for every such child:

Provided further that if, as a result of *Isqat-i-janin*, any hurt is caused to the woman or she dies, the offender shall also be liable to the punishment provided for such hurt or death, as the case may be.

338-D. Confirmation of sentence of death by way of qisas or tazir etc:

A sentence of death awarded by way of qisas or tazir, or a sentence of qisas awarded for causing hurt, shall not be executed, unless it is confirmed by the High Court.

Isqat-i-haml concerns abortion before the child's organs have been formed, which can be within eight weeks and, according to some authorities, within twelve weeks of the pregnancy. The change in law permits abortion within eight/twelve weeks of pregnancy, not only to save the life of the woman but also to provide the woman with necessary treatment.

Causing miscarriage without the woman's consent carries severe punishment by maximum imprisonment for ten years, if the *Isqat-i-haml* is caused without the consent of the woman. In the case of *Isqat-i-janin*, after the limbs or organs of the child have been formed, abortion is legally allowed only for the purposes of saving the life of the woman.

Section 323. Value of Diyat:

(1) The court shall, subject to the injunctions of Islam as laid down in the Holy Quran and Sunnah and keeping in view the financial position of the convict and the heirs of the victim, fix the value of diyat which shall not be less than the value of 30 630 grams of silver.

(2) For the purpose of subsection 1 the Federal government shall, by notification in the official Gazette, declare the value of silver on the first day of July each year or on such date as it may deem fit, which shall be the value payable during a financial year.

The minimum diyat which a court can fix is 30,630 grams of silver. The diyat is to be fixed by the court keeping in view the financial position of the convict and that of the heirs of the victim.

The Federal government declared Rupees 270,493.53 only, to be the value of 30,630 grams of silver for the financial year 1999-2000. [17]

With the changes in law, especially the inclusion of the provision 'providing necessary treatment to the woman in good faith' makes conviction for *Isqat-i-haml* (abortion before the limbs are formed) quite difficult. In cases of complaint or prosecution, several defences would become available, especially if the consent of the woman is also available. The scope of legal abortion for family planning purposes has expanded considerably. 'Providing necessary treatment' can include several reasons for abortion. Weak health, mental anguish, and emotional disturbances can be pleaded as reasons for the treatment by abortion. If the pregnant woman's health is the primary concern of the law, providing the treatment as abortion can be an absolute defence. The amendment being recent there is little case law.

Widening the Scope for Abortion

Formerly abortion was a criminal offence in Pakistan, except when undertaken to save the life of the woman. The Pakistan Women's Rights Committee considered this problem and noted, 'There are many good reasons for narrowing down the scope for the offence of abortion. It has been noticed that in actual practice illegal abortions are resorted to by paying exorbitant amounts to incompetent medical practitioners and semi-trained midwives. In such cases abortions are caused under unhygienic conditions which either prove fatal for the women or seriously affect their health.' The Committee recommended that abortion should be permissible for preventing serious danger to the physical or mental health of the pregnant woman. It also recommended that for the purpose of the penal laws 'an embryo of less than 120 days shall not be deemed to be a child'.[18]

The latter was based on strong juristic opinion that abortion performed up to 120 days of pregnancy is not a crime and not forbidden under Islamic Law. A similar recommendation was made in the Report of the Commission of Enquiry for Women 1997.[19]

There are several cases of abortions by unqualified practitioners causing serious health problems. 'Providing the treatment of septic and incomplete abortions (TSIA), the Marie Stoppes Society had saved the lives of over 10,000 women who had tried unsafe methods. The NGO had begun its work in Pakistan in the 1990s.'[20]

It has been the practice in some family planning clinics to perform abortions under the pretext of correction of 'irregular menstruation'. Besides, several doctors and women agree to perform abortion under cover of D and C (Dilatation and Curettage), which is a common procedure performed for a number of reasons. Unfortunately the procedure of D and C is performed even by *dais* or neighbourhood midwives who do not have the expertise and hygiene. As a result several women die following these illegal abortions.

The crime of killing an illegitimate infant is also resorted to because of apprehension of being jailed and convicted under the Zina Ordinance.[21] A recent report from Karachi stated that: 'The dead bodies of twenty-five newborn babies were picked up and buried by the volunteers of Edhi Foundation in different parts of the city during the first three months of the current year'.[22]

Abortions are often performed by untrained persons. In rural areas there are few doctors, and hospitals with equipment are few and far between. Pregnant women, particularly poor women living in far-flung areas are victims to the tricky practices of quacks masquerading as medical practitioners.

Untrained *dais*, midwives, and quacks cause a large number of maternal deaths. 'Hospitals receive two to three cases a week of women with severe infection and bleeding as a result of abortions carried out by non-professional people. Infected material, chemicals, and even limestone and cement were used by unscrupulous people.'[23] Dr Sadiqua Jafarey, President of the National Committee of Maternal Health, reportedly stated that 'such cases continued mainly as people were not aware of the measures for preventing such tragedies. If people go in for unprotected sex the women could still use drugs known as emergency contraception. In a survey conducted in 1997-98 of three katchi abadis of Karachi city it was reported that out of one thousand women 25.5 per cent women had gone for abortion in their life and about 60 per cent faced complications.' According to official reports, 11 per cent of maternal deaths occur due to abortions.

'Though the Penal Code of Pakistan makes provision for abortion if the life of the mother is endangered, the fact that no data is available concerning legally induced therapeutic abortion, indicates restrictive interpretation of the law by the medical profession.'[24]

To quote from another study, 'In Pakistan abortion is illegal except when the life of the mother is at risk.'[25] These quotes from studies published in the year 2000-01, clearly indicate that the change in law has not reached the family planning promoters. It definitely points to the need to publicize the amendment so that the doctors and health workers can give relief by abortion not only to save the mother's life but also to provide necessary treatment to the woman in early pregnancy, before the organs of the child have formed.

Abortion being a controversial subject, both health workers and women are secretive concerning the facts of abortion. There is insufficient response in studies. 'Only 3 per cent of women admitted to have induced abortion. Cases may be underreported for obvious reasons of disapproval by religion. Yet the prevalence of abortion which at times can be fatal, is significant and needs the attention of both policy makers and service providers.'[26] Women who already have a number of children or have become pregnant due to premarital affairs and extramarital affairs usually resort to illegal unsafe abortions. Attitudes towards induced abortion are negative and a majority of health care providers (67.3 per cent) had unfavourable attitudes. Only 25 per cent favoured induced abortion while 7.7 per cent did not even answer the question.[27] This may be due to reluctance on the part of health care workers when questioned to air their true feelings, especially as induced abortions are usually resorted to illegally. They may not wish to be termed as part and parcel of the illegal trade of abortion or even deemed to be encouraging it.

A large number of abortion clinics abound all over the country. Most of them are considered to be performing illegal abortions. Untrained *dais* perform abortions daily. Creating awareness about the changes in the law can legalize most of the abortions done by these clinics, making abortions safer for women in need, performed by trained health care providers. Doctors are naturally afraid of performing abortions, except to save a woman's life. They must be made aware that an abortion is legally allowed for a woman with child whose organs have not been formed for providing necessary treatment to the woman, with her consent.

In Pakistan, the figures as stated by health providers are: 58 per cent of abortions are carried out due to unwanted pregnancies, 23.8 per cent due to contraceptive failures, 15.2 per cent for medical reasons, and 4.8 per cent due to premarital affairs and 1 per cent due to extramarital affairs.[28]

The reasons as listed by abortion clinics are different: 64.4 per cent cited too many children, 20.8 per cent contraceptive failure, 8.6 per cent cited premarital affairs, 4.9 per cent medical factors, and 1.3 per cent extramarital affairs.[29]

Considering that abortion is against the law and not available legally, thousands of women are forced to adopt unsafe methods of abortion.

> About 75,000 more die from attempting to abort their pregnancy themselves. Some will take drugs or submit to violent massage. Alone or assisted, many choose to insert a sharp object, a straightened coat hanger, a knitting needle, or a sharpened stick through the vagina into the uterus. Some 50,000 women and girls attempt such procedures every day. Most survive though often with crippling discomfort, pelvic inflammatory disease, and a continuing foul discharge. And some do not survive: with punctured uterus and infected wound, they die in pain and alone, bleeding and frightened and ashamed.[30]

Contraceptive Use

The most widely used method of preventing conception or impregnation is contraception. Commonly used contraceptives include condoms, withdrawal, oral pills, IUCDs, injectables, and sterilization. Contraceptives legally fall under the Drug Act 1976.[31] The Pharmacy Act 1967,[32] the Pakistan College of Physicians and Surgeons Ordinance 1962,[33] Pakistan Nursing Council Act 1973,[34] and the Allopathic System Ordinance 1962[35] all affect population control programmes indirectly.

There is no legal bar to advocating or persuading individuals or groups of individuals to adopt family planning methods such as contraception and voluntary sterilization. It is legal to buy, sell, advertise, or use contraceptives in Pakistan. However, the advertisements have to be indirect.

Contraceptive use is limited. A survey was conducted in 1994-95, where one-fourth of the respondents had attended school, half of them had been regularly exposed to TV and one-third to radio. The results of the survey revealed that knowledge of family planning methods and sources of modern methods have increased substantially over the last ten years. Ninety-one per cent of the respondents could name at least one method. Respondents knew less about male methods of contraception than of female methods. In the five-year period from 1990-91 to 1994-95, the use of contraception had increased by 50 per cent.

> Despite this, in 1994-95 the Contraceptive Prevalence Rate (CPR) was as low as 17.8 per cent in currently married women. This was substantially higher in urban than in rural areas. The highest CPR was reported from the Punjab and the lowest from Balochistan. Female sterilization is the most prevalent method. Fifty-two per cent of women interviewed said they did not want any more children ....[36]

The survey reveals that a very high proportion of women of reproductive age—72 per cent—have never used contraceptive methods and these have not been available to many. There also appeared to be many weaknesses in the care and quality provided for family planning. Today, in the year 2001, the survey results are outdated. There must have been a substantial increase in the CPR.

Recent Survey

To collect data on fertility, childhood mortality, family planning, and their determinants, a Pakistan Fertility and Family Planning Survey (PFFPS) was carried out from October 1996 to March

1997. Seven thousand eight hundred and forty-eight ever-married women between the ages of 15 to 49 years were interviewed.[37]

> Twenty per cent of current married women are current users of contraceptives, continuing the rise from the 1991 survey of 11.9 per cent and 17.8 per cent of the 1995 Pakistan Contraceptive Prevalence Survey.... Modern methods, including condoms, IUDs, and injectables contribute to the CPR. Traditional methods, particularly withdrawal, make up a third of current use.
>
> Sixty per cent women have a need for family planning, comprising 43 per cent who would like to limit their family and do not want any more children and 19 per cent women who would like to space the next child. Of these more than 60 per cent are not current users, indicating the unmet need of 37.5 per cent.[38]

The survey shows that women know about family planning. Even in rural areas in Balochistan, 75 per cent of women were aware of at least one modern method of family planning. At the national level over 93 per cent of women had heard some family planning message on TV or radio. Fifty-eight per cent of women find it acceptable for family planning messages to be broadcast on television and radio. Two-thirds of women interviewed approved of family planning, though less than half think their husbands approve.

Creating Awareness

The practice of contraception or use of contraceptives naturally depends on knowledge about contraception and the availability of contraceptives.

The Penal Code makes obscenity punishable by imprisonment, which may extend to three months, or with fine, or with both. For sale, hire, exhibition, or circulating obscene material to persons under the age of 20 years, the law doubles the punishment to a term, which may extend to six months plus fine. Obscene acts or songs performed in public are punishable.[39]

Therefore, advertisements for contraceptives must be effective without being vulgar. According to the TV Code of Advertising Standards and Practice (1995), the law and the best traditions must be conformed to. It excludes mention of products such as female pills. It requires that scenes depicting acts of perversion, abortion, and childbirth should be avoided and contraceptives are to be advertised as medicines.[40]

Today many more households own TVs and radios. Forty-one per cent of households have television. Even in rural areas, over a quarter of households have radios. Media campaigns through television and radio would effectively convey the importance of the use of contraceptives to both men and women. Knowledge of the need for family planning, the availability of contraceptives and services, Islamic permission, and the change in the law can be thus conveyed to the public. An unabashed marketing approach, which appeals directly to the consumer, is advocated. Zee TV and Star TV of India have very effective advertisements for contraceptives. Awareness must be created about contraception. The law limits the showing of contraceptives on TV, but it must be reconsidered.

Sterilization

For sterilization the law requires that the person performing the operation must be qualified to do so. Sterilization is being performed on both men and women though on larger numbers of women. Written permission is required from the husband for the tubal ligation of his wife. But the wife's consent is not required for the vasectomy of the husband. However, it is recommended that the consent of the person undergoing sterilization and of the spouse should be obtained. By law the person giving the consent must be adult and of sound mind and the person must fully understand the consequences and purposes of sterilization.

Voluntary sterilization in Pakistan is legal because no law prohibits it. Forcible sterilization is a crime. Female sterilization was again found to be the most accepted method: 11 per cent of women aged over 35 years, with more than four living children, opt for sterilization. In comparison, male sterilization is extremely low, that is 0.2 and 0.1 per cent for men with more than five or six children and 0 for those with fewer children.[41]

These figures are discouraging as they indicate that sterilization is resorted to after the women have already borne a number of children, though it does protect women from the hazards of childbirth, which increases with age and after the fifth child. The sterilization procedure for men is simple and under the new method no stitch is required. Efforts need to be made to enlighten and persuade large numbers of men to undergo sterilization. Information about sterilization needs to be widely disseminated through the mass media.

Inadequate Health Facilities

Discrimination against women starts from the womb. Child mortality for girls is much higher than for boys. Medical care for female infants is often neglected. The food available and allocated to girls and women in the household is less and inferior to that for boys and men. Malnutrition follows the woman from birth to the grave. The indicators are that nearly 40 per cent of pregnant women are malnourished and anaemic, resulting in babies with low weights at birth.

Antenatal care is either not available or not accessible to most women in rural areas. Eighty per cent of deliveries are conducted at home. Only 11 per cent of women get postpartum care. Maternal mortality in Pakistan is one of the highest in the world and has not declined significantly. Studies have shown that newborns whose mothers die are eight times more likely to die than those whose mothers live, bringing to light a dismal picture of maternal mortality in Pakistan. It is a senseless waste of women's lives. It is difficult to estimate maternal mortality, as death registration is far from being universal. Maternal mortality for Pakistan has been officially reported at 400 per

100,000 live births.[42] It has also been quoted at 905 per 100,000,[43] or three deaths occurring every hour.[44]

Most of these deaths can be avoided. Women die because trained midwives are not available. This illustrates the urgent need for training of midwives. Women die because even when abnormalities are diagnosed they do not reach the hospital because it is far away, they are denied autonomy to take decisions, there is a lack of mobility and transport, and absence of emergency obstetrical care at accessible places. Tertiary health centres are not equipped and the necessary medicines are not available. There are no blood banks in most rural areas. Quacks and criminals undertake termination of the pregnancy because of ignorance and illiteracy of the family who are not willing to seek professional help.[45]

In developed countries, maternal mortality was reduced when competent midwives conducted deliveries.

Dr Shershah Syed and Ms Imtiaz Kamal stress the importance of making properly qualified midwives and health workers available to provide care at the time of delivery of the child, as well as neonatal care and postpartum care. In Pakistan today, the majority of women bearing children are attended to by untrained *dais* who cannot even diagnose any problems to refer to the proper facilities.

'Maternal death has a very close and unfortunate relationship with poverty. In the poor community, their women basically represent the mass of those who fall victim to pregnancy-related complications and maternal death.'[46]

Alarmingly high levels of maternal mortality persist in Pakistan. The situation has not changed so far. Pakistan has utilized precious resources on training thousands of TBAs and *dais*, but no attention has been paid so far to promote midwives as a replacement strategy.

Some Facts About Pakistan
- For every maternal death 27 women suffer from morbid conditions.
- Total fertility rate per woman is 5 (Bangladesh 3.7, Sri Lanka 2.3).
- 82 per cent of babies are born at home, only 5 per cent of them are delivered by skilled birth attendants.
- Infant mortality rate is 95/1000 live births (Indonesia 50, Sri Lanka 15).

Some Positive Changes
- Desire for ideal family size has decreased from 4.9 to 3.6.
- Contraceptive prevalence rate has increased from 12 per cent to 30 per cent.

The Silver Lining
- Awareness of the need to make motherhood safe has definitely increased.[47]

Low Literacy

The literacy rate for the population aged 10 years and above increased from 22 per cent in 1972 to 26 per cent in 1981. According to the 1998 figures, the literacy rates were estimated at 45 per cent, 56.6 per cent for males and a considerably lower percentage of 32.6 for females. In rural areas the gender differences increase, 48.6 per cent males are literate and only 19.1 per cent of females are literate.[48] Though literacy rates have improved, this is hardly sufficient.

In primary education, differences between boys and girls persist. Despite an increase over the years, serious disparities continue. At primary schools, for every 100 boys only sixty-eight girls are enrolled. At the secondary level even less girls are found, that is fifty-two girls are enrolled compared to every 100 boys. Even with the recent spread of education women lag behind, 43 per cent women and 24 per cent men aged 15 to 19 have no schooling.[49]

A number of studies have clearly indicated that educating women has a direct influence on reducing fertility and unwanted births. The statistical data depicting the poor educational status of women is not conducive to population control. Unfortunately, in Pakistan there are false notions of women's needs and roles inhibited by orthodoxy, which keep most women not only uneducated but also illiterate and unaware of their basic human rights.

There can be no gainsaying that educated women make better mothers. Though the Prophet (PBUH) advised that men and women must go far and wide to obtain knowledge, misguided Muslim countries lag behind. Experience in other countries indicates that educating girls keeps the population growth down, as, for example, in Kerala in south India and Sri Lanka, where the population growth is 1.04 per cent.

It is interesting to note that the fertility rates of Pakistani women are lower among educated women. The 1996-97 figures show that the TFR (Total Fertility Rate) is 5.36 children per woman. With no education it is 6.4, with primary education it is 4.92, for women with middle education it is 4.42, with secondary education and above it is 3.1.

The contraceptive prevalence rate (CPR) rises with the level of education: with no education it is 18.9, with middle/lower secondary education it goes up to 35.4, with secondary school education and above the CPR goes up to 43.5.[50] As high fertility can be reduced by educating women, the emphasis on education has to be doubled not only in plans and policies, but more importantly in their implementation.

A large number of schools are dormant. They need to be rehabilitated and restarted. Teachers need to be trained from and posted to backward areas. Budgetary allocations for education are extremely low and uneven. They need to be substantially increased. *Madaris*, which are now being allocated funds, must be required to impart a positive attitude to family planning. Convincing the students of religion can bring positive results.

Women Earners

Another factor influencing the number of children women have is their work outside the home. There is a wide variance in the male and female representation in the labour force. A Labour Force Survey indicates that in 1997 about 70 per cent of males ten years and above were employed, compared to only 13.6 per cent for females. This does not take into account the unreported labour of women, particularly unpaid work and family labour in farms where women contribute as family workers, or the work of women in the home. Besides, there is gross under-reporting of women working outside the home.

Apart from domestic labour of cooking, cleaning, looking after the sick and the infirm, carrying home fuel and water, bearing and rearing children, women also take care of the animals and storing of food in rural areas.

This means that a large percentage of women are not engaged in gainful employment outside the home. Women wage earners are inclined to be more aware and assertive for their own well-being. The number of children a woman bears affects her lifestyle. With the additional responsibility of work outside the home, as wage earners women have more autonomy and are naturally inclined to have smaller families.

'The employment of women has important implications for their economic independence. Overall, 20 per cent of ever-married women are currently working for money compared with 17 per cent reported in PDHS 1990-91.'[51]

Male Decision Makers

An important factor for the failure of population planning is that the programme is catered for women. Women are the objects and targets. Men have been bypassed. In Pakistan it is the males who are the decision makers.

Though a majority of women are consulted about domestic matters, very few women are decision makers; especially concerning use of contraceptives by them or by their husbands. The most common reason for women not using contraception is the lack of awareness and availability, fear of the husband's disapproval, and socio-cultural religious taboos. Population control programmes must cater to the males also.

PAWLA's Experience

Cases have been reported to the Pakistan Women Lawyers' Association (PAWLA) Legal Aid Centre where the husband refuses to use or allow the wife to use birth control methods, resulting in serious marital discord and even threat of divorce. Based on one case, the Pakistan Women Lawyers' Association in its project for legal awareness, produced a touching video drama titled *Such ki Jeet*,[52] depicting two sisters. The husband of the elder sister believes in family planning and they have two well-cared for children. On the other hand the husband of the younger sister refutes birth control on Islamic religious grounds. They have five children, who are underfed, with no schooling. His wife is weak and ill. The doctor recommends sterilization. The husband threatens his wife that he will divorce her if she insists on contraception.

    She comes to PAWLA for advice. Conciliation processes are started by a PAWLA law officer. The husband is brought to PAWLA by his brother-in-law. He is difficult and refuses to bend even with counselling, including quoting from the Hadith. The wife refuses to have more children and decides to leave home. On the night before she is to leave, she tells her children the story of a she-goat, who goes away to the woods, leaving the children with the father. The children, sensing disaster, create a commotion. They tell their father that their mother is not telling the truth as no mother would leave her children and in any case the children would have followed their mother to the woods and not remained with the father. The father is touched and tells his wife that she is not going anywhere. They will together care for the children and not have any more.

This video film promotes acceptance of family planning. In the video, several authorities, especially Islamic jurists and Quranic verses supporting population control, have been quoted. For family planning to become popular it is important that the target population be both men and women.

Age at Marriage

It would be useful for the government to seriously consider legal measures for increasing the minimum age for marriage for women to 18 years and men to 21 years. No marriage before these ages should be accepted as valid.

There are strong reasons for advancing the minimum age at marriage. This will influence the social aspects of family life and will also have a positive effect on the physiological growth of girls. Women marrying at a later age will have become physically, emotionally, and mentally more mature, and they will benefit as individuals. Physiologically, a woman may be mature enough to become pregnant, but physically her body is not sufficiently developed until the age of 18 and the birth canal is not mature until approximately 20 to 21 years of age—although these ages vary with nutritional levels.[53]

Advancing the minimum age will definitely deter child-bearing, which is adversely affecting the girl child in early marriages. The earlier a girl marries, the more children she will have by the end of her reproductive years. Infant mortality rates are higher where the mothers are younger. Early marriage is incompatible with formal education.

For females the singulate mean age at marriage (years) has substantially increased. In 1990 it was 21.6, in 1997 it increased to 22.0, in 2001 it went up to 22.7.[54] Yet there are several young girls in their early teens getting married and suffering. They have several pregnancies before the age of 25 years, their children suffer and their bodies deteriorate, and they age prematurely.

Poverty

There is a close link between poverty and population growth. The poor have more children. In Pakistan almost 40 per cent of the population lives below the poverty line. The recent UN Report on Demographic Dynamics and Sustainability records that 'the world population growth rate has declined from a peak of 2 per cent in 1963 to 1.7 per cent in 1980 and 1.3 per cent in 2000. The report points out that the world's poorest countries tend to have the highest population growth rates, undermining their efforts to invest in human development.'[55]

Apart from other measures to alleviate poverty in Pakistan it is essential to improve the programme to reduce population growth. A positive and extensive family planning programme is needed. The interdependence of raising the contribution of women in national development and family planning is well known.

Violence Against Women

In South Asia 15 per cent of deaths of women occurring during pregnancy and delivery are related to violence and injury. In Pakistan men are accepted as the controllers of women's lives. From birth a girl is dominated by her father, and she has little freedom in the choice of her marriage partner. After marriage she is under the control of her husband and in-laws. There has been a constant increase of domestic violence against women. Men control the sexuality of women. Honour killing has become rampant. Violence against women has far-reaching harmful effects on their bodies and minds. Rape of women is increasing. The law needs to be amended so that a woman who becomes pregnant by rape must be entitled to legal safe abortion to be provided by the State. Honour killing, domestic violence, and any abuse of women must be declared a punishable crime.

Awareness and Availability of Contraceptives

Availability of contraceptives with a wider base of distribution and sale is a basic requirement. Though contraceptives are already subsidized, the government can by law require a minimum sale of subsidized contraceptives by pharmacies, cooperative and general stores, and by *paan* (betel)/cigarette/*bidi* vendors. Laws must be enacted to give incentives to stimulate the manufacture, distribution, and sale of contraceptives. Presently, over half the current users obtain their method from public sector outlets, 45 per cent from the private sector, and less than 2 per cent from NGOs.[56]

Religious Preachers

The religious propaganda against family planning must be countered through special measures such as training of religious scholars and speakers on the Islamic acceptance of family planning. It is strongly recommended that the programme for family planning should include training and orientation workshops for maulanas and maulanis to inculcate a positive approach to birth control as being allowed in Islam. This will deter them from consistently creating a negative environment against the practice of birth control. Awareness of the true Islamic concepts supporting family planning must be propagated through research and the media.

Preference for Sons

Numerous studies show that there is a strong preference for sons in Pakistan. This is attributed to socio-economic and cultural factors. According to a study conducted by NIPS, sons are preferred because they protect the family name and offer economic support to parents in their old age. Girls on the other hand require the arrangement of costly dowries, and without a brother's protection are regarded as socially insecure.

Overall, 48 per cent of currently married women want their next child to be a boy, compared with only 9 per cent who want a daughter. As the number of living sons increases, the preference for a son decreases. Among women with one daughter, 67 per cent want their next child to be a boy, while the remainder (33 per cent) are indifferent about the sex of the next child. If the only child is a son, over half (57 per cent) of the women are indifferent about the sex of the next child, 25 per cent want another boy and only 18 per cent want a girl. Among women with two daughters and no sons, almost all (94 per cent) want their next child to be a boy. Conversely, among those with two boys and no daughter only 49 per cent want a girl.[57] All this data reveals a strong preference for a son, even by women. The men are all for sons, especially if they do not have any.

Technology has devised the means to determine the sex of the child in the mother's womb through ultrasound scans. Abuse of these scans is rampant. Though no exact statistics are available in Pakistan, considering the prevalent preference for sons, a large number of women must be taking these tests to determine whether the foetus is male. In Pakistan, it is estimated that a considerable number of female foetuses are being aborted. In India there are continued reports of abortion of female foetuses. The female is considered a burden on the family in the social/cultural milieu of dependency of the female. A girl child is not always welcome. Giving birth to more than one girl child often results in abuse and rejection of the mother by the family. In several cases the husbands have married again for a male heir. There is little knowledge of the fact that it is the male sperm that determines the sex of the child. Technology is misused to work against the female foetus.

Women with no children consider the ideal family size to be 3.4 children. Among those with three or more children the ideal family size increases steadily.[58] Nearly four children is double the ideal of two children projected by the family planning campaign for a happy family.

'Over 11.7 million children are suffering from stunting (less height for age) and wasting (low weight for height), official reports revealed.... (due to).... malnutrition and high rate of infectious disease among children. This phenomenon exists more in girls particularly those living in rural areas.'[59]

Population Planning

During 1965-70, the Third Plan period, the population planning programme was initiated.

> It was based upon the efficient distribution of supplies and the motivation of potential acceptors. Implementation of the programme faltered for a variety of reasons. The programme was introduced on a large scale without the groundwork, which was needed to overcome cultural and social constraints. In 1969, after four years, only 6 per cent of couples used contraceptives.... In 1973, the Continuous Motivation System was introduced, shifting the focus from targets to client motivation and follow-up. One of the major problems of this phase was the unstable political climate....
>
> *Dawn*, 4 January 2002

With a change in leadership of the government and the family planning programme, a new Contraceptive Inundation Scheme was initiated in 1975. The objective of this scheme was to overcome any contraceptive supply bottlenecks and to allow supply to create demand. This was also poorly implemented, mainly due to inadequate distribution systems. Contraceptive use and knowledge were unchanged from 1969 levels.

> During 1977-80, family planning activities were suspended due to the after-affects of the 1977 general elections and resulting transition to a military government. Family planning clinics tried to continue to function, but without promotional support...
>
> The Continuous Motivation System was discarded in 1981. The population programme restarted with a multisectoral approach and was transferred to the Ministry of Planning and Development...

Under the Sixth Five-Year Plan (1983-88), the multi-sectoral approach was continued...emphasis was put on MCH, female education, broad-based IEC programmes... Major problems were inadequate technical support and lack of political support. In 1986, a social marketing project began subsidised retail sales of condoms with the assistance of USAID...

During the Seventh Five-Year Plan (1988-93), the policy and strategy of the Sixth Plan were continued. Mobile service units were added to the programme to increase coverage... But also during the Seventh Plan period, the population programme only had a small impact: in 1990-91, contraceptive prevalence had slightly increased to a level of 14 per cent... In 1990 the Population Welfare Division was given an independent status of the Ministry of Population Welfare...

During the Eighth Plan (1993-98), efforts to increase the coverage continued, as it was realised that only 20-25 per cent of the total population had access to family planning services and only five per cent of the rural population...

During the current Ninth Plan (1998-2003), a reproductive health package through the MOH and MOPW was introduced. Efforts will be undertaken to bring the community-based workers (VBFWWs and LHWs) of both sectors under one umbrella... The major demographic objectives in the Ninth Plan are:

- Increase contraceptive use from 23.9 per cent to 40.3 per cent in 2003;
- Reduce the annual population growth rate from 2.4 per cent to 2.1 per cent in 2003;
- Reduce TFR from 5.1 to 4.2 in 2003.[60]

Financial Flow

Funding for population welfare activities as a share in the total five-year plans has been at a low level of 1 per cent. Allocations to related population activities were low as well. The share of women's development activities has been less than 0.5 per cent, and health and nutrition activities have been fluctuating and are now hovering at a level of 4 per cent of the total five-year plan allocation.

Historically, Pakistan's public expenditure on population has been modest, at between 0.06 per cent to 0.07 per cent of GNP.

The population programme is financed from the government's annual development budget, rather than the regular budget, with unfavourable implications on staff recruitment and development.... Since the inception of the population welfare programme, total funding for the Division of Population Welfare, and later the Ministry of Population Welfare has been rising slowly until the early eighties. A decline is noticeable during 1978-83, the period during which family planning activities were suspended. Since then funding is increasing from Rs 1.7 billion (roughly US $182 million) to Rs 9.1 billion (about US $288 million) during the Eighth Plan, and is allocated for Rs 15.9 billion (US $318 million) in the Ninth Plan.

Although funding for the population programme rose during the five-year plans, actual releases, and final expenditures were much lower.[61]

The Prime Minister's Programme on Primary Health Care and Family Planning and AIDS Programme

The Prime Minister's vertical health and family planning programme was launched in 1994. During 1994-95, Rs 402 million (US $13 million) was allocated, of which Rs 371 million (82 per cent) was spent. For 1995-96, Rs 1 billion (US $32 million) was allocated, of which almost 100 per cent was spent.... During the Eighth Five-Year Plan, Rs 901 billion (US $288 million) was allocated for this programme, of which Rs 4.28 billion was released, with only Rs 3.7 billion or 41 per cent actually spent.

The AIDS programme (1994-97) was allocated Rs 774.35 million (US $24 million) by the government. The actual releases until 1998 came only to Rs 271 million, of which Rs 183 million was spent. Forty per cent of the budget goes to the media campaign.... Since 1995-96, when 100 per cent of the allocations were spent, expenditures are decreasing continuously. In 1998-99 only 44 per cent of the budget was spent. In addition to government funding, the international donor community contributes significantly to the HIV/AIDS programme, especially through UNAIDS (US $420,000 in 1999), WHO (US $250,000), and UNICEF (US $200,000 in 1999).[62]

Total expenditure for population activities in 1997 (roughly Rs 4 billion) comes to a per capita expenditure of US $0.75, of which US $0.57 is contributed by the Government of Pakistan, and the remaining US $0.17 from the international community. When one relates the expenditures in 1997 to GNP (of US $490), it means that 0.20 per cent of GNP is spent on population, of which 0.15 per cent comes from national sources, and 0.05 per cent from international....

Ninety-five per cent of the government expenditure goes to family planning/reproductive health activities, 4 per cent to STD, HIV/AIDS, and only 1 per cent to research activities.

The programme suffered when USAID (the largest donor to the population programme during the 1980s) cut off all bilateral aid to Pakistan in 1993 following a dispute over nuclear policy. USAID has been the most important donor for the population programme, accounting for roughly 60 per cent of total foreign assistance. Support from other donors, especially UNFPA and Department for International Development (UK) tried to balance this cut.[63]

Relations between the US and Pakistan have improved following the signing of the new agreement in November 2001 resulting from Pakistan's support in the war against terrorism. A grant of Rs 36 billion has also been promised to help Pakistan in its social sector priorities, including education, job creation, and health. US $17.4 million is allocated for ongoing support to the NGOs involved in education, health, women's empowerment, and micro-finance and US $1.8 million to support democracy and governance programmes through NGOs.[64]

Role of National NGOs

Less than 5 per cent of the family planning services are supported by NGOs. The technical and absorption capacity of national NGOs is low and they are very dependent on international donors. They serve in indirect ways by training local women to become motivators or field workers who do most of the outreach work.

Their life attitudes have changed, too. 'It is evident that budgetary allocation is very low and utilization of funds is limited. The coverage of the population for Family Planning Services especially in rural areas is a serious handicap in achieving the objectives. More emphasis and encouragement of the private sector is essential. NGOs with community communication have to be strengthened for a wider role in making family planning services available to women in Pakistan.'[65]

Ninth Five-Year Plan, 1997-98—2002-03

The public health sector has failed to provide adequate family planning services. According to the planners, this is due to lack of coordination between the two concerned ministries and the shortage of female staff at primary health care units.

The long-term policy of the Ninth Five-Year Plan is to merge family planning activities in the health sector at all levels of implementation and collaboration between the health department and local bodies. It envisages integration of Family Planning Services (FPS) in the health sector at the service delivery level i.e. district level and merger of two cadres of community worker, that is Lady Health Worker (LHW) and Village-Based Family Welfare Worker (VBFWW). The plan will aim for universal coverage with emphasis on rural areas.

The plan's targets are to reduce the crude birth rate to 29.0 per 1000 population, the crude death rate to 07.2 per 1000 population; the TFR to 4.2 per woman; to spread knowledge of AIDS to 90 per cent of the population; to raise the CPR to 41 per cent; and to reduce the population growth to 2.1 per cent.[66] The President of Pakistan, General Pervez Musharraf, has called for reduction of the population growth to 1.9 per cent.

Female Paramedics (LHW)

A recent survey indicates a large unfulfilled demand. Fifty-two per cent of women of childbearing age do not want more children and only 17.8 per cent practised family planning in 1994-95. However, the situation has improved recently with the deployment of LHWs. The Ninth Plan required that all the RHCs and BHUs provide family planning services along with the 100,000 LHWs working at the community level.[67]

Each BHU covers 10,000 people. Each RHC gives primary health coverage to 25,000 to 50,000 population. A tehsil headquarters hospital (THQ) with 40 to 50 beds and district headquarters hospital (DHH) with 100 or more beds (announced in June) will provide health coverage to over 2 million people.

In the wake of the shortfall of 4000 LHWs and female paramedics, training facilities are to be improved and upgraded. It is also planned that one Traditional Birth Attendant will be trained and made available in every village and for each urban slum. At present most of the deliveries are conducted at home by untrained *dais* or family members with no training. The government is taking steps to implement reproductive health care and primary health care plans. The tehsil headquarters hospital and district headquarters hospital are to be made functional to provide reproductive health services.

The National Population Planning Programme in 1998 is aimed at making the population issue a national cause. Its objective is to create public awareness of the adverse consequences of rapid and unchecked population growth, and to reduce the mortality and fatality rate through gender equality and equity. It also emphasizes targeting both men and women, and including family planning for both men and women.[68] Little activity has been noticed on this front.

National Health Policy

The National Health Policy 2001 was formulated for 2001 to 2010. It is based on the high-sounding national health vision of

'Health for All', a dream that is a long way away. Among the key factors of the policy are good governance and gender equity.

The implementation modality is to have trained Lady Health Workers (LHW). Under the National Programme for Family Planning and Primary Health Care, 50,000 Lady Health Workers under the Ministry of Health and 13,000 Family Welfare Workers under the Ministry of Population Welfare will be integrated from July 2001 to create a cadre of 71,000 Family Health Workers. This cadre will be increased to 100,000 by the year 2005. To promote gender equity, focused reproductive health services, emergency obstetric care, and referral systems are to be established under the Women's Health Project.

The project aims to provide reproductive health services universally with an integrated approach for primary health care (PHC). It plans to expand reproductive health services in urban and rural areas in Pakistan. It expects to accelerate family planning by decreasing maternal mortality, infant mortality, and the incidence of morbidity in children.

The National Health Policy of 2001 envisages giving adequate financial and administrative powers to the district health officer under the Devolution Plan to effectively manage priority programmes at district level.[69] The Devolution Plan of Power Policy requires that the population and health programmes be decentralized to the district level.

Local Monitoring

The Devolution Plan was introduced by President Pervez Musharraf in the year 2000. Elections to local councils were completed in 2001. This is a new concept for Pakistan, as in the past the powers and functions of local bodies were limited, and the local bodies were time and again disbanded for political reasons. An innovative feature of the plan has been that 33 per cent of seats were reserved for women and for the first time several women have been elected to the local government. The Nazims and Naib Nazims who head the councils and wield the powers are mostly men, and only two women have been elected as Nazims. There is confusion concerning the powers and functions of the local government personnel and it will take considerable time and experience to unravel the tangles. At present it is unclear as to how the local government functionaries will control and coordinate the work of the health sector. The Local Government Ordinances so far promulgated leave a lot of blank areas.

In a recent case of complaints by the locals of absence of doctors and hospital staff at a district hospital, the Governor of Sindh personally visited the hospital to verify the complaint. Finding several doctors and staff absent, the Governor directed the Nazim and Naib Nazim to conduct an enquiry and present their findings to him. If the Nazim had defined functions and powers it would not need the Governor of the province to spearhead the monitoring.

> The most disorganized departments are those of health and education....
>
> The newly-born district government is, therefore, facing problems all over the province. Squeezed and frozen funds have resulted in a difficult situation for the Zila Nazims and others.
>
> Over 400 primary schools are closed in the district. The reasons are that local teachers are either not available or the schools are built in far-flung areas or are occupied illegally by influential people... Now an example of how many Basic Health Units, falling under the purview of the executive district office (Health), work: EDO (Executive District Officer) Health, Dr Mohammad Sharif Sheikh, in a letter to the Sindh Home Secretary on 10 September 2001 revealed that 16 BHUs, dispensaries, and rural health centres in the Larkana district had been illegally occupied by the police and other agencies for a long time... The EDO Health in his letter had made a request to the Home Secretary to take personal interest to get these centres vacated because in the absence of health facilities, it is the people of the area who suffer most. The cruel joke is that no action has been taken in this regard although, according to district Nazim Khursheed Junejo, Gen. Pervez Musharraf too was told about these illegal occupations....

Not only this but millions of rupees may go down the drain if work on 22 BHUs, maternity homes, and dispensaries started in 1988 and 1992 is left halfway. Work on BHUs has already stopped, either because of the inaccessibility of the location, or because of the exhausted funds allocated during the PPP government. The buildings department was given the job to construct these health facilities but almost all the projects have been left halfway. Sources said work in a number of BHUs had been left halfway.

Five dispensaries are decaying due to the non-availability of funds.... The need of the hour is to make operational these illegally occupied BHUs for the general good of the people.[70]

Recent Statistics

The Pakistan Reproductive Health and Family Planning Survey 2000-01 (PRHFPS) undertaken during August 2000 to April 2001 reveals the latest status of socio-economic, demographic, reproductive health and family planning indicators. Infant mortality of females is higher than that of males in the first year of life. This shows that females are neglected from their infancy. The overall infant mortality rate has fallen from 92 per 1000 live births in the period 1992-96 to 85 per 1000 live births in the period 2000-01. Neonatal mortality rate (within the first month of life) is higher than the post-neonatal rate (within the first year). During this period child mortality has declined from 21 to 20 (from first to fifth birthday).[71]

According to the RHFP Survey 2000-01, of the 6370 currently married women in the sample 20.9 per cent have expressed a desire for no more children and are current users of contraception, 6.7 per cent want to delay the next birth and are currently using some method, and 33.0 per cent do not want another child but are not using any contraception, indicating the magnitude of the unmet need for family planning.[72]

Maternal Mortality

As a vital registration system is virtually non-existent estimation of maternal mortality is problematic. The sisterhood method, with a TFR of 4.8 implies a maternal mortality ratio of 533 per 100,000 live births in Pakistan.[73]

Present Situation

The budgetary allocation for health is extremely low. Over the years the government has spent 1 to 1.5 per cent of the GNP on health, mostly for hospitals. The provincial governments spent between 5 to 9 per cent of their annual budget on health. The budget for the financial year 2001-02 for the public sector development programme is Rs 75.2 billion. Of this, only Rs 2.5 billion has been allocated to health.

Health insurance coverage is low. There are no direct laws protecting the patient's rights. Only 2.5 million individuals were insured in the country, while 4.5 million people had insurance coverage through group insurance.[74] Besides, the Employees Social Security Institution (ESSI) provides health care for one million registered members. It is employer financed. The standard of health care at government facilities is very poor. Only a small percentage of the people utilize it. Private sector clinics provide health care to nearly 75 per cent of the population.

Sexuality

The norm of virginity is ancient. In Greece and Rome the term was used for a woman (or a Goddess) who was independent, autonomous, not owned by anyone. Over time it has come to mean sexual virginity and it reflects the concept of property. To uphold family honour, a woman must remain a virgin until she gets married. An unmarried girl passes from the father's home to her husband a pure virgin. Nothing less is acceptable in our society. Women's sexuality is circumscribed by marriage.

Girls are born and develop feelings, sexual awareness, and natural desires in a familial environment of suppression and domination. They are conditioned to be embarrassed and ashamed of their sexual feelings, leading to denial and guilt. Family and society shape and suppress women's sexuality.

The myth is that men have strong sex drives, women are only passive recipients. The fact that women have sexual needs is taboo. Our culture values husbands much more than wives. The wife is expected to be ready and willing to have intercourse whenever the husband wants to. A wife is expected to do everything to please her husband. There is no direct law giving a woman the right to refuse sex to her husband. Even forced intercourse or rape by the husband is not a crime under the Zina Ordinance.

Many women are abused. Sexual violence is a weapon used by men. Women are vulnerable to rape, incest, and sexual harassment with little protection from the State. Families often expect women to remain silent and bear these atrocities so that family honour is not publicly maligned.

Reproductive Rights

Reproductive rights are hardly discussed or heard about. Sexual awareness is limited. The duty and obligation of the State to make women aware of rights over their bodies and provide the means of utilizing these for their personal welfare and protection is not even countenanced.

The vast majority of women have little knowledge or awareness that they have rights over their bodies. The right to decide whether or not to bear children, the right to determine how many children she will bear, the right to space the children, the right to health services, and the right of protection from sexually transmitted diseases are denied to the majority of poor, uneducated, suppressed women in Pakistan. The rights to use contraception are only considered by a minority of women. Little debate or media news is available on the question of a woman's rights over her body. In the male dominated family life, the male partner considers only his desires and makes the decisions. The woman/wife is expected to cater to his needs. Crucial services such as sex education, protection from early and unplanned pregnancies and sexually transmitted diseases, legal abortion as and when necessary, and guarding against bearing abnormal, maimed babies are not available.

Connected with the issue of reproductive rights is the question of how much knowledge people have about reproductive health. Sex education is not allowed. Culturally sex is a taboo topic. Adult women or adult men discuss issues relating to sex if at all, separately. It embarrasses even adults to discuss sex.

Sexually Transmitted Disease

Reproductive health education is not available, and the consequences are harmful. At a workshop on reproductive health education for adolescents it was suggested that sex education should be given by parents and teachers. There is no reproductive health education in schools at present.

In a survey it was reported that 73 per cent students who believed that they had sexual problems never consulted doctors, five per cent went to the so-called sexologist, nearly 80 per cent had obtained information about sex from friends, movies, and books.

Parents and teachers are shy to give them information. According to WHO estimates, 15 to 18,000 people suffer from HIV in Pakistan. Ninety per cent of them did not know about HIV/AIDS since there was no sex education. They were unaware of the nature of the disease and how it is transmitted. Safe sex practices need sex education.... Only 50 per cent girls and 30 per cent boys said that this information comes from parents.[75]

The crucial service of sex education to prevent sexually transmitted disease is denied. Wives contract these diseases from their husbands.

> According to the latest statistics of the Sindh AIDS Control programme, till June 2001 there were 517 cases of HIV/AIDS. Out of these 10 per cent are women while 90 per cent are males. According to estimates of the WHO and UNAIDS, there are about 70 to 80,000 hidden cases of HIV/AIDS in Pakistan and about 20 to 25,000 hidden cases in Sindh alone....
>
> Trafficking in women has been flourishing in the SAARC countries and particularly in Pakistan.... However, all at the AIDS Control programme have agreed that awareness is the best way to combat this problem. An essential tool is the media, which they must take along with them.[76]

Women's Reproductive Rights Denied

There is little discussion in Pakistan of the right-based perspective, or life-saving intervention, or the premise of women's human rights. The magnitude of maternal mortality in Pakistan reflects the denial to women of the right to life, the right to safe pregnancy and childbirth. Maternal mortality is a blatant denial of women's rights to life as health technology is now available.

In South Asia less than one per cent of women experiencing complications during pregnancy or childbirth receive treatment in health facilities providing emergency obstetric care.... One quarter of the cases reaching emergency obstetrics die.[77]

Within South Asia, Pakistan is practically at the lowest rung of human rights. The lack of care for women is phenomenal. Millions of women die as the facility to have safe pregnancy and childbirth is not available. There is a real need to change the situation of women in Pakistan.

NOTES

1. Pakistan Statistical Yearbook 2000, Federal Bureau of Statistics, Government of Pakistan, published by the Manager of Publications, Karachi, April 2000.
2. 1998 census bulletin. (Ibid).
3. Financial Resources Flow for Population Activities, Report of a case study in Pakistan, May/ June 1999, 'Concluding Remarks', Chapter 5, p. 47.
4. Fatwas of Sheikh Jadel Haq Ali Jadel Haq, the Grand Imam of Al-Azhar, in 1979 and 1980, quoted by Abdel Rahim Omran, *Family Planning in the Legacy of Islam*, pp. 6-9, published by Routledge, II New Fetter Lane, London EC4P 4EE with support from United Nations Population Fund, 1992.
5. Ansar Burney vs. Federation of Pakistan, PLD 1983, FSC, p. 73.
6. Abdel Rahim Omran, *Family Planning in the Legacy of Islam*, pp. 206 and 207, published by Routledge, II New Fetter Lane, London EC4P 4EE with support from United Nations Population Fund, 1992.
7. Abdul Hakim, John Cleland, and Mansoor ul Hassan Bhatti, *Pakistan Fertility and Family Planning Survey 1996-97*, December 1998, published by National Institute of Population Studies, Islamabad and Centre for Population Studies, London School of Hygiene & Tropical Medicine, p. 163.
8. PLD 1997 CS, p. 326.
9. PLD 1991 CS, p. 93.
10. PLD 1989, Supreme Court, p. 633.
11. Ibid.
12. Ibid.
13. 'The Constitution of Islamic Republic of Pakistan': [As Amended up to April 1998]. Compiled by Sheikh Ebrahim, published by PLD Publishers, Nabha Road, Lahore, Pakistan.
14. PLD 1991 CS, p. 521.
15. Criminal Law Amendment Act II of 1997, PLD 1997 CS, p. 326.
16. The Pakistan Penal Code (XLV of 1860) with Provincial Amendments published by All Pakistan Legal Decisions, Nabha Road, Lahore. 1964.
17. PLD 1999 CS, p. 431.
18. Report of the Pakistan Women's Rights Committee 1976, published by the Government of Pakistan, Ministry of Law, Islamabad.
19. Report of the Commission of Enquiry for Women 1997, published by Government of Pakistan.
20. 'Contraception awareness must for women's health', *Dawn*, 25 April 2001, published by Pakistan Herald Publications, Dr Ziauddin Road, Karachi, Pakistan.

21. PLD 1979, Central Statutes, p. 51.
22. *Dawn*, 15 April 2001, p. 15, published by Pakistan Herald Publications (Pvt.) Ltd., Dr Ziauddin Ahmed Road, Karachi.
23. 'Quacks play havoc with lives of abortion patients', *Dawn*, 12 May 2001.
24. Unsafe Abortion, Magnitude and Perceptions 1998, Chapter 2, Rationale of Study, p. 14, published by Family Planning Association of Pakistan, 3/A, Temple Road, Lahore, 1998.
25. Abdul Hakim, Mehboob Sultan, and Faateh ud din, *Pakistan Reproductive Health and Family Planning Survey 2000-01*, published by National Institute of Population Studies, Islamabad, July 2001, p. 31.
26. Ibid.
27. UA, M&P 1998, ante 20, p. 29.
28. UA, M&P 1998, ante 20, p. 29.
29. UA, M&P 1998, ante 20, p. 33.
30. Peter Adamson, 'Deaf to the Screams', p. 2, *The Medical Spectrum*, March/Apr 2000, published by Pakistan Medical Association, Karachi.
31. The Drug Act 1976, PLD 1976 CS, p. 317.
32. The Pharmacy Act 1967, PLD 1967 CS, p. 210.
33. The Pakistan College of Physicians and Surgeons Ordinance 1962, PLD 1962 CS, p. 320.
34. Pakistan Nursing Council Act 1973, PLD 1973, p. 239.
35. The Allopathic System Ordinance 1962, PLD 1962 CS, p. 614.
36. Pakistan Contraceptive Prevalence Survey 1994-95, Final Report, March 1998, published by Population Council, Pakistan, 55, Street 1, F-6/3, Islamabad, Pakistan.
37. PFFPS 1996-97, ante 5, p. 4.
38. Ibid., p. xxi.
39. The Pakistan Penal Code 1860 SS 292 and 293, published by the Nadeem Law Book House, 7, Turner Road, Lahore, 2000.
40. TV Code of Advertising Standards and Practice in Pakistan, PTV Limited 1995, p. 19.
41. PFFPS 1996-97, ante 5, Table 7.8, p. 145.
42. Ninth Five-Year Plan 1997-98–2000-03, Government of Pakistan, Chapter Health Sector, p. 4.
43. N.S. Qureshi, A. Sarwar, M. Aslam, 'An Audit of Maternal Deaths', *The Medical Spectrum*, January 2001, published by Pakistan Medical Association, Karachi. Quoted from Abou Zahr, Roystan E. (1991), *Maternal Mortality: A Global Factbook*. Geneva. WHO.
44. S. Syed (2000), 'Emergency Obstetrical Care and Family Physicians', *The Medical Spectrum*, Vol. 21, pp. 37-43, published by Pakistan Maternity and Health Association, Karachi.
Note: There is a stark difference in the government figures, which are much lower than the non-government figure.

45. Shershah Syed, 'Let's talk sense', *The Medical Spectrum*, Jan 2001, p. 1, published by Pakistan Maternity and Health Association, Karachi.
46. Shershah Syed, 'Poverty and maternal death', p. 1, *The Medical Spectrum*, March/April 2000, published by Pakistan Medical Association, Karachi.
47. Imtiaz Kamal, Editor, National Committee for Maternal Health Newsletter, July 2001.
48. PSYB 2000, ante, 1998 census bulletin.
49. Ante 20, PRHFPS 2000-01, p. xi.
50. PFFPS 1996-97, p. xxiii.
51. Ibid., p. xxi.
52. Video Films for Legal Awareness, Brochure, published by the Pakistan Women Lawyers' Association, 710, Kashif Centre, Shahrah-e-Faisal, Karachi, Pakistan.
53. Sarwat Fatima, 'Prisoners of ignorance', *The Medical Spectrum*, March/April 2000, p. 7.
54. PRHFPS 2000-01, p. 12.
55. UN Report on Demographic Dynamics and Sustainability, *Dawn*, 15 April 2001.
56. PFFPS, p. 147.
57. Ante 5, PFFPS, 1996-97, December 1998, p. 205.
58. Ibid., p. 206.
59. Zahra Syed, 'Over 11.7m children suffer from stunting, wasting', *Dawn*, 4 January 2002.
60. Financial Resources Flow for Population Activities, Report of a case study in Pakistan, May/June 1999, National Population Policy, Chapter 3, p. 7.
61. Ibid., p. 17.
62. Ibid., p. 22.
63. Ibid., p. 25.
64. 'Pakistan, US sign $600m agreement', *Dawn*, 16 November 2001, p. 1.
65. FRFPA ante, p. 37
66. Ninth Five-Year Plan 1997-98–2002-03, Ministry of Planning and Development Division, Government of Pakistan, Islamabad.
67. Ibid.
68. Ibid.
69. National Health Policy, Ministry of Health, Government of Pakistan, June 2001.
70. M.B. Kalhoro, 'Restarting the illegally occupied BHUs', *Dawn*, 22 November 2001.
71. Abdul Hakim, Mehboob Sultan, and Faateh ud din, *Pakistan Reproductive Health and Family Planning Survey 2000-01*, published by National Institute of Population Studies, Islamabad, July 2001, p. 39.
72. Ibid., p. 72.
73. Ibid., p. 41.

74. Nadeem Malik, 'State Life of Pakistan to launch health insurance scheme.' Download http://www.ifds.net/artlin2_16022000.html
75. 'Better sex education of adolescents urged', *Dawn*, 20 May 2001.
76. '10pc women HIV/AIDs cases', *The Nation*, 28 September 2001.
77. 'Saving Women's Lives', A Call to Right-Based Action, UNICEF (Regional Office for South Asia) 2000.

GLOSSARY

Alim	Learned person. Knowledgeable, well informed in religion.
Adal/adl	Justice or equity.
Afw	Waiver; pardon; forgiveness; remission of sins.
A'imma	Jurists.
Al-azl	Where the man ejaculates outside the vagina to prevent pregnancy.
Al-Hadith/ Hadis/Hadith	The collection of traditions/records of what the Hazrat Muhammad (PBUH) did, what he enjoined, and that which he did not forbid. They also include the authoritative sayings and doings of the companions of the Hazrat Muhammad (PBUH).
An-nisa	The women—the name of a Quranic chapter.
Ar-rijal	The men.
Ayat	A verse.
Badal-i-sulh	Mutually agreed compensation in cash or kind.
Bait-ul-mal	Government treasury for charitable purposes.
Baradari/beradari	Brotherhood; group relationship; caste; tribal attachment; fraternity.
Batil	That which is false in doctrine, void.
Challan	Prosecution, invoice.
Choola	Stove.
Dais	Untrained women who aid at childbirth.
Daman	The compensation determined by the court to be paid by the offender to the victim for causing hurt not liable to *Arsh*.
Diyat	Blood money or compensation for murder or manslaughter, or other injury. Compensation specified under the law

	payable to the heirs of the victim by the convict, his family, or any other person liable for the payment thereof.
Eid	Muslim festival; festivity.
Eidi	The gift given to youngsters by elders on Eid (the Muslim festival).
Ejab-o-Qabool	Offer and acceptance in a contract of marriage.
Faqihs	A Muslim lawyer or theologian. A person well-versed in religious law.
Fasad-fil-arz	Mischief on the earth. The past conduct of the offender as being a previous convict, habitual or professional criminal, and the brutal manner in which the offence is committed.
Fateha	Prayers for the dead or the saints; name of the opening chapter of the Holy Quran.
Fatwa	A religious or judicial sentence/opinion pronounced by the *Khalifah*, or by the *Mufti*, or qazi. It is generally written.
Fiqah Jafria	A school of Islamic jurisprudence which is traced back to its founder Imam Jafar Sadiq.
Fuqaha	Jurists.
Ghairat	Modesty, shame, self-respect, sense of honour.
Ghairat-mand	Modest, bashful; self-respecting; honour-bound person.
Ghayr Kufu	Inequality.
Hadd	A kind of fixed punishment prescribed by God in the exercise of His exclusive right. *Hadd* is fixed punishment for the reason that this can neither be increased nor decreased by anybody [Ibn Nujaim, Bahur Raiq, v. 8, p. 286].
Haj	Pilgrimage to Mecca by Muslims (at due date and as directed in Islam).
Hajjatul-Wida	Last Haj. The last Haj (pilgrimage) performed by the Prophet Muhammad (PBUH).

Hakams	An arbitrator appointed by a qazi to settle disputes.
Halala	A divorced woman's marriage with another man, followed by a divorce before she can remarry her first husband according to most Islamic jurists. Halala is not required in case of dissolution of marriage by khula.
Hanafi	A member of the sect of Sunnis founded by the Imam Abu Hanifa.
Haq-bakshwai	The right of pardon or forgiveness.
Haram	Prohibited, that which is unlawful.
Hizanat	The right of fosterage, nourishment, and nursing of a child from birth till the age of two years, as the duty of the mother, and custody of a minor child.
Hudood	Plural of *Hadd*.
Huq Mehar	Dower.
Ibadat	Divine worship, prayer.
Iddat	The period which a divorced woman or a widow must wait before remarrying according to Muslim Law. After a divorce the period is three months, and after the death of her husband, four months and ten days.
Ijma	The literal meaning is collecting or assembling. Unanimous consent of the learned. General agreement or unanimity; consensus of issues of Muslim Law by learned Muslims of the highest degree.
Ijtehad	The literal meaning is exertion, diligence, or striving to accomplish something. Exposition of Muslim laws. The logical deduction on a legal or theological question by the learned.
Ikrah-i-Naqis	Any form of duress which does not amount to *Ikrah-i-Tam*.
Ikrah-i-Tam	Putting any person, his spouse or blood relations within the prohibited degree of marriage in fear of instant death, or instant permanent impairing of any organ of the

	body, or instant fear of being subjected to sodomy or *Zina-bil-jabr*.
Ila	A form of divorce in Muslim Law.
Imam	One whose leadership or example is to be followed. Leadership of a community.
Isqat-i-Haml	Abortion before the limbs are formed.
Isqat-i-Janin	Abortion after the limbs of the child have been formed.
Izzat	Honour; reputation; esteem.
Jaiz	Permissible.
Jirga	Sect; tribe; assembly; gathering; company; literally meeting or *faisla* (a Sindhi term) for both the meeting and the decision of the tribal *jirga* justice system.
Jumhour	Majority.
Jurh	Hurt, cause pain, do harm to, bodily injury.
Katchi Abadi	Squatter settlements.
Khairul Baloogh	Option of puberty for divorce.
Khata	Offence of murder or mistake.
Khula	Release from the marriage tie at the instance of the wife, for consideration to the husband.
Kismet	Fate, destiny, luck.
Kitabia	Belonging to the revealed religion having a revealed book (Christians).
Lian	Mutual cursing. A form of divorce which takes place under circumstances where a man accuses his wife of adultery and does not prove it by four witnesses and the wife denies the allegation four times resulting in divorce.
Madaris	Religious institutions for learning.
Madhahib	Legal schools.
Mahr	Dower.
Majlis-e-Shura	Consultation council or committee. Under the Federal Council (Majlis-e-Shura) Order 1981, Majlis-e-Shura means the Federal Council. Under the Revival of the Constitution of 1973 Order 1985, vide article 50, Majlis-e-Shura (Parliament) of Pakistan consists of the President and two

	Houses to be known as the National Assembly and the Senate.
Makrouh	Disliked but not forbidden.
Masoom-ud-dam	Murder during loss of self-control on sudden provocation.
Matta	Maintenance.
Maulana/Maulvi	A preacher of Muslim religion; or a title of respect. A religious leader.
Maulani	Feminine gender for maulana.
Mayar	Name of a Code (law).
Memon	Muslim sect.
Milad	Religious prayer meeting in praise of the Holy Prophet (PBUH).
Mohajir	An emigrant; a refugee.
Mubah	Action which a person may do or let alone, being attended with neither praise nor blame.
Mubarat	Mutual discharge. Divorce by mutual agreement.
Mullah	A teacher of Muslim religion. A religious leader.
Nafka	Maintenance.
Nazim	An administrator, a director, a governor.
Nikah	Literally, conjunction. Marriage or marriage contract.
Nikah khawan	Nikah registrar. A person entitled to perform nikah (marriage).
Nikahnama	Marriage contract.
Nuss	Text (of the Quran).
Pakhtoonwali	Code of honour and conduct. Law followed by the Pakhtoons.
Pashto	The language of the Pathans of the North West Frontier Province of Pakistan.
Pathan	Ethnic designation.
Qatl	Murder, unlawful killing of a person.
Qatl-i-amd	Wilful murder, homicide. Intentionally causing death of a person.
Qatl-i-khata	Without any intention to cause the death of, or cause harm to, unintentionally causing

	death of a person, either by mistake of act or by mistake of fact.
Qatl-Shibh-ul-amd	Causing death by means of a weapon or act which ordinarily is not likely to cause death.
Qawwam/Qawwma	Protector or provider; person in charge.
Qazi	A judge or a magistrate or one appointed to perform marriage among the Muslims.
Qisas	Retaliation/punishment by causing similar hurt to the same part of the body of the convict as he has caused to the victim or by causing his death if he has committed *qatl-i-amd* in exercise of the right of the victim or a *wali*.
Quran	The sacred Book of Islam revealed to Prophet Muhammad (PBUH) in the Arabic language.
Rishta	To form an alliance; proposal for marriage; relationship for marriage.
Riwaj	Customs; usage; practice.
Rukhsati	The wedding ceremony of the bride leaving the home of her parents.
Sahaba Kiram (RZA)	Companions of Hazrat Muhammad (SAW).
Sardar	Head of community or tribe.
Sarkari	Official; belonging to government, state, or any superior authority.
Sayyaba	A woman who had once been married and lived with her husband.
Sega	Formal words for divorce in Shia Law.
Shibh-ul-amd	Murder without sharp instrument.
Such ki Jeet	Truth prevails.
Sulh	Reconciliation, to come to terms, compromise; settle differences by mutual concessions.
Sunnah	Literally, a path or way. Record of the sayings or doings of Prophet Muhammad (PBUH).
Talaq-i-Tafwiz	Delegation of the right of divorce by the husband.
Tauba	Repenting; penitence; renouncing; abjuring.

Tauhid	A term used to express the oneness of God in Islam.
Tazir	Punishment other than *hadd*.
Trimizi	Name of a Jurist.
Tuhr	The period during which a woman is not menstruating.
Uhad	The famous battle between Muslims and non-believers in early Islam.
Ulema	Plural of *Alim*; in the plural form the word is used as the title for those bodies of religious leaders who by their fatwas or decisions on questions of religious importance regulate the life of the Muslim community. In the modern state with democratic and legislative institutions the bodies act as non-governmental bodies unless included in State institutions.
Ummah	A people, a nation, a sect.
Vakil	An attorney, an agent.
Wali	Guardian, heirs.
Wakf/Waqf	An endowment. A term which in law signifies the dedication of property to charitable uses and to the services of God.
Watta-Satta	Exchange marriages.
Zakat	Regulated poor-rate to be given every year compulsorily according to Islam, specified as 2.5 per cent of a person's property.
Zamin	Land; estate; region; earth; site; grounds.
Zamindar	Land holder.
Zan	A woman; a wife.
Zar	Wealth; money; gold; riches; lands; property.
Zihar	A form of divorce in Muslim Law.
Zila	District.
Zina	Adultery or fornication.
Zina-bil-jabr	Rape.

BIBLIOGRAPHY

Abdel Rahim Omran, *Family Planning in the Legacy of Islam*, Routledge, with the support of the United Nations Population Fund, 1992

Abdul Hakim, John Cleland, and Mansoor ul Hassan Bhatti, *Pakistan Fertility and Family Planning Survey 1996-97*, National Institute of Population Studies, Islamabad, and Centre for Population Studies, London School of Hygiene & Tropical Medicine, December 1998

Abdul Hakim, Mehboob Sultan, and Faateh ud din, *Preliminary Report, Pakistan Reproductive Health and Family Planning Survey 2000-01*, National Institute of Population Studies, Islamabad, July 2001.

Abdullah Yusuf Ali, *The Holy Quran. Text, Translation and Commentary*, explanatory note no. 509 published by Shaikh Ashraf, Hashmi Bazar, Lahore. First Edition, April 1934. Note: All Quranic verses quoted by the author in this book are from the above.

Awan, Hakim Amir Bakhsh, *Comprehensive Manual of Family Laws*, Comprehensive Publishers, Lahore, 1999.

Baxter, Craig, Charles H. Kennedy, *Pakistan 2000*, Oxford University Press, Karachi, 2001.

Beijing Plus 5 Update, issued by UNDP, Islamabad, July 1999.

Beijing Plus 5 Update, Shirkat Gah, Women's Resource Centre, Lahore, Pakistan. Issued by UNDP, 2nd Issue, October 1999.

Beijing Plus 5 Update, Shirkat Gah, Women's Resource Centre, Lahore, Pakistan. Issued by UNDP, 3rd Issue, January 2000.

Conference Report, South Asian Conference on Women Legal Aid, Legal Awareness, Law Reforms, and Lobbying, Pakistan Women Lawyers' Association (PAWLA), Karachi, Pakistan.

Crime or Custom? Violence Against Women in Pakistan, Oxford University Press, Karachi, Edition 2001.

Effective Enforcement of Maintenance Decrees, Pakistan Women Lawyers' Association (PAWLA), Karachi, April 2000.

Engineer, Asghar Ali, *Islam Women and Gender Justice*, Gyan Publishing House, India, 2001.

Engineer, Asghar Ali, *Islam Women and Gender Justice, Modern Society*, Sterling Publishers Private Limited, India, 1999.

Esposito, John L., *Islam, The Straight Path*, Third Edition, Oxford University Press Inc, New York, 1998.

Family Law Court Act 1964, West Pakistan Act No. XXXV of 1964, Gazette of Pakistan Extraordinary, 18 July 1964.

Final Draft Report: Reproductive Health Project, Pakistan and annexure I to VIII ADB TA No. 3387, Government of Pakistan, Ministry of Population Welfare, Asian Development Bank, and Options Data-line.

Financial Resources Flows for Population Activities, Report of a case study in Pakistan, May/ June 1999.

Gender on the Agenda, A Guide to participating in Beijing Plus 5, published by United Nations Development Fund for Women (UNIFEM) and United Nations Non-Governmental Liaison Service (UN/NGLS).

Hassan, Dr Riffat, 'The Effect of Marriage Preferences on Women's Autonomy: A Case Study', School of Health, University of New England, Australia. Presented at the Conference on Pakistan's Population Issues in the 21st Century at Karachi, 2001.

Jafarey, Sadiqua N., 'Women's Health', revised 19 March 2001, Professor of Obstetrics and Gynaecology, Ziauddin Medical University, Karachi and President, National Committee on Maternal Health (unpublished).

Jafarey, Sadiqua, Talat Rizvi, and Imtiaz Kamal, 'Safe Motherhood Situational Analysis', Pakistan, country paper for Workshop on Strengthening Safe Motherhood Programmes, 7, 8 February 2000, Bangkok (unpublished).

Jayasuriya, Shanti, D.C. Jayasuriya, *Women and Development—The Road from Beijing*, Har-Anand Publications Pvt. Limited, India, 1999.

Mahmood, Naushin, 'Gender Perspectives on Population and Development in Pakistan,' Pakistan Institute of Development Economics, Quaid-i-Azam University. Presented at the Conference on Pakistan's Population Issues in the 21st Century.

Mahmood, Tahir, *Personal Laws in Crisis*, Metropolitan Book Co. (Pvt.) Limited, India.

Malik, Dr Hafeez, *Pakistan Founders' Aspirations and Today's Realities*, Oxford University Press, Karachi.

Mernissi, Fatima, *Women and Islam—An Historical and Theological Enquiry*, Basil Blackwell Limited, UK, 1991.

Moghissi, Haideh, *Feminism and Islamic Fundamentalism, The Limits of Postmodern Analysis*, Oxford University Press, 1999.

National Feedback Report, Health Management Information System, National HMIS Cell, Ministry of Health, Government of Pakistan, Islamabad.

National Health Policy, Approved by Federal Cabinet on 17 December 1997, Ministry of Health, Government of Pakistan.

NCMH Newsletter, published by National Committee for Maternal Health, July 2001.

Ninth Five-Year Plan 1997/98 - 2002/3 Chapter on Health Sector, Ministry of Planning, Government of Pakistan.

Our Bodies Ourselves for the New Century—A Book by and for Women, Touchstone, New York, 1998.

Pakistan Contraceptive Prevalence Survey 1994-95, Final Report, Population Council, Islamabad, Pakistan, March 1998.

Pakistan National Report, Fourth World Conference on Women, Beijing, September 1995, Government of Pakistan, Ministry of Women Development and Youth Affairs, Islamabad.

Pakistan NGO Review, Beijing Plus 5, Women 2000: Gender Equality, Development, and Peace for the 21st Century, NGO Coordinating Committee for Beijing Plus 5, Shirkat Gah, Women's Resource Centre, Lahore, 1999.

Pakistan Penal Code (XLV of 1860), Nadeem Law Book House, Lahore, Pakistan.

Pakistan, Country Report on Human Rights Practices–2000. Released by the Bureau of Democracy, Human Rights, and Labor, US Department of State, February 2001.

Pakistan, Reproductive Health Service Package, Ministry of Health and Ministry of Population Welfare, Government of Pakistan, Islamabad, August 1999.

Pakistan, Violence Against Women in the Name of Honour, Amnesty International, United Kingdom, September 1999.

Pakistan's Population Issues in the 21st Century, concerning proceedings 24-26 October 2000, Karachi, Population Association of Pakistan, 2001.

Patel, Rashida, *Islamisation of Laws in Pakistan*, Faiza Publishers, Karachi, 1986.

Patel, Rashida, *Socio-Economic Political Status and Women and Law in Pakistan*, Faiza Publishers, Karachi, 1991.

Patel, Rashida, *Women and Law in Pakistan*, Faiza Publishers, Karachi, 1979.

President Order No. 18 of 1959, Gazette of Pakistan, Extraordinary, Government of Pakistan, Islamabad, 27 October 1959.

Progress Report January 1995–June 1996, Prime Minister's Programme for Family Planning and Primary Health Care, Ministry of Health, Government of Pakistan.

Rehan, Dr N., *Unsafe Abortion, Magnitude and Perception*, Family Planning Association of Pakistan, Lahore, 1998.

Rizvi, Hasan Askari, *The Military & Politics in Pakistan 1947-1997*, Sang-e-Meel Publications, Lahore, 2000.

Sardar Ali, Shaheen, 'A Comparative Study of the United Nations Convention on the Elimination of all Forms of Discrimination Against Women, Islamic Law and The Laws of Pakistan', supported by the Royal Norwegian Embassy, Development Cooperation (NORDAN), Islamabad.

Sather, Zeba A., Shahnaz Kazi, *Women's Autonomy, Livelihood Fertility, A Study of Rural Punjab*, Pakistan Institute of Development Economics, Islamabad, 1997.

Serajuddin, Alamgir Muhammad, *Shari'a Law and Society, Tradition and Change in South Asia*, Oxford University Press, Karachi.

Special Issue on Women's Health, *The Medical Spectrum*, January 2001, Pakistan Medical Association, Karachi.

Special Issue, *The Medical Spectrum*, March/April 2000, Pakistan Medical Association, Karachi.

Statistical Pocket Book of Pakistan 2001, Federal Bureau of Statistics, Statistics Division, Government of Pakistan, Islamabad, January 2001.

Taking up the Cairo Challenge, Country Studies in Asia Pacific, Asian Pacific Resource & Research Centre for Women (ARROW), Malaysia.

Time to Speak Out: Illegal Abortion and Women's Health in Pakistan, Special Bulletin–December 1996, Shirkat Gah, Coordination for Asia, Lahore, Pakistan.

West Pakistan Rules under Muslim Family Laws Ordinance 1961, Gazette of West Pakistan, 19 July 1961.

Women: Challenges to the Year 2000, United Nations Department of Public Information, New York.

Women's Health in Pakistan, Fact Sheets, prepared for Pakistan National Forum on Women's Health, 3-5 November 1997, United Nations Children's Fund, Pakistan.

INDEX

INDEX OF CASES AND STATUTES CITED

STATUTES